Fro

P O R T A B L E

California Wine Country

2nd Edition

by Erika Lenkert and Matthew R. Poole

with John Thoreen

IDG Books Worldwide, Inc.
An International Data Group Company
Foster City, CA • Chicago, IL • Indianapolis, IN • New York, NY

ABOUT THE AUTHORS

Native San Franciscan **Erika Lenkert** returned home from a 4-year-stint in her favorite town—Los Angeles—where she wrote a restaurant column for *Los Angeles Magazine* and contributed to *InStyle, Travel & Leisure, Bon Appétit, California Homes,* and dozens of travel guides to California. Why return north? To get in on the dot-commercialization of the City By The Bay, of course. As editor-in-chief of WineShopper.com she now brings her passion for food, wine, travel, and overall celebration to the Web. She also continues to write magazine articles and remains subservient to her owners—two Siamese cats.

Freelance travel writer and photographer **Matthew R. Poole** has authored more than two dozen travel guides and magazine articles on California and abroad. He currently lives in San Francisco and is an ardent fan of Ravenswood Zinfandels.

In addition to this guide, Erika and Matthew co-author a number of other Frommer's guides to California, including *Frommer's California, Frommer's San Francisco from $60 a Day,* and *Frommer's Memorable Walks in San Francisco.*

IDG BOOKS WORLDWIDE, INC.

An International Data Group Company
919 E. Hillsdale Blvd.
Suite 400
Foster City, CA 94404

Find us online at **www.frommers.com**

ISBN 0-02-863682-1
ISSN 1093-9776

Editor: Margot Weiss
Production Editor: Robyn Burnett
Photo Editor: Richard Fox
Production Team: John Bitter and Kendra Span
Design by Michele Laseau
Staff Cartographers: John Decamillis and Roberta Stockwell

SPECIAL SALES

For general information on IDG Books Worldwide's books in the U.S., please call our Consumer Customer Service department at 1-800-762-2974. For reseller information, including discounts, bulk sales, customized editions, and premium sales, please call our Reseller Customer Service department at 1-800-434-3422.

Manufactured in the United States of America

5 4 3 2 1

Contents

List of Maps

AN INVITATION TO THE READER

In researching this book, we discovered many wonderful places—hotels, restaurants, shops, and more. We're sure you'll find others. Please tell us about them, so we can share the information with your fellow travelers in upcoming editions. If you were disappointed with a recommendation, we'd love to know that, too. Please write to:

Frommer's Portable California Wine Country, 2nd Edition
IDG Travel
1633 Broadway
New York, NY 10019

AN ADDITIONAL NOTE

Please be advised that travel information is subject to change at any time—and this is especially true of prices. The authors, editors, and publisher cannot be held responsible for the experiences of readers while traveling. Your safety is important to us, however, so we encourage you to stay alert and be aware of your surroundings. Keep a close eye on cameras, purses, and wallets, all favorite targets of thieves and pickpockets.

WHAT THE SYMBOLS MEAN
✪ Frommer's Favorites

Our favorite places and experiences—outstanding for quality, value, or both.

The following abbreviations are used for credit cards:

AE	American Express	EC	Eurocard
CB	Carte Blanche	JCB	Japan Credit Bank
DC	Diners Club	MC	MasterCard
DISC	Discover	V	Visa
ER	enRoute		

FIND FROMMER'S ONLINE

www.frommers.com offers up-to-the-minute listings on almost 200 cities around the globe—including the latest bargains and candid, personal articles updated daily by Arthur Frommer himself. No other Web site offers such comprehensive and timely coverage of the world of travel.

The Best of the Wine Country

Whether you're on a budget or blowing your annual bonus, there's no way around it: a Wine Country experience epitomizes indulgence. Literally all that's expected of you is to eat, drink, relax—and then do it all over again. The rest—wine tastings, spa treatments, hot-air balloon rides, horseback tours—is mere icing on an already idyllic itinerary. In fact, you don't even have to like wine to love the Wine Country; anyone who enjoys lounging in a hammock on a warm summer's day will succumb, because the Wine Country is just that: the country. The verdant expanses of rolling hills patterned with grape-garnered trellises, hued with mustard and wildflowers, and dotted with farmers plowing the soil and vintners tending to their vines is country life at its picture-perfect best.

Of course, there's a whole lot more: wineries both great and small producing some of the world's finest wines, nationally renowned chefs serving exceptional cuisine, luxury resorts and soothing mineral hot springs. Yes, the world may be falling apart elsewhere, but not here—for this eternal Eden of indulgence is where we go when we feel the need to be pampered, when it's time to whip out the charge card for that $200 dinner or a 1996 Joseph Phelps Insignia and say, "Frankly, my dear, I don't give a damn."

Which is why you're holding *Frommer's Portable California Wine Country.* Consider it your personal passport to the best that the Napa and Sonoma valleys have to offer. Follow our suggestions and you'll know why this is one of our favorite vacation spots on the planet; in time, it's bound to become one of yours, too.

1 The Best Wineries

- **Domaine Chandon** (Yountville, Napa Valley): Founded by Moët et Chandon, the valley's most renowned sparkling winery has all the grandeur of a world-class French champagne house. Strolling with a glass of bubbly in hand through this estate's beautifully manicured rose gardens—complete with swan pond—is a quintessential Wine Country experience. See page 66.

- **PlumpJack Winery** (Oakville, Napa Valley): The proprietors of San Francisco's PlumpJack restaurant and wine shop have transformed the former Villa Mount Eden's winery into a hip, playful, energetic place—a welcome diversion from the attitude you'll come to expect from Napa Valley wineries. But it's not just about atmosphere: They're making some very impressive wines here, including some killer Cabernets. No tours or picnic spots are available, but this refreshingly stylized and friendly facility will make you want to hang out for a while nonetheless. See page 68.
- **V. Sattui Winery** (St. Helena, Napa Valley): Nowhere else can you taste small-volume wines (only sold here), stock up on gourmet lunch supplies (free tastes!), and join in on a huge ongoing picnic all at the same time. The crowds are mighty, but as the saying goes: If you can't beat 'em. . . . See page 74.
- **Joseph Phelps Vineyards** (St. Helena, Napa Valley): Intimate, comprehensive tours and knockout tastings make this one of our favorite wineries to visit. An air of seriousness hangs heavier than harvest grapes when you first arrive, but the mood lightens as your knowledgeable guide explains the ins and outs of wine making and you begin to taste five to six wines. These range from Sauvignon Blanc to what's bound to be terrific Cab (*Wine Spectator* regularly awards Phelps's Cabernets and blended reds with scores in the high 90s, and aficionados have been known to come close to brawling over bottles of the coveted Insignia Cab). Don't forget to reserve ahead; tours and tastings are by appointment only. See page 76.
- **Prager Winery & Port Works** (St. Helena, Napa Valley): If you want a real down-home, off-the-beaten track Wine Country experience, this place can't be beat. A cozy clapboard tasting room is where owner/winemaker Jim Prager, a sort of modern-day Santa Claus, will pour you samples of his yummy after-dinner wines and a few other selections (including a very good Chardonnay and Cab). The whole experience is so wonderfully unique that it makes the $5 tasting fee seem like a bargain. See page 77.
- **Clos Pegase** (Calistoga, Napa Valley): Viewing the art at this temple to wine is as much the point as tasting the wines themselves. Renowned architect Michael Graves designed this incredible oasis, which integrates an impressive modern art collection—including a sculpture garden—with a state-of-the-art wine-making facility that features 20,000 square feet of aging caves. See page 82.

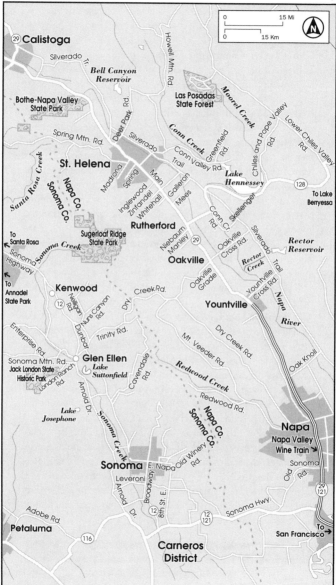

The **Hess Collection** winery also houses a noteworthy display of museum-quality artwork that's worth checking out. See page 64.

- **Gloria Ferrer Champagne Caves** (Carneros District, Sonoma Valley): Gloria is the grande dame of the Wine Country's sparkling wine producers. On a sunny day, it's impossible not to enjoy sipping a glass of dry Brut on the terrace of this palatial estate as you take in the magnificent views of the vineyards and valley below. If you're unfamiliar with the *méthode champenoise,* make time for the 30-minute tour, which takes you past the fermenting tanks, the bustling bottling line, and into the dark caves brimming with rack after rack of fermenting wine. See page 138.

- **Gundlach-Bundschu Winery** (Sonoma, Sonoma Valley): Gundlach-Bundschu is the quintessential Sonoma winery: nonchalant about appearance, obsessed with wine. Oenophiles in the know covet G-B's reds, particularly the Zinfandels, which are remarkably inexpensive for such well-crafted wines. Tours include a trip into their 430-foot cave. They also have the best picnic grounds in the valley here. And if you're in the valley on a summer weekend, plan on catching one of the Shakespearean plays staged at the winery's outdoor theater—they're loads of fun. See page 139.

- **The Benziger Family Winery** (Glen Ellen, Sonoma Valley): As soon as you arrive here, you'll know you're at a family-run winery—in fact, you'll feel instantly like part of the Benziger clan. This low-volume, high-quality winery offers an exceptional self-guided tour, a free 40-minute tram tour through its pastoral grounds, free tastings, and many excellent, reasonably priced wines. See page 143.

- **Matanzas Creek** (Santa Rosa): It's not technically in Sonoma Valley, but if there's one winery that's worth the drive up to Bennett Valley, it's Matanzas Creek, one of the prettiest wineries in California (particularly when the lavender fields are in bloom near the end of June). And their wines are pretty spectacular, too: Their Journey 1990 Chardonnay has been hailed by wine critics as the finest Chardonnay *ever produced in the United States*—and we think their Merlot is easily the finest you'll taste in the Wine Country, too. See page 146.

2 The Best Winery Tours for First-Timers

- **Domaine Chandon** (Yountville, Napa Valley): Not only are the grounds sublime, but the comprehensive tour walks you through the high-tech facilities and the entire champagne-making process, from the history of the winery to the cellars, riddling room, and bottling line. Tours are free and no reservation is necessary, but if you want to taste, it'll cost you: $8 to $12 for a full glass (sorry, no free sips). Come during high season, though, and you can supplement your bubbly with a few appetizers and kick back on their garden-front patio. See page 66.

- **Robert Mondavi Winery** (Oakville, Napa Valley): As one of the most prominent wineries in the valley, it's only appropriate that Robert Mondavi would offer a guided tour for every sort of wine taster. The basic 1-hour comprehensive production tour covers all aspects of the wine-making process and gives you a look at the destemmer-crusher, the tank room where fermentation is done, the bottling room, and the vineyard, all accompanied by a top-notch narrative—the guides are great at making sure you know what you're looking at. Your reward at the end? A free tasting, of course. If you find yourself inspired, you can then move on to one of the other offered tours, such as the 3- to 4-hour advanced wine-growing tour. Make your reservations in advance, if possible; these tours get booked up, especially in high season. See page 66.

- **St. Supéry Winery** (Rutherford, Napa Valley): This straightfor-ward winery is a great place for first-time tasters to learn more about oenology. Their nifty self-guided tour comes complete with "SmellaVision," an interactive display that teaches you how to identify different wine aromas and attributes; there's also a dem-onstration vineyard that you can wander through to learn about growing techniques. See page 70.

- **Frank-Rombauer Cellars** (Calistoga, Napa Valley): While this isn't the Wine Country's most comprehensive tour, it may be its most unintimidating. Staff members Dennis, Bob, Chris, and Rich claim to run one of the friendliest wineries in the valley, which includes taking the time to explain *anything* you want to know about wine. They also serve you all the bubbly you want and guarantee that you'll never wait more than 10 minutes to take the 20-minute tour. See page 81.

- **Schramsberg** (Calistoga, Napa Valley): The label that presidents serve when toasting with dignitaries from around the globe also serves up the Wine Country's best introduction to the méthode champenoise process of making sparkling wine. The excellent tour is both comprehensive and non-threatening, and an experi-ence you won't soon forget; the highlight is the visit to the

2¹/₂ miles of hand-carved champagne caves—you'll feel like you've landed in the middle of a *Tom Sawyer* adventure. And the tasting room is positively gothic. Be sure to book a spot on the tour in advance, as they fill up quickly. See page 81.

- **Sterling Vineyards** (Calistoga, Napa Valley): This dazzling white Mediterranean-style winery, perched high above the rest of the valley atop a rocky knoll (you'll arrive via aerial tram), offers the most comprehensive self-guided tour in the entire Wine Country. It's great for getting to know the entire wine-making process at your own pace. See page 82.

- **The Benziger Family Winery** (Glen Ellen, Sonoma Valley): *Wine Spectator* magazine hailed this family-run winery as having "the most comprehensive tour in the wine industry." The exceptional self-guided tour, which includes a free 40-minute tram ride, is both informative and fun; it winds through the estate vineyards before making a champagne-tasting pit stop on a scenic bluff. Tour tickets are a hot commodity, so be sure to plan ahead for this one. See page 143.

3   The Best Experiences Beyond the Wineries

- **Hot-Air Ballooning over Napa's Vineyards:** Admit it: Floating over lush green pastures in a hot-air balloon is something you've always dreamed of but never got around to actually doing. Here's your best chance, because Napa Valley is the busiest hot-air balloon "flight corridor" in the *world*—and what more romantic place to sail up, up, and away? For recommendations on the best Napa hot-air balloon companies, see page 85.

- **Spreading Out Your Picnic Blanket for a Gourmet Alfresco Feast:** You've been with the crowds all day—sitting with them in traffic and sipping elbow-to-elbow in the tasting rooms. If the thought of joining the masses for a meal after all that seems about as romantic and relaxing as a New York subway ride, cancel your restaurant reservations and pack a picnic instead. Both Napa and Sonoma have some of the most spectacular picnic spots on the planet, not to mention excellent places to fill your basket, including the legendary **Oakville Grocery Co.** (☎ 707/944-8802), a West Coast outpost of New York's **Dean & DeLuca** (☎ 707/967-9980), and the **Sonoma Cheese Factory** (☎ 707/996-1000), which offers more kinds of house-made jack cheeses than you ever imagined were possible. See pages 127-129 for details on picnicking in Napa, pages 172-173 for Sonoma.

- **Pampering Yourself at a Spa:** The Wine Country is the perfect place to relax—so what better place to indulge in a tension-relieving massage, a purifying facial, or a rejuvenating body wrap? Our favorite spots to spa it are St. Helena's **White Sulphur Springs Retreat & Spa** (☎ 707/963-4361) and **Health Spa Napa Valley** (☎ 707/967-8800), and the **Sonoma Mission Inn & Spa** (☎ 800/862-4945). See page 87 for details on Napa spas, page 149 for Sonoma.

- **Horseback Riding through the Wine Country:** If you like horses and venturing through cool, shaded forests, then consider seeing the countryside from the saddle. **Napa Valley Trail Rides** (☎ 707/996-8566) will lead any level of rider on a leisurely ride (with the occasional trot thrown in for excitement) through beautiful Bothe-Napa Valley State Park. On the other side of the hills, the **Sonoma Cattle Company** (☎ 707/996-8566) will take you through lovely Jack London State Historical Park. Both companies also offer sunset, full-moon, barbecue, and box-lunch rides as well. See pages 89 and 151.

- **Touring Sonoma's Wineries on Two Wheels:** With quiet, gently sloping country roads and lots of bucolic scenery, Sonoma is perfect for cycling. **Goodtime Bicycle Company** (☎ 888/525-0453) can take you on one of their organized excursions to Kenwood-area wineries or to south Sonoma's wineries; not only do they provide a gourmet lunch featuring local Sonoma foodstuffs, they'll also carry any wine you purchase and even help with shipping it home. They'll happily rent you a bike and point you to easy trails if you'd rather set out on your own. See page 133.

- **Getting Your Thrills in the Skies:** If you're the thrill-seeking type, catch a panoramic ride in an authentic 1940 Boeing-built Stearman biplane with **Vintage Aircraft Company** (☎ 707/938-2444), which depart from the south end of Sonoma Valley. You can also try a glider ride, which will take you soaring over the vineyards—simply breathtaking. See page 148.

4 The Best Luxury Hotels & Inns

- **Auberge du Soleil** (Rutherford, Napa Valley; ☎ 707/963-1211): This spectacular Relais & Châteaux member is quiet, indulgent, and luxuriously romantic. The *bathrooms* are celestial; let alone the views. This is one of our favorite places on earth—and always our first choice in the Wine Country. See page 100.

- **Meadowood Napa Valley** (St. Helena, Napa Valley; ☎ **800/ 458-8080**): Tucked away in its own private valley is this ultra-luxurious resort, a favorite retreat for Hollywood celebs and corporate CEOs. Spend your days hiking the private trails or playing golf, tennis, or croquet, and follow up with a trip to the health spa and whirlpool. Top it all off with dinner in the excellent restaurant, and you'll have a tough time finding a reason to leave. See page 102.

- **Sonoma Mission Inn, Spa & Country Club** (Sonoma, Sonoma Valley; ☎ **800/862-4945**): Another popular retreat for the wealthy and the well-known, this multimillion-dollar resort is the last word in spa luxury. Naturally heated artesian springs are the place's coup de grace. Sauna, steam room, whirlpool, outdoor exercise pool, weight room, tennis courts, a whole menu of spa treatments—you can pamper yourself in myriad ways, and retire to your superluxe suite when the day is done. Excellent restaurant, too. See page 154.

- **Gaige House Inn** (Glen Ellen, Sonoma Valley; ☎ **800/ 935-0237**): When we visited this gorgeous inn, we were not merely impressed—we didn't want to leave. This is the finest B&B in the Wine Country. First-class service, an abundance of amenities, luxurious rooms outfitted with top-quality goods—everything you'd expect from an outrageously expensive resort, but at much more reasonable prices (and with a much more intimate atmosphere). See page 158.

- **Kenwood Inn & Spa** (Kenwood, Sonoma Valley; ☎ **800/ 353-6966**): The honey-colored, Tuscan-style buildings, flower-filled flagstone courtyard, and pastoral views of vineyard-covered hills are enough to make any northern Italian homesick. The lavishly done rooms come with just about every extra you could want (except TV, which would interfere with the tranquil ambiance), the full-service spa is to die for, and the staff is as friendly and welcoming as they can be. See page 160.

5 The Best Moderately Priced Accommodations

- **Wine Country Inn** (St. Helena, Napa Valley; ☎ **707/ 963-7077**): This attractive wood-and-stone hideaway, complete with a French-style mansard roof and turret, offers lovingly and individually decorated rooms and copious amounts of hospitality. It's also very well priced, considering the outrageous rates usually charged in St. Helena. One of the inn's best features is its attractively landscaped outdoor pool (heated year-round); in fact, the whole charming place overlooks a pastoral landscape of Napa Valley vineyards. See page 104.

- **Deer Run Bed & Breakfast** (St. Helena, Napa Valley; ☎ 800/ 843-3408): If romantic solitude is a big part of your vacation plan, this place had better be on your itinerary—regardless of your budget. Each of the wood-paneled rooms looks onto innkeepers Tom and Carol Wilson's 4 acres of forest; each one comes outfitted with gorgeous antiques and a slew of amenities, not to mention all the solitude you could possibly desire. The ultimate heavenly hideaway. See page 105.

- **White Sulphur Springs Retreat & Spa** (St. Helena, Napa Valley; ☎ 707/963-8588): This woodsy hideaway is a short winding drive away from downtown St. Helena. Established in 1852 and set among 330 acres of creeks, waterfalls, hot springs, hiking trails, and redwood, madrone, and fir trees, White Sulphur Springs claims to be the oldest resort in California; it's geared toward nature-retreat types, who will appreciate both the cozily rustic cabins and the untrammeled surroundings. A full menu of spa treatments rounds out the relaxation. See page 106.

- **Cottage Grove Inn** (Calistoga, Napa Valley; ☎ 800/799-2284): This romantic cluster of cottages is our top affordable pick for doing the Calistoga spa scene in comfort and style. Each brand-spanking-new cottage comes complete with a wood-burning fireplace, homey furnishings (perfect for curling up in front of the fire), cozy quilts, and an enormous bathroom with a skylight and a deep, two-person Jacuzzi tub. See page 107.

- **El Dorado Hotel** (Sonoma, Sonoma Valley; ☎ 800/289-3031): Designed by the same folks who put together Napa's exclusive Auberge du Soleil, this place may look like a 19th-century Wild West relic from the outside, but inside it's all 20th-century deluxe. French windows offer lovely views of the courtyard, which features a heated lap pool. Breakfast, served either inside or out in the courtyard, is heavenly. See page 155.

- **Glenelly Inn** (Glen Ellen, Sonoma Valley; ☎ 707/996-6720): With verdant views of Sonoma's oak-studded hillsides, this former 1916 railroad inn is positively drenched in serenity, and it has everything you'd expect from a Wine Country retreat. Bright, immaculate rooms have old-fashioned claw-foot tubs and Scandinavian down comforters, a hearty country breakfast is served beside the large cobblestone fireplace, and there's a long veranda where you can curl up in a comfy wicker chair to admire the idyllically bucolic view. See page 159.

6   The Best Restaurants

- **La Toque** (Rutherford, Napa Valley; ☎ **707/963-9770**): Chef Ken Frank's dining room is one of our favorite places to go for special occasions. But even when the celebration is simply to honor an insatiable appetite for truly memorable French-inspired cuisine, we recommend reserving a table here—so long as you don't mind the utterly formal atmosphere. See page 115.

- **Bistro Jeanty** (Yountville, Napa Valley; ☎ **707/944-0103**): The locals' favorite newcomer is also one of ours. Cheery and casual atmosphere and outstanding French bistro classics from long-reputed chef Phillipe Jeanty are an absolute must-try. We love dropping by on a whim and eating at the bar. See page 117.

- **The French Laundry** (Yountville, Napa Valley; ☎ **707/ 944-2380**): If you've got the cash, are a serious food lover, and can get a reservation, you have no choice: Dine here and find out for yourself why chef/owner Thomas Keller's restaurant continues to be hailed the best restaurant in the world. Dinner at this intimate restaurant is an all-night affair, and when it's finally over, you'll be ready to sit down and do it all over again—it's that good. See page 116.

- **Catahoula** (Calistoga, Napa Valley; ☎ **707/942-2275**): Celebrity chef Jan Birnbaum runs one of the best restaurants in the Wine Country. Catahoula is both funky and fun, and the Southern food that comes out of the wood-burning oven—such as the gumbo ya ya with andouille sausage—is spicy and exciting. You'd have to travel all over Louisiana to find another place like this. See page 125.

- **Cucina Viansa** (Sonoma, Sonoma Valley; ☎ **707/935-5656**): For a quick gourmet lunch in Sonoma, there's no better place to go than Cucina Viansa. This suave deli and wine bar, run by the same people responsible for the success story that is Viansa Winery, is the sexiest thing going in Sonoma. It's a visual masterpiece, with shiny black-and-white-checkered flooring, long counters of Italian marble, and an enticing display of cured meats and cheeses. See page 167.

- **The Girl & The Fig** (Glen Ellen, Sonoma Valley; ☎ **707/ 938-3634**): The cuisine at this modern, attractive cafe is nouveau-country with French nuances—and, yes, figs: They appear in such wonderful creations as the winter fig salad made with arugula, pecans, dried figs, and Laura Chenel goat cheese, tossed in a fig-and-Port vinaigrette. Nonfiggy dishes include pan-roasted pork tenderloin with a potato leek pancake and roasted beets and sea scallops with lobster scented risotto. Both tourists and locals pack the place nightly, so try to reserve ahead. See page 170.

- **Meritage** (Sonoma, Sonoma Valley; ☎ **707/938-9430**): Chef Carlo Cavallo has put his heart and soul into this exciting Sonoma newcomer that combines the best of Southern French and Northern Italian cuisines. What's not to like about wild boar chops in a white truffle sauce, handmade roasted pumpkin tortelloni, and Napoleon of escargot in a champagne and wild thyme sauce—all at surprisingly reasonable prices? Check it out. See page 165.

- **Café La Haye** (Sonoma, Sonoma Valley; ☎ **707/935-5994**): This small, sophisticated Sonoma cafe is a must-stop on your Wine Country dining binge. You'll enjoy the simple yet savory dishes emanating from the tiny open kitchen, such as their thick grilled pork chop spiced with hot sweet mustard and accompanied with mashed sweet potatoes. Add a friendly wait staff and reasonable prices and it's easy to see why Café La Haye is one of our favorites. See page 162.

2

The Wine Country Experience

by John Thoreen, Wine Tutor at Meadowood Napa Valley

Over the past 20 years, John Thoreen has built
an international reputation as wine lecturer and
writer. Presently he is director of the Wine
Center at the prestigious Meadowood Napa
Valley resort. You can reach John at
Meadowood at ☎ **707/967-1205** or
online at **vintuteur@aol.com**.

*S*eeing the Wine Country can be an enormously pleasant day trip. However, investing at least a full day in each valley will reward you with multiple hedonistic dividends—and put you near the head of the class in understanding the ultrapremium wines of California. In the pages that follow, we'll give you a head start on your trip by introducing you to the Napa and Sonoma valleys and the exciting world of wine making.

1 Introducing the Napa & Sonoma Valleys

If you see San Francisco as a charming yet congested metropolis, the two rural valleys just an hour to the north, Sonoma and Napa, offer by contrast a delightfully calming and rustic retreat. In the Wine Country, the focus is mainly on gastronomy: adventures with wine and food augmented by a setting of charming villages and towns, sunny afternoons, striking mountain landscapes, carefully presented works of art and architecture, and seas of the world's tidiest vineyards.

The mix of sophistication and rusticity can be peculiar: Dusty pickups park outside some of the finest restaurants in the country. Vintners clad in denim jackets carry bottles of First Growth Bordeaux Chateaux into local bistros. Barns both small and large are more likely to house wine barrels than bales of hay. Many of the homes that pepper the region, tucked back among the vines or perched on hillsides, appear in the pages of *Architectural Digest.* And these are small towns!

While Napa and Sonoma view each other as competitors (Sonoma produced a bumper sticker that reads "NAPA makes auto parts, SONOMA makes wine"), and while you can sense a difference in attitude traveling from one valley to the other, together as the Wine Country they differ from any other region in California. This uniqueness is based on several factors: a tumultuous geology comprised of 50 or 60 perfectly poor soils; a colorful yet disjointed historical record; a climate unique to growing world-class grapes; legions of entrepreneurs who have often misunderstood the wine business; resilient farmers who once grew wheat and prunes before switching to grapes; and you, one of five million folks who visit each year. (Some years ago, a journalist claimed that Napa is second only to Disneyland as a tourist attraction—an exaggeration that has been perpetuated ever since.)

QUALITY, NOT QUANTITY In the odd jargon of marketing, "premium" refers to those wines selling for under $7, "super premium" wines run between $7 and $14, and "ultrapremiums" cost $15 and up. The majority of California's premium wines come not from Napa and Sonoma, but from the state's vast Central Valley—still, most of America thinks of Napa and Sonoma as *the* Wine Country. In fact, the seemingly endless spread of vines in Napa and Sonoma comprise only a small part of California's total vineyard acreage. Because the yields per acre here are much lower than in the Central Valley, Sonoma produces only about 7% of the wine made in the state; Napa only around 5%. In short, the Wine Country north of San Francisco gained its fame not from quantity, but quality.

Though the Wine Country's total acreage is small, the intensity of its wine-making activity is remarkable. Sonoma Valley claims to be home to 150 wine producers, Napa Valley to 250, which places almost *half* of California's 900 wine producers in just two relatively small regions. Even more remarkable is the fact that many of the hot boutique labels selling for $50 or more per bottle are housed as "tenants" in larger wineries and are not counted as wineries per se. When you combine the wineries you can visit with those that thrive as "labels," Napa and Sonoma are probably home to 60% or 70% of the ultrapremium labels in California. Thus, when you visit the Wine Country, you're sure to experience many of the very best wines that California has to offer.

THE KEY: GEOGRAPHY

Why does the Wine Country produce such a disproportionate amount of the ultrapremiums in the state? What makes the wines of Sonoma and Napa so good? Mother Nature can take most of the credit: The local climate and geology are the primary factors for the region's wine-making success. Beyond these fortuitous geographical features, the flow of history and twists of politics also come into play, though to a much lesser degree. If not for the ocean, the mountain ranges, the earthquakes, and the volcanoes, the valleys of Napa and Sonoma would never have been formed.

Heading into the Wine Country from San Francisco, you traverse a range of Mediterranean-like climates. Each differs significantly based on its distance from the ocean or San Francisco Bay, and on its proximity to the small mountain ranges that parallel the coast and block the passage of cold ocean air inland. Grapes love this particular climate, as do numerous other crops ranging from olives, walnuts, apples, and citrus fruits to wild herbs like fennel, bay, sage, and mustard.

The climatic differences are subtle, yet significant. While the Wine Country will never know such weather extremes as the snows of Buffalo, New York, or the humidity of Washington, D.C., everyone who lives here knows that Napa, the city, is cooler by 10 or more degrees on a warm summer day than Calistoga, 20 miles to the north. Because the south end of the Wine Country—referred to as the Carneros District—is cooled by the breeze off the bay, it works best for Chardonnay and Pinot Noir, delicate grapes of Burgundy that cannot thrive in hot climates. Farther north, around Kenwood in Sonoma and St. Helena in Napa, the warmer climate suits Bordeaux grapes such as Cabernet Sauvignon, Merlot, and Sauvignon Blanc.

THE IMPORTANCE OF PLACE: APPELLATIONS   In both Sonoma and Napa, the latest refinements occurring in the wine world involve discovering a "sense of place" for each style of wine. This critical understanding of soils and slopes happened years ago in Bordeaux, Burgundy, Chianti, and other classic wine-growing regions. Those areas' legally recognized, specific place-names say "This soil planted to this grape on this hillside makes a distinctive style of wine." The United States started such a system only recently. As a result, "Napa" was recognized as an appellation, a "named place," in 1981; the area designated "Sonoma" received its approval in 1983. Finer distinctions have sliced these larger regions into smaller pieces, each of which makes further claims to unique qualities in their wines. Today, Sonoma has 11 subappellations; Napa has 10. Thus, you might see a wine label that reads: "Kenwood Vineyards, Cabernet Sauvignon, Sonoma County, Sonoma Valley," the terms becoming increasingly more specific about the source of the grapes. In Napa it might be "Saintsbury, Pinot Noir, Napa Valley, Carneros."

Over the last 10 years, players in the local wine scene have debated the merits of appellations and subappellations. One school says that the words "Napa" and "Sonoma" carry tremendous good-will, and that diluting them with numerous new terms will only con-fuse the consumer, who's often confused enough already about wine. The visionaries argue that as long as "Napa" and "Sonoma" appear on the label, additional specifics will only help the wine drinker. Only time will tell in this latest twist in the history and politics of the Wine Country.

A LOOK AT THE PAST

Sonoma and Napa valleys were latecomers to the California vineyard scene. Around 1780, Franciscan missionaries, establishing the first of their 21 missions in California, planted the first vineyard in the state near San Diego. The first commercial vineyards were estab-lished in Los Angeles around 1825. Around the same time, the 21st and last Franciscan mission, Mission San Francisco Solano, planted its vines near present-day Sonoma; the same vines became the first commercial vineyard in the region about 15 years later, when the missions became secularized. Napa saw its first vineyards in 1838, but had yet to produce commercial wine until 1858, when Charles Krug made a few gallons for John Patchett.

Los Angeles continued to dominate California's wine industry until the 1870s, when Sonoma took over the leadership in total acres around 1875. In turn, Napa replaced Sonoma in acreage a decade later. Not only did Napa and Sonoma grow in size, but tasters noticed their wines were demonstrably superior simply because the climates of Sonoma and Napa were (and still are) distinctly cooler than those in the Los Angeles region.

Somewhat sadly, in terms of today's viticultural and wine-making successes, the delightfully colorful history of wine of early California is rather short-lived. In one sense, the wine business in California is only 30 or 40 years old. Unlike Europe and other New World wine-growing regions, which have enjoyed continuous gen-erations of wine making, we lived through a terrible break in our development—Prohibition—and had to start all over again.

Most of California's wineries shut down during Prohibition, though a few remained in operation to produce wine for sacramental and medicinal purposes. But in the years of temperance, the United States had all but lost whatever palate it had acquired for dry table wines. For 35 years after Prohibition, more than half the wine consumed in this country was dessert (a.k.a. "fortified") wine, so-called ports and sherries, which contain 18% to 20% alcohol and loads of sugar.

Of course, this perversion of good taste has since been reversed, but oddly so. Each wine generation has been dramatically shorter than its predecessor: The first lasted almost 100 years (1825–1919), the second (after the break for Prohibition) only 30 years (1934–1965), and the third just 15 years (1966–1980). From hereon the path swerves from wine making to growing grapes, and necessarily slows down, as the Wine Country has—albeit cautiously—hit its stride.

THE FIRST GENERATION (1825–1919)   This fascinating period in wine making involves the entangling of a variety of ethnic groups over several generations: Spanish Fathers, native Americans, European immigrants (the first settlers in Napa and Sonoma were mostly Germanic, followed later by Italians and French), and Chinese (the main labor force; even today you can see the miles of stone walls they built and visit caves they carved out with picks). One of the major struggles of this generation involved breaking away from the grape variety used by the missions (and therefore called "Mission"), but only a few growers possessed such vision: Count Agoston Haraszthy at Buena Vista, T. Belden Crane and Charles Krug in St. Helena, Jacob Schram at Schramsberg (a historical monument now making champagne), and, later, Gustaf Niebaum at Inglenook (now Niebaum-Coppola).

Between 1870 and 1890, Sonoma and Napa wines won medals with some frequency in international competitions; most of the region's wines, however, were not even bottled at the wineries but rather sold in bulk to merchants, who often blended them badly. Not infrequently, they were even labeled with European names for sale on the East Coast! Regardless, these years laid a solid basis for a regional wine industry: In 1889, Sonoma could claim around 100 wineries, Napa around 140.

Unbeknownst to wine makers, however, a disaster was in the works. A plant louse the size of a pinhead, *phylloxera vastatrix,* began attacking vineyards in the 1880s. As a result, Napa lost roughly 75% of its acreage in the 1890s.

The Looming Shadow of Prohibition   The business managed to hold its own after the turn of the century, only to encounter a far more formidable foe—the cries of Carrie Nation and the Temperance Movement, whose Prohibition stance had been gaining ground with the moral majority in the last decades of the 19th century. Even in Napa, the Anti-Saloon League made inroads with voters as early as 1912, 7 years before Prohibition became a national fact. During this dry era, the number of wineries dwindled from 600 to a few remaining stragglers. (Ironically, the grape acreage *exploded* to satisfy the need for home wine makers across the country who could legally make 200 gallons per household. Unfortunately, the thick-skinned grape varieties that ship well in railcars do not make fine wine.)

THE SECOND GENERATION (1934–1965)   Whoopee! After 13 years of speakeasies, bathtub gin, and phony sherry, Americans could legally drink real wine!

Well, not at first. The few hundred entrepreneurs who rushed in to make a killing in wine found they had essentially no market, and quickly went bankrupt. Americans had almost no interest in dry European-style table wines. A few producers who had made wine during the last years of Prohibition and aged it throughout the Prohibition period had some success. Growers such as Louis Martini and Cesare Mondavi had survived and flourished by shipping their grapes to home winemakers (legal during Prohibition), and were ready to start promoting their California wines in the late 1930s and early 1940s.

In trying to revive the wine business, one of the major battles was fought over varietal labeling—the labeling system we now take for granted that makes the name of the grape variety (Cabernet Sauvignon, Chardonnay, and so on) the most important word on the label after the name of the producer. All through the 19th century and fully into the 1960s, huge volumes of wine were called Burgundy, Chablis, Chianti, Rhine Wine, and such, referring wistfully to some vague growing region or type of grape, and usually delivering wine that only accidentally resembled the stated product. One grower argued vociferously against the new labeling because if the law passed, he would have to actually put some Riesling grapes in his wine labeled "Riesling." To him, Riesling was just a style or a marketing tool. Who cared if it actually tasted like Riesling?

It was a pretty grim era for American wine making in general, and California's Wine Country wasn't faring much better. In 1937, Napa had 37 wineries, while Sonoma was flush with 91. Collecting accurate statistics is a challenge, but apparently the number of Napa wineries decreased from 47 in 1945 to 25 in 1960. According to one source, only 12 wineries of those 25 made enough wine to sell outside of Napa County; the same source reports that Sonoma's count had dwindled to seven wineries in 1950 and grew only to nine by 1960. If these numbers are even close to reality, it's clear that recovery from Prohibition was painfully slow, backsliding a few times along the way.

Nonetheless, a handful of well-grounded wineries sailed through this sluggish period, and a few of their wines can still be appreciated today. Most came from Napa, including Inglenook, Beaulieu, Beringer, Christian Brothers, and Louis Martini. Sonoma, in contrast, had a stronger bulk wine-making tradition and a more casual attitude about the role of wine in the good life (subsequently, long-winded arguments have been—and probably always will be—held about the casual Italian-Sonoma approach versus the more northern-European, image-conscious, award-bent Napa approach).

Ironically, in recent years, Sonoma has been touting its ability to garner more gold medals. Whatever the significance of a wall festooned with ribbons and awards, Sonoma has certainly caught up with Napa when it comes to making fine wines.

THE THIRD GENERATION (1966–1980)   It's impossible to draw hard lines in the flow of time, but no other single event marks the modern era of wine making like Robert Mondavi's 1966 move away from Charles Krug, a family-owned winery since 1943, to found his own winery in Oakville. Joe Heitz had launched his own label in 1961 and, in Sonoma in 1959, James Zellerbach at tiny Hanzell had revived traditional Burgundian wine-making techniques. At around the same time, Peter Newton acquired the first land holdings for Sterling Vineyards. But unlike his peers in the field, Mondavi combined a push toward new wine-making technology with an aggressive marketing flair that has grown ever since, and now extends to several brands and international alliances.

Compared to previous generations of wine makers, third-generation vintners looked like grade-schoolers, a bunch of kids (many of whom were graduates of U.C. Davis or Fresno State) in playgrounds filled with new toys: stainless-steel tanks, small oak barrels, a panoply of yeast cultures to ferment their wines, new vineyards planted to the best grape varieties, and, in several senses, the freedom to play and experiment. In 1972 and 1973, a remarkable cluster of wineries came on the Napa scene: Chateau Montelena, Clos du

Val, Burgess Cellars, Mt. Veeder Vineyards, Silver Oak, Caymus, Diamond Creek, Stag's Leap Wine Cellars, Carneros Creek, Franciscan, Silver Oak, Trefethen, Clos du Val, Stonegate, Joseph Phelps, and Domaine Chandon. These seasoned players now share a quarter of a century of wine-making experience—and the beginnings of a legacy.

In Sonoma Valley, Kenwood, Chateau St. Jean, and St. Francis all sprang up in the early 1970s. For these wineries, and the many that followed, the 1970s can be considered the decade that wine makers discovered their styles of wine. With all the new wine-making equipment and new vineyards, styles changed almost annually: one year a crisp, appley Chardonnay with moderate oak; the next, a very fleshy, soft wine dominated by a heavy oak bouquet. In the third year, a third style. The poor consumer took a wild ride through these years, but as wine makers matured, their styles stabilized.

Napa and Sonoma had often compared their wines with international benchmarks, and favorably so. The French pooh-poohed the comparison; that is, until an English wine merchant staged a tasting in Paris in 1976. There, French wine experts on French soil gave top places in a blind tasting to the Chardonnay from Chateau Montelena, as well as the Cabernet from Stag's Leap Wine Cellars. The results shocked France and tickled the California Wine Country. At last, they were approaching the big leagues.

THE FOURTH GENERATION (1980–present)   The most recent phases of change in the Wine Country have been marked by signs of caution—both in the vineyard and in the marketplace—mingled with a few fantastic vintages. Since 1990, we have lived in a golden age of good vintages and astonishing sales, especially for more expensive wines ranging from $50 to $150 per bottle. Throughout the 1980s and 1990s, the number of new labels has grown steadily, as if there were no problems and never will be. Wine creates optimists, and always has.

Wine sales leveled off in the early 1980s, when both Napa and Sonoma vintners discovered that phylloxera, scourge louse of the 1880s and 1890s, had returned, requiring replanting of most acreage in both counties. (Actually, phylloxera was never really exterminated; it's permanently in the soil. Rather, the solution to fix the problem went awry.) The prospects of pulling out 70% to 80% of the vines hit growers and wineries hard, both emotionally and financially. A vineyard is a long-term investment, taking 30 to 40 years to fully mature—and that's only if nature, always a temperamental partner, behaves. Add to that the staggering costs—$20,000 to $25,000 per acre to plant a vineyard—and you'd best tell your banker you need another $2,000 per year per acre just to cover farming costs before you get a full crop in 4 or 5 years. Most growers worked out the financing, and by the late 1990s, over half of the replanting had been finished. Now, with thousands of acres coming on stream, a few voices talk about overproduction. Welcome to the ever-cyclical wine business.

While Napa and Sonoma make both white wines and red wines extremely well, the 1990s saw a breakthrough in the styling of reds, a higher level style change than those of the 1970s and early 1980s. Using a couple of techniques that you'll likely hear discussed on tours (for example, "presoaking" and "extended maceration"), wine makers are coming up with richly flavored wines that are supple and approachable, even when young. One enthusiast of the new style, Dennis Johns at St. Clement Vineyards, says he wants his red wines to be "sweet, round, and juicy, even in the barrel." Don't look for these wines to have true sweetness. The difference lies in their having a very fine grade of tannin, which in the past could make wines so puckery they went down like liquid nails. If a decade ago you were ever turned off by red wines, it's time to retaste—and hopefully, enjoy.

2 Wine Making 101

In the flush of today's golden age of California's Wine Country, one might forget that California, let alone Napa and Sonoma, did not invent wine. Credit for this discovery goes to a woman who probably lived around 7,000 years ago: At least one cultural anthropologist suggests that a cave-dwelling woman brought into her cave clusters of wild grapes and put them in a concavity on a rock ledge. Her child, or children, walked over them a few times (or, worse, sat on them), breaking open many berries. The busy cave keeper neglected the grapes for a few days. When she finally noticed the pool of juice (caves *are* dark, after all), it was frothing and giving off strange, but not unpleasant, aromas. It's hard to imagine why she would cup the juice in her hand and drink it, but she did—and it affected her most strangely. Let's assume it was pleasantly tasty, if not a little bit too sweet. In any case, she'd discovered wine—and Sonoma and Napa, as well as the rest of the world, owe her a debt of gratitude.

Amazingly, her techniques saw only a few improvements in the next millennia. First, wine makers learned that wine must be stored in sealed containers—clay amphora or wooden barrels—or it spoils, turning into vinegar. Second, cool storage also prevents spoilage, hence the use of caves and cellars. The wines of the Greeks and Romans were probably as good, or as bad, as those made by monks in the Middle Ages, and only a bit improved by secular wine makers from the Renaissance to the Industrial Revolution.

The science called "enology," which has given the world the highest overall quality of wine ever, was developed after Louis Pasteur's work with fermentation and bacteriology around 150 years ago. Only in the last few generations have wine makers acquired very technical training and earned PhDs in viticulture (the science of grape growing) in a concentrated effort to understand wine and vineyards.

Even with this recent development of science applied to wine, the catch phrase today for many wine makers in Sonoma and Napa is "I want the wine to make itself." The desired image is wine maker as midwife, whose role is to merely assist the mother (grape) in a very natural process—not much different from the cave dweller and her young assistants. It sounds so simple: 1) harvest ripe grapes; 2) put the juice from the grapes in a container with some yeast; 3) watch the juice ferment into wine; 4) clarify and age the new wine; and 5) drink!

Obviously, making wine is much more complex than that. From arguing about the very meaning of "ripe" to controlling the "ferment" in order to affect flavors and textures of the wine, the contemporary "natural" wine maker must incorporate his or her knowledge of fermentation, microbiology, and even such vagaries as the proper barrel (French, American, or Hungarian oak) for aging. These wine makers enjoy the powerful position of being able to make wine simply, naturally, and without spoilage simply because they know, scientifically, what can go wrong. Our cave dweller didn't have a clue.

On your tours of wineries, you'll hear differing stories about the "right" way to make wine, for each vintner harbors strong opinions—almost like a creed—on his or her wine styling. Be prepared for some inconsistencies; ferreting them out can be half the fun. To help you sort through the claims, here's a brief but broad sketch of the ABCs for making white wines, red wines, and sparkling wines.

WHITE WINES   For white wines, the wine maker wants only the juice from the grapes. (For red wines, both the juice and skins of the grapes are essential; using the white wine–making technique, you can make a *white* wine from a *red-skinned grape*—White Zinfandel, for example.) Grapes are picked either by hand or machine and brought to the winery as quickly as possible. Just as a sliced apple turns brown when left on the kitchen counter, grapes oxidize—and can even start fermenting—if not processed quickly. At some wineries, the clusters go through a "destemmer-crusher," which pops the berries off their stems and breaks them open (not really crushing them). The resulting mixture of juices, pulp, and seeds—called "must"—is pumped to a press. At other wineries, the whole clusters are put directly into a press (a new and widely used technique called, logically, "whole cluster pressing").

Most presses these days use an inflatable member, like a balloon, and gently use air pressure to separate the skins from the juice, which is then pumped into fermenting vessels. In the recent past, most white wines were fermented in stainless-steel tanks fitted with cooling jackets. Cool, even cold, fermentations preserve the natural fruitiness of white grapes. More recently, many Napa and Sonoma producers have begun using small wooden barrels for fermentation of white wines, especially Chardonnay. This practice reverts to old-style French wine-making techniques, and captures, so it's believed, fragrances, flavors, and textures not possible in stainless steel. Barrel fermentation is labor intensive (each only holds 45 to 50 gal. for fermentation), and the barrels are expensive ($600 to $700 each for French barrels, $250 to $300 for American barrels).

After white wines are fermented, they are clarified, aged (if appropriate), and bottled, usually before the next harvest. For the simpler white wines—Chenin Blanc, Riesling, and some Sauvignon Blancs—bottling occurs in the late winter or early spring. Most Sauvignon Blancs and Chardonnays go into the bottle during the summer after the harvest. A few white wines, usually Chardonnays, take the slow track and enjoy 15 to 18 months of aging in small barrels with prolonged aging on the lees, the sediments from the primary fermentation. Those treatments are unusual, but they produce Chardonnays that are richly flavored, complex, and expensive.

RED WINES　The chief difference between white wines and red wines lies simply in the red pigment that's lodged in the skins of the wine grapes. So while for white wines the juice is quickly pressed away from the skins, for rosés and reds the pressing happens after the right amount of "skin contact." That can be anywhere from 6 hours—yielding a rosé or very light red—to 6 weeks, producing a red that has extracted all the pigment from the skins and additionally refined the tannin naturally occurring in grape skins and seeds.

Almost all red wines are aged in barrels or casks for at least several months, occasionally for as long as 3 years. In the past, casks in California were usually made from redwood and were quite large (5,000 gal. to 25,000 gal.). Only a few wineries still use redwood today. Most of the wooden containers—collectively called "cooperage"—are barrels now made of American or French oak, holding roughly 60 gallons each.

The aging of red wines plays an important role in their eventual style, because several aspects of the wine change while in wood. First, the wine picks up oak fragrances and flavors (yes, it is possible to "overoak" a wine). Second, the wine, which comes out of the fermenter murky with suspended yeast cells and bits of skin, clarifies as the particulate material settles to the bottom of the barrel. Third, the texture of the wine changes as puckery compounds called "tannins" interact and round off, making the wine more supple. Deciding just when each wine in the cellar is ready to bottle challenges the wine maker every year. And, to make the whole process even more challenging, every year is different.

Unlike white wines, which are usually ready to drink shortly after bottling, many of the best red wines will improve with aging in the bottle. Napa and Sonoma Cabernet Sauvignons, for example, often reach a plateau (try not to think "peak") of best drinking condition that ranges from 7 to 12 years after the vintage, the year that appears on the label. However, there are no rigid rules. Some self-proclaimed Cabernet freaks prefer their reds rather rough and ready. Only by tasting, tasting, tasting will you find your own comfort zone. Such a trial!

SPARKLING WINE & CHAMPAGNE   In Sonoma and Napa, sparkling wine plays the role of a serious specialty—serious enough to have drawn major investments from four of the best-known French houses from Champagne as well as two from Spain, in addition to 10 or 12 local producers.

Whether the bubbly wine in the fancily dressed bottle is called "sparkling wine" or "champagne" (it *is* legal for wineries in America to call their product "champagne," though it galls the French, pun intended), the key to the pervasive high quality of all these wineries lies in their using the *méthode champenoise* as their production technique. In Champagne, it takes the form of step-by-step regulations that, for the most part, codify practices learned by trial and error for making the best wine. Those regulations have no force here, but the best producers follow most of them and put the words "méthode champenoise" on their labels. For quality assurance, those are the words to look for (as opposed to "bulk" or "Charmat" process).

There is no better way to understand the fascinatingly intricate "champagne method" than to see it firsthand, to walk through the process with a knowledgeable guide. The harvest begins in August in Napa and Sonoma with the picking of Pinot Noir, Chardonnay, Pinot Blanc, and Pinot Meunier, the grape varieties of champagne. The grapes are picked a bit underripe by "still" (nonbubbly) wine standards, both to retain crispness and to avoid excessive body and flavors. The grapes are then pressed and the juice fermented into plain—austere, in fact—still white wines. That takes 2 weeks. By November and December, the new wines (each variety and vineyard kept as a separate lot) are clear, or "bright."

Now the wine makers *really* go to work, because they need to blend the new wines in preparation for a second fermentation—this one taking place right in the bottle, the very bottle that eventually comes to your table. That's how we get the bubbles.

The second fermentation takes 4 to 6 weeks. After that, we have primitive champagne, 90 to 100 pounds per square inch of carbon dioxide (CO_2) in each bottle. And we also have a yeasty sediment in each bottle. That's a bit of a mess and must be cleaned up eventually. But for now—and perhaps for as long as 3 to 7 years—it's a benign mess. Yeast plays two virtuous roles in making sparkling wine: first, it produces the bubbles; second, as the dead yeast cells decompose over time, they release flavor products that give sparkling wines made by méthode champenoise their special fragrances and flavors. The amount and depth of flavor varies widely from producer to producer. Each house has its own style, light or heavy, and tries to replicate it each year. That's why people say, "I'm a Mumm drinker," or "I'm a fan of Krug."

Making fine sparkling wine, and making it well, constitutes the ultimate wine-making challenge. The general rule among wine makers is that great white wines and great red wines are derived mostly from their place of origin: the right grape planted in the right soil and right climate. Sparkling wine involves artifice and finesse at every step, making it all the more remarkable that we drink it so freely, at times even carelessly. But the producers wouldn't have it any other way—if only we would drink more of it.

GROWING GRAPES

Somehow wine making seems much more glamorous than growing grapes. Growing grapes is farming; it's dusty and hard manual labor.

In contrast, wine making is almost ethereal (except for rolling and stacking barrels around and hosing grape skins out of the press).

In truth, most wine makers in Sonoma and Napa spend more time in the vineyards than at the winery. It took 20 or 30 years to learn that quality starts, absolutely, in the vineyard, and that the wine maker can do nothing to compensate for bad fruit. There's simply so much to learn about wine making that decisions can be revised, even reversed, annually; not so with vineyard decisions.

MODERN GROWING AS GARDENING   Just as wine makers had worked their way up the learning curve for wine making, and as winery owners had turned to acquiring vineyards as the next source of quality control, everyone in the Wine Country learned that the *phylloxera vastatrix,* a soil-based plant louse, would be wiping out most of the vineyards, just as it had done a century ago, first in Europe and then in California (for more on this, see "A Look at the Past" earlier in this chapter). The "fix" was to plant rootstocks that resisted phylloxera and to graft desirable grape varieties above the soil, which worked for several decades.

Unfortunately, it seems that the choice for the principal rootstock was somewhat vulnerable, or phylloxera mutated and developed new appetites, or perhaps a combination of both occurred. Since the mid-1980s, replanting has been a major focus, almost a preoccupation. In hindsight, phylloxera might be seen as a small (but enormously expensive) blessing. It has indeed refocused our attention to the soil; it's no exaggeration to say that today much of the excitement in Napa and Sonoma lies in the vineyards. And we're showing that farming here isn't agribusiness; rather, it could almost be called microfarming. Warren Winiarski, founder of Stag's Leap Wine Cellars, eloquently insists that for himself and the others in Napa, grape growing is not agriculture, it's horticulture-gardening.

As you drive through Sonoma and Napa, you'll pass hundreds of experimental "gardens." If you look closely at the shape of the vines, the density of the planting, the height of the trellis system, even the orientation to the compass, you'll perceive a playground in the earth just as the wine makers of the 1970s had a playground of fancy wine-making toys. It's too early to assess the results of this replanting, but the "silver lining" attitude common to farming sees higher grape quality than ever, and thus higher wine quality.

CLIMATE CONTROL   Because you will visit the Wine Country for a day or two in one particular season, you might want to know how the Wine Country looks in other seasons. While the climate is benign, the changes from season to season still have a drama about them. In the winter, the rainy season in Mediterranean climates, the nights can be cold, dropping to 30°F to 40°F, but a sunny winter day sees highs in the 60s—picnic weather if you're wearing a light wool sweater.

Winter also can be confused with spring elsewhere. Camellias might bloom on New Year's Day, azaleas shortly thereafter, along with the blue and yellow acacias. From December through April, the vines are dormant, stark outlines of trunks and arms, but the valley floors and hillside are lush green with common weeds and a few seeded ground covers. One of the common weeds is mustard: In good years, you'll find acres and acres of bright-yellow mustard, celebrated each season with the Napa Valley Mustard Festival.

The vines burst from dormancy in mid-March for the earliest varieties (Chardonnay, Pinot Noir, Gewürztraminer) and in April for the later blooming varieties (Cabernet Sauvignon, Zinfandel). The growth is rapid, sometimes almost an inch a day. Until mid-May, there's a danger of frost. By late May and early June, the new shoots, called "canes," have grown 3 or 4 feet in length; flower clusters start to blossom. The success of the "bloom and set," as it's called, makes for some nervous moments: uncontrollable elements such as hot weather and rain can compromise the crop. But, especially compared with the vagaries of weather in continental Europe, the benign Mediterranean weather goes sour only occasionally.

In midsummer, usually around late July, the first signs of color show up in red grape varieties, a pretty blush at first that in a couple weeks becomes a deep purple, a sure sign that the grapes are ripening. White grapes change from a lime green to a golden green as they ripen. They get delectably sweeter and sweeter until the wine maker decides they are ripe for the picking, as the saying goes.

From August through October, you'll probably see every available hand in the Wine Country harvesting the grapes. For a single vineyard it takes only a day—perhaps just a few hours—to pick the grapes, since they need to be as fresh and cool as possible. Once the grapes are harvested, the vines hopefully have the chance to grow for a few more weeks, now storing energy in the form of carbohydrates that will sustain them to the next spring.

After cold nights in November and December, the first winter rains knock and blow the vibrant-colored leaves off the vines, which then go dormant until March and April, when they'll start the cycle again.

THE LIFE OF THE VINE   Unless soil problems or vineyard pests intervene, a vineyard should have a commercial life of 30 to 40 years. In Sonoma, a number of producing vineyards are approaching the 100-year mark, and though the quantity of the harvest falls off in old vines, the quality seems to improve. As the Italian proverb goes, "You plant a vineyard for your son; you plant an olive grove for your grandson." Regardless of the latest technological advances in viticulture, vineyards will not be rushed—which gives much-needed consolation to grape growers, and a sense of permanence to the Wine Country.

3   How to Wine-Taste Like a Pro

Stopping at tasting rooms to sample the goods, otherwise known as wine tasting, ranks as one of the top rituals in Wine Country touring. It provides pleasure for everyone, as well as the chance to learn why the wines of Sonoma and Napa rank high among the wines of the world.

Precautionary notes would say "taste moderately," for there are literally 200 or so tasting rooms, and the virtues in wine take time to notice. Most of the attendants in tasting rooms know that, generally speaking, Americans drink very little wine (20% of the population drinks over 80% of the wine consumed). Because we're all on a very pleasant learning curve, our goal as wine educators is to help you discover wine at many levels. If you should encounter a winery staffer with "attitude" (unfortunately, it happens), don't buy *any* of that wine and simply move on to the next stop.

The time-honored techniques for tasting wine involve three steps: a good look, a good smell, and a good sip of each wine. You'll learn about wine most quickly if you compare them, ideally side by side. Almost any comparison will reveal features of wines you might not see by tasting one wine at a time. You might think of it as the wines talking to one another ("I'm smoother than you are"; "I'm way more puckery than all of you"). By listening to these little conversations, you can discover just how smooth or how puckery you want your wines to be. Tasting rooms in Napa and Sonoma have their own regimens, usually offering a series of wines. When it seems appropriate, and when the tasting room is not too busy, ask your host if you can do some comparisons.

THE VISUALS OF WINE

Take a moment to look at the wine for its clarity and for its hue. With just a couple of glances, you'll see that red wines reveal many shades of red: ruby, garnet, purple, and variations. White wines also differ in hue, from white gold to straw to dark gold, sometimes laced with a light green. For the most part, wines ought to be clear, even brilliant, though a few unfiltered wines now bear a light haze as a badge of courage that says, "I was not heavily filtered." (Filtration for clarification is standard practice and benign if not overdone.)

Color can be a sign of a wine's condition, of its health, even of its age. White wines that show any browning might be going "over the hill" and have a musty, baked smell. Red wines that show a lot of rusty red might also be past their prime, while reds that show a lot of purple are probably young.

THE AROMAS & BOUQUET OF WINE

Some wine professionals will tell you the olfactory aspect of wine is more important than the taste. Saner heads remind you that wine is a *beverage,* not a perfume; it comes home to rest in the mouth. It's true that our noses work better as tools of perception than our mouths. We can smell several thousand scents, but can taste only four: sweet, sour, bitter, and salty. But it's also true that we smell the wine (via the retro nasal passages) when it passes through our mouths.

A decently shaped wineglass will direct a lot of aromas to your nose. Swirling the glass helps excite the fragrances. Comparing the "nose" of two or three wines can be very revealing, but possibly a bit frustrating, too: You "see" differences with your nose, but might stumble when you try to describe them. The words are on the tip of your tongue, if there at all. What comes to mind may seem silly: "apple," "coconut," "cherries," "mushrooms," "dirt," "cheese," and the like.

If this is the case, then you've hit the Wall of Wine Tasting: **vocabulary.** It's not easy to describe the fragrances and flavors in wine. We are mostly reduced to similes and metaphors, to comparing wines with more familiar substances. A lot of wine writing is inadvertently humorous; some of it qualifies as bad poetry. That's neither your fault *nor* the fault of the wine. We must simply get over the inadequacies of language to describe wine—and get on with our tasting. Have fun with your verbal fantasies!

For all the ambiguity in wine descriptors, the words "aroma" and "bouquet" do possess widely recognized, distinct meanings (though on the street we use them almost interchangeably). **Aroma** points to the characteristic smell of the various grape varieties, which can be quite distinct. Just as you would probably not confuse a Pippin apple with a Golden Delicious, once you are familiar with Sauvignon

Blanc, it will not remind you of Chardonnay. **Bouquet,** in the academy of wine, refers to fragrances that come from sources other than the grapes, such as the vanillalike fragrance of French oak.

During your trip to the Wine Country, you can learn the basics of aroma simply by comparing a Sauvignon Blanc side by side with a Chardonnay. Or, in terms of bouquet, a younger Cabernet beside an older Cabernet. Not every tasting room will be able to arrange all the comparisons, but you will find many opportunities.

THE TASTE OF WINE

Tasting wine—literally putting it through our mouths—can be seen as something quite different from *drinking* other beverages. (Of course, we can drink wine, too. Indeed, *most* of the time we should just drink wine.) Tasting, as opposed to drinking, has built-in dynamics. In fact, it helps to focus on the wine moving through the mouth: something that happens in a measured sequence, like listening to a musical phrase. It's not like taking a snapshot— "Click, I've got it."

One of the legendary tasters in California at the turn of the century, Henry Lachman, merchant and international judge of wines, wrote a monograph in which he discussed each sip of wine as having "a first taste, a second taste, and the good-bye." That's a cute way of dealing with the physiology of our mouths: In the front of the mouth we taste for **sweetness** and **feel the body** of the wine; in the middle we find **acidity** and the **flavors** of the grape; and in the back, the **finish** or "good-bye," which can be long or short, supple or astringent. Imagine a tasting as having checkpoints in your mouth: front, middle, and back.

In the abstract, wine dynamics sound odd. With practice, however, especially as you compare the taste of two or three wines, they become obvious, and the observational skills quite easy to pick up. After you see how a wine can be full and lush in the front of your mouth, then turn fresh and tasty, and finally linger nicely (or fail to linger), it remains for you to decide what "shapes" you prefer in your wines.

Red wines in particular show fairly clear **shapes.** One of the additional challenges in tasting red wines lies in knowing that the shape changes with age. Rough, puckery young red wines can age into supple, subtly flavorful, pleasing liquids. Which red wines will age well and over what period of time is, again, something you can learn by comparison. It's best done by arranging a "vertical" tasting: several vintages of the same wine. ("Horizontal" tastings are several producers tasted from the same vintage.) Even three to five wines from vintages spread over, say, 10 years will give you a good idea of how much age you want to have on your red wines. Tasting rooms often have "Reserve" wines or "Library" wines that you can acquire for tasting.

Tastings of several wines—either vertical or horizontal tastings—make for marvelous evenings of gourmandizing when you return home. Have a few friends over to taste the wines "blind" (without labels visible). Get everyone's preference. Then sit down to dinner and finish them off, now with the labels in full view. Inevitably, opinions will change, often in amusing reversals.

It's up to you to decide how seriously you want to engage the Wine Country. If it's a first visit, consider it an introduction. You can't do it all in a single visit, of course, which is all the more reason to schedule a return trip to the Wine Country.

Finally, two important tips for a healthy day in the Wine Country: Be moderate in your wine tasting and generous in drinking water. Cheers!

4 The Wine Country's Major Grape Varieties

by Erika Lenkert and Matthew R. Poole

MAJOR GRAPE VARIETIES

CABERNET SAUVIGNON This transplant from Bordeaux has become California's most well-known varietal. The small, deep-colored, thick-skinned berry is a complex grape, yielding medium- to full-bodied red wines that are highly tannic when young and usually require a long aging period to achieve their greatest potential. Cabernet is often blended with other related red varieties, such as Merlot and Cabernet Franc (see below), into full-flavored red table wines. Cabernet, whose most distinctive character is a lush black-currant aroma, is best matched with red-meat dishes and strong cheeses. If you're looking to invest in several cases of wine, Cabernet Sauvignon is always a good long-term bet.

CHARDONNAY Chardonnay is the most widely planted grape variety in the Wine Country, producing exceptional medium- to full-bodied dry white wines. In fact, it was a California Chardonnay that revolutionized the world of wine when it won the legendary Paris tasting test of 1976, beating out France's top white Burgundies.

You'll find a range of Chardonnays in the Wine Country, from delicate, crisp wines that are clear and light in color to buttery, fruity, and oaky (no other wine benefits more from the oak aging process) wines that tend to have deeper golden hues as they increase in richness. This highly complex and aromatic grape is one of the few grapes in the world that doesn't require blending; it's also the principal grape for making sparkling wine. Chardonnay goes well with a variety of dishes, from seafood to poultry, pork, veal, and pastas made with cream and/or butter.

MERLOT   Traditionally used as a blending wine to smooth out the rough edges of other grapes, Merlot has gained popularity in California since the early 1970s—enough so that wineries such as Sonoma's St. Francis are best known for producing masterful Merlots. The Merlot grape is a relative of Cabernet Sauvignon, but it's fruitier and softer with a pleasant black-cherry bouquet. Merlots tend to be simpler and less tannic than most Cabernets and drinkable at an earlier age, though these wines, too, gain complexity with age. Serve this medium- to full-bodied red with any dish you'd normally pair with a Cabernet (it's great with pizza).

PINOT NOIR   It has taken California vintners decades to make relatively few great wines from Pinot-Noir grapes, which are difficult to grow and vinify. Even in their native Burgundy, the wines are excellent only a few years out of every decade, and are a challenge for wine makers to master. Recent attempts to grow the finicky grape in the cooler climes of the Carneros District have met with promising results. During banner harvest years, California's Pinot grapes produce complex, light- to medium-bodied red wines with such low tannins and such silky textures that they're comparable to the finest reds in the world. Pinots are fuller and softer than Cabernets and can be drinkable at 2 to 5 years of age, though the best will improve with additional aging. Pinot Noir is versatile at the dinner table, but goes best with lamb, duck, turkey, game birds, and semisoft cheeses. It's also one of the few red wines that pairs well with many types of fish dishes.

RIESLING   Also called Johannisberg Riesling or White Riesling, this is the grape from which most of the great wines of Germany are made. It was introduced to California in the mid-19th century by immigrant vintners and is now used mainly to produce floral and fruity white wines of light to medium body, ranging from dry to very sweet (it's often used to make late-harvest dessert wine). Well-made

Rieslings, of which California has produced few, have a vivid fruitiness and lively balancing acidity, as well as a potential to age for many years. Suggested food pairings include crab, pork, sweet-and-sour foods, and anything with a strong citrus flavor. Asian-influenced foods also pair well with Riesling.

SAUVIGNON BLANC   Also labeled as **Fumé Blanc,** Sauvignon Blanc grapes are used to make crisp, dry whites of medium to light body that vary in flavor from slightly grassy to tart or fruity. The grape grows very well in the Wine Country, and has become increasingly popular due to its distinctive character and pleasant acidity; indeed, it has recently become a contender to the almighty Chardonnay. A few of California's premier makers of Sauvignon Blanc (at least in our opinion) are Grgich Hills, Matanzas Creek, and Cakebread. Because of their acidity, Sauvignon Blancs pair well with shellfish, seafood, salads, olive oil–based dishes, and vegetarian cuisine.

ZINFANDEL   Zinfandel is often called the "mystery" grape because its origins are uncertain. The first "Zinfandel" label appeared on California labels in the late 1800s; hence, it has come to be known as California's grape. In fact, most of the world's Zinfandel acreage is planted in Northern California, and some of the best Zinfandel grapes grow in cool coastal locations and on century-old vines up in the Gold Country. Zinfandel is by far the Wine Country's most versatile grape, popular as blush wine (the ever-quaffable **White Zinfandel,** a lighter, more fruity wine, usually served chilled), as dark, spicy, and fruity red wines, and even as a port. Premium Zins, such as those crafted by Ravenswood winery in Sonoma (the Wine Country's Zeus of Zins), are rich and peppery, with a lush texture and nuances of raspberries, licorice, and spice. Food-wise it's a free-for-all, though premium Zins go well with beef, lamb, venison, hearty pastas, pizza, and stews.

LESSER-KNOWN GRAPE VARIETIES

Here are also a few lesser-known grape varieties that you might encounter as you explore the Wine Country. In addition to these, California's wine makers are beginning to experiment with a number of French varietals from the Rhône region and the Italian **sangiovese** grape with some success.

CABERNET FRANC   A French black grape variety that's often blended with and overshadowed by the more widely planted Cabernet Sauvignon, Cabernet Franc was actually recently discovered to be one of the parent grape species that gave rise to Cabernet

Sauvignon. The grape grows best in cooler, damper climatic conditions and tends to be lighter in color and tannins than Cabernet Sauvignon and therefore matures earlier in the bottle; these wines have a deep purple color with a herbaceous aroma.

CHENIN BLANC   Mainly planted in France, Chenin Blanc runs the gamut from cheap, dry whites with little discernible character to some of the most subtle, fragrant, and complex whites in the world. In the Wine Country, the grape is mostly used to create fruity, light- to medium-bodied and slightly sweet wines. Chenin Blanc lags far behind Chardonnay and Sauvignon Blanc in popularity here, though in good years it's known for developing a lovely and complex bouquet, particularly when aged in oak. It's often served with pork and poultry, Asian dishes with soy-based sauces, mild cheeses, and vegetable and fruit salads.

GEWÜRZTRAMINER   The Gewürztraminer grape produces white wines with a strong floral aroma and lychee nut–like flavor. Slightly sweet yet spicy, it's somewhat similar in style to the Johannisberg Riesling, and is occasionally used to make late-harvest dessert-style wine. The grape grows well in the cooler coastal regions of California, particularly Mendocino County.

PETITE SIRAH   Widely grown throughout the warmer regions of California, Petite Sirah's origins remain a mystery. The grape, which produces rich red wines high in tannins, serves mainly as the backbone for Central Valley "jug" wines. Very old vines still exist in cooler northern regions, where the grapes are often made into a robust and well-balanced red wine of considerable popularity.

PINOT BLANC   A mutation of the Pinot-Gris vine, the Pinot-Blanc grape is generally grown in France's Alsace region to make dry, crisp white wines. In California, Pinot Blanc is used to make a fruity wine similar to the simpler versions of Chardonnay. It's also blended with champagne-style sparkling wines thanks to its acid content and clean flavor.

SYRAH   This red varietal is best known for producing France's noble and age-worthy Rhône Valley reds such as Côte-Rôtie and Hermitage. California is just starting to plant new vineyards and importing wine makers who can tame the tannins and coax out Syrah's earthy flavors. Syrah vines produce dark, blackish berries with thick skins, resulting in typically dark, rich, dense, medium- to full-bodied wines with distinctive pepper, spice, and fruit flavors (particularly cherry, black currant, and blackberry).

3

Planning a Trip to the Wine Country

*I*n the pages that follow, we've compiled everything you need to know to plan your trip—how to get there, the best times to go, how much you can expect to spend, strategies for touring the region, and more. If you're visiting from outside the United States, be sure to check out section 5, "For Foreign Visitors," for entry requirements and other pertinent information.

1 Visitor Information

There's so much to see and do in the Wine Country that it's best to familiarize yourself with what's available before you start your trip. Both Napa and Sonoma offer very informative visitor guides that provide information on everything each valley has to offer.

The slick, comprehensive *Napa Valley Guide* includes listings and photos of hotels, restaurants, and hundreds of wineries, as well as hours of operation, tasting fees, and picnicking information. The **Napa Valley Conference and Visitors Bureau,** 1310 Town Center Mall, Napa, CA 94559 (☎ 707/226-7459), offers a $10 package that includes the guide plus a bunch of brochures, a map, a *Four Perfect Days in The Wine Country Itinerary,* and hot-air balloon discount coupons. If you want less to recycle, call **Vintage Publications,** 2929 Conifer Court, Napa, CA 94558 (☎ 800/651-8953), to mail-order just the guide ($6, plus $3 for shipping within the U.S.). If you don't want to pay the bucks for the official publications, point your browser to **www.napavalley.com/nvcvb.html**, the NVCVB's official site, which has lots of the same information for free.

Like the town itself, the *Sonoma Valley Visitors Guide* is far less fancy—no glossy photos, and far less information. But the free pocket-size booklet does offer important lodging, winery, and restaurant details; contact the **Sonoma Valley Visitors Bureau,**

10 E. Spain St., Sonoma, CA 95476 (☎ **707/996-1090**), to order one, or check out their Web site at **www.sonomavalley.com**.

2 When to Go

THE SEASONS   The beauty of the valley is striking at any time of the year, but it's most memorable in **September** and **October,** when the grapes are being pressed and the wineries are in full production. Another great time to come is **spring,** when the mustard flowers are in full bloom and the tourist season is just starting; you'll find less traffic, fewer crowds at the wineries and restaurants, and better deals on hotel rooms. While **winter** promises the best budget rates and few crowds, it often comes with chilly days and the threat of rain; the valleys, while still lovely, become less picturesque as miles of bare vines lay dormant over the cold months. **Summer?** Say hello to hot weather and lots of traffic.

THE CLIMATE   While the valleys claim a year-round average temperature of 70°F, if you come with a suitcase packed with T-shirts and shorts during the holiday season, you're likely to shiver your way to the nearest department store to stock up on winter clothes. In summer, rent a car without air-conditioning, and you're liable to want to make a pit-stop at every hotel swimming pool you pass. And don't let that morning fog and those early cool temperatures fool you; on most days, come noon, that big ol' ball of flames in the sky sends down plenty of rays to bless the vineyards and your picnic spot. For the most comfortable experience no matter what time of year, dress in layers and keep in mind that the temperature can drop dramatically at night.

Average Seasonal Temperatures

	Spring (Mar–May)	Summer (June–Aug)	Fall (Sept–Nov)	Winter (Dec–Feb)
Average Highs (in °F)	78	92	85	72
Average Lows (in °F)	64	81	74	61

Packing Tip

If you're visiting the Wine Country between December and March, be sure to pack an umbrella and a pair of durable walking shoes. The rainy season isn't usually fierce, but it is wet.

Festivities to Plan Your Trip Around:
The Wine Country's Best Annual Events

A few years back, February and March were considered the slow season in Napa. So, to drum up interest in visiting the valley, the **Napa Valley Mustard Festival** was born. The idea was to celebrate the blossom of the mustard flowers that coat the valley and mountains with their rich yellow petals—and of course, to generate a few dollars along the way. The result is 6 weeks' worth of events ranging from a kick-off gourmet gala featuring more than a dozen local restaurants at the CIA Greystone to a wine auction, golf benefit, recipe and photography competition, and plenty of food and wine celebrations. For information or a schedule of events, call ☎ **707/259-9020,** point your browser to **www.winery.com/ mustardfest,** or write to P.O. Box 3603, Yountville, CA 94599.

The **Napa Valley Wine Auction,** held each June, is the area's most renowned event. The annual charity affair brings close to 2,000 deep-pocketed wine aficionados to the Napa area. The schedule includes a weekend of culinary events, barrel tastings, a live auction, and a vintners' ball. But don't pack your bags yet: tickets to the event are $2,000 per couple—and they sell out every year. For information, call ☎ **707/963-3388.**

One of our favorite festivals in the Sonoma Valley is the **Heart of the Valley Barrel Tasting,** held in late March. This event, born 8 years ago to give the public a glimpse of Sonoma Valley's finest

3 Money Matters

WHAT THINGS COST IN THE WINE COUNTRY

North America's recent economic prosperity has made wine drinkers and high-lifers feel like celebrating again—and northern California's Wine Country is one of their favorite places to do it. Unfortunately, the region's ever-growing popularity has resulted in a reputation as one of the most expensive vacation destinations in the state. Nowadays, because hotels are booked almost year-round, innkeepers have the confidence to charge an average of $180 a night in Napa Valley, and things aren't much cheaper in the less touristy towns of Sonoma. It's gotten to the point where a charmless motel or a basic B&B can easily get $150 a night for a room.

And that's just the beginning. If you want to eat in any of the more renowned dining spots, you can pretty much count on shelling out future releases, has since turned into a 2-day-long fiesta of barbecues, food pairings, demonstrations, and all the world-class wine you can drink—all for only $25 a ticket. For details and this year's schedule, call the St. Francis Winery at ☎ **707/833-4666.**

Sonoma Valley's other major celebration is the Vintage Festival, held the last weekend in September at Sonoma's central plaza. This is a real blowout of a party, complete with live music, dancing, parades, arts-and-crafts shows, and—of course—copious wine tasting. Earlier in summer, Gundlach-Bundschu Winery presents its annual Shakespeare Festival, held Friday through Sunday from Memorial Day through Labor Day. You're encouraged to bring a blanket and picnic basket to the winery's outdoor amphitheater, which is set in a beautiful wooded area surrounded by vineyards; call the winery at ☎ **707/938-5277** for this year's schedule.

For more information on these and other Sonoma Valley events, contact the Sonoma Valley Visitors Bureau at ☎ **707/996-1090,** or check out their Web site at **www.sonomavalley.com**. If you want to find out what's going on in the Napa Valley when you're in town, contact the Napa Valley Conference and Visitors Bureau at ☎ **707/226-7459,** or point your browser to **www.napavalley. com/nvcvb.html**.

at least $35 per person just for food—not including even one glass of wine. And don't even think of stepping foot in a high-end haunt like the French Laundry without at least $90 per person to burn—and we're just talking lunch.

Is that cash register ringing in your head yet? Well, keep the tab open, 'cuz there's more. While some wineries offer free wine tastings, many—particularly in the Napa Valley—charge between $2 and $6; Niebaum-Coppola charges a whopping $7.50 per person. Stop by three or four in a day and—cha-ching!—they start to add up. Of course, you'll also want to buy a few bottles of your favorite vino. Cha-ching, cha-ching, cha-ching—it just keeps going. We're not telling you this to try to scare you away from the Wine Country; we just want you to know what to expect.

MONEY-SAVING TIPS   If you're starting to think that you just can't afford a Wine Country visit, don't despair yet: There are a few things you can do to keep your costs down and still enjoy the region to its fullest.

If you're on a budget, be sure to reserve your accommodations months in advance to secure the cheapest room; don't expect much more than a clean room and bed, and you won't be disappointed—but you're not planning to hang out in your room anyway, right? Other money-saving tips:

- **Travel between December and March,** when accommodations rates are at their lowest. Stay at a place whose rates include breakfast and afternoon hors d'oeuvres, which will save you big bucks on dining out.
- **Visit wineries that don't charge to taste;** plenty of wineries are happy to get you drunk without asking you for even one hard-earned cent.
- If you want to dine at one of the Wine Country's more expensive restaurants, **have a late lunch** there and make it the day's biggest meal. The lunch menu is often served until mid-afternoon, and main courses usually cost several dollars less than the same dishes at dinner.
- There's no better place to **picnic** than the Wine Country. Stop at a grocery or gourmet shop—each valley has lots of wonderful ones, which we've recommended in the chapters that follow—and pick up the picnic fixings for breakfast, lunch, or dinner. Head to one of the fabulous picnic spots we recommend, pop the cork on a bottle you've picked up in your travels, and you've got the perfect alfresco feast—for a fraction of what it would cost you to eat in a restaurant.
- **Buy wines from local wine shops,** not from the wineries. Believe it or not, prices in the shops are better, and they're likely to have that extra-buttery Chardonnay or that perfectly balanced Merlot that you fell in love with earlier in the day in stock. In Sonoma, your best bet is the **Wine Exchange,** on the plaza at 452 First St. E. (☎ **707/938-1794**), which boasts more than 700 domestic wines and a remarkably savvy staff. In Napa, head to St. Helena, where both **Dean & DeLuca,** 607 S. Main St. (☎ **707/ 967-9980**), and **Safeway,** 1026 Hunt Ave. (☎ **707/963-3833**), have enormous wine selections; Safeway tends to offer some of the best deals around.

LIVING THE HIGH LIFE　If you're not on a budget, we recommend you go for broke. Reserve a room at one of Napa's or

Sonoma's fabulous luxury resorts, such as St. Helena's Auberge du Soleil or the Kenwood Inn & Spa, and schedule massages twice a day; gorge yourself in gourmet fashion at the French Laundry, Pinot Blanc, and Tra Vigne; and drink yourself silly. The Wine Country may be hyped, but not without justification—there may be no place in the country that's more conducive to luxurious living.

PAYING YOUR WAY

Banks throughout the Napa and Sonoma valleys have automated teller machines (**ATMs**), which accept cards connected to networks like Cirrus and PLUS. For specific ATM locations, call ☎ **800/424-7787** for the Cirrus network, ☎ **800/843-7587** for the PLUS system. You also can locate Cirrus ATMs on the Web at **www.mastercard.com**, and PLUS ATMs at **www.visa.com**.

Traveler's checks are still the safest way to carry currency—Visa and American Express are the kinds most widely accepted. Wine Country businesses are pretty good about taking traveler's checks, but you're better off cashing them in at a bank (in small amounts, of course) and paying in cash. *Remember:* You'll need identification, such a driver's license or passport, to change a traveler's check. And be sure to record the numbers of the checks, and keep that information separate from your checks in the unlikely event that they get lost or stolen. Note that there are no American Express offices in either valley.

Rather than fussing with traveler's checks, it's easier to just use **credit cards**—most notably American Express, MasterCard, and Visa—which are almost as good as cash and are accepted in most Wine Country establishments. Also, ATMs will make cash advances against MasterCard and Visa cards; make sure you have your PIN (personal identification number) with you.

4 Getting There

BY PLANE

Commercial planes don't fly into Napa's private airport, so unless you're traveling by corporate jet, your best bet is to fly into either **San Francisco International Airport (SFO),** which is 60 minutes away by car, or **Oakland International Airport (OAK),** which is 45 miles south of Napa. It's pretty much the same deal for Sonoma; though **United Express** (☎ **800/241-6522**) accesses the Santa Rosa Airport (a few miles north of Sonoma) via San Francisco, you don't save time—or money—by taking the additional flight.

Both SFO and OAK airports are serviced by the following major domestic airlines:

Airline	Phone number	Web address
Alaska Airlines	☎ 800/426-0333	www.alaskaair.com
American Airlines	☎ 800/433-7300	www.americanair.com
America West Airlines	☎ 800/235-9292	www.americawest.com
Continental Airlines	☎ 800/525-0280	www.continental.com
Delta Air Lines	☎ 800/221-1212	www.delta-air.com
Northwest Airlines	☎ 800/225-2525	www.nwa.com
Southwest Airlines	☎ 800/435-9792	www.iflyswa.com
TWA	☎ 800/221-2000	www.twa.com
United Airlines	☎ 800/241-6522	www.ual.com
US Airways	☎ 800/428-4322	www.usair.com

Regardless of which airport you fly into, you should rent a car and drive to the Wine Country (see "By Car", below, for driving directions). Although for $18 you can hitch a ride to Napa Valley from SFO with **Evans Airport Service** (☎ **707/255-1559**), and the **Sonoma Airporter** (☎ **707/938-4246**) offers door-to-door service six times daily from SFO to hotels and inns in most areas of Sonoma ($28 for home pickup, $23 for standard downtown pickup locations), there's no public transportation in either valley, which makes it almost impossible to explore the region without wheels.

RENTING A CAR   All the major companies have desks at the airports. Currently, you can get a compact car for about $200 a week, including all taxes and other charges (but remember that rates are always subject to change). Some of the national car-rental companies operating in San Francisco include:

Airline	Phone number	Web address
Alamo	☎ 800/327-9633	www.goalamo.com
Avis	☎ 800/331-1212	www.avis.com
Budget	☎ 800/527-0700	www.drivebudget.com
Dollar	☎ 800/800-4000	www.dollarcar.com
Enterprise	☎ 800/325-8007	www.pickenterprise.com
Hertz	☎ 800/654-3131	www.hertz.com
National	☎ 800/227-7368	www.nationalcar.com
Thrifty	☎ 800/367-2277	www.thrifty.com

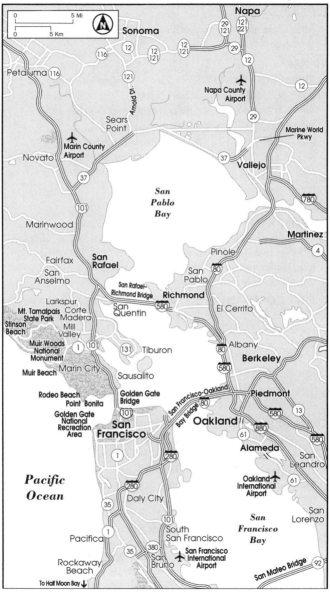

The San Francisco Bay Area

Napa

Sonoma

Petaluma

Arnold Dr.

Sears Point

Napa County Airport

Marine World Pkwy

Marin County Airport

Novato

Vallejo

San Pablo Bay

Martinez

Marinwood

Pinole

Fairfax

San Anselmo

San Rafael

San Pablo

Larkspur

San Rafael–Richmond Bridge

Richmond

El Cerrito

Corte Madera

San Quentin

Mt. Tamalpais State Park

Mill Valley

Stinson Beach

Muir Woods National Monument

Tiburon

Albany

Berkeley

Muir Beach

Marin City

Sausalito

Rodeo Beach

Point Bonita

Golden Gate Bridge

San Francisco–Oakland Bay Bridge

Piedmont

Golden Gate National Recreation Area

San Francisco

Oakland

Alameda

San Leandro

Pacific Ocean

Daly City

Oakland International Airport

San Lorenzo

Pacifica

South San Francisco

San Francisco Bay

Rockaway Beach

San Bruno

San Francisco International Airport

San Mateo Bridge

To Half Moon Bay ↓

0   5 Mi
0   5 Km

BY CAR

All of these routes are very well marked, with plenty of signs along the way.

TO NAPA

FROM SAN FRANCISCO   Cross the Golden Gate Bridge and go north on U.S. 101; turn east on Highway 37 (toward Vallejo), then north on Highway 29, the main road through Napa Valley.

FROM OAKLAND   Head eastbound on I-80 toward Sacramento; a few miles past the city of Vallejo (and after paying a $2 toll fee to cross the Carquinez Bridge), exit on Highway 12, which, after a few miles, intersects with Highway 29 and leads directly into Napa.

TO SONOMA

FROM SAN FRANCISCO   From San Francisco, cross the Golden Gate Bridge and stay on U.S. 101 north. Exit at Highway 37; after 10 miles, turn north onto Highway 121. After another 10 miles, turn north onto Highway 12 (Broadway), which will take you directly into the town of Sonoma.

FROM OAKLAND   Head eastbound on I-80 toward Sacramento. A few miles past the city of Vallejo (and after paying a $2 toll to cross the Carquinez Bridge), exit on Highway 12, which, after a few miles, intersects with Highway 29 at the southern foot of Napa Valley. Just before entering the city of Napa, you'll come to a major intersection, where Highway 29 meets Highway 12/121. Turn left onto Highway 12/121, which will take you directly to the Sonoma Valley.

CROSSING FROM VALLEY TO VALLEY

The easiest way to get from Napa to Sonoma and vice versa is to head to the southern end of either valley (the Carneros District) and cross over along the Sonoma Highway (Calif. 12/121). From Napa to Sonoma, the trip will take about 20 minutes, assuming there's no traffic. Another option is to take the Oakville Grade (a.k.a. Trinity Road) over the Mayacamas Range, which links Oakville in Napa with Glen Ellen in Sonoma. It's an extremely steep and windy road, but a real time-saver if you're headed to the northern end of either valley. There is a way to cross from Calistoga to the Sonoma Highway along Calistoga and St. Helena roads (at the northern end of Napa and Sonoma valleys), but the circuitous route takes so long that it isn't worth the effort.

5 For Foreign Visitors

BASIC ENTRY REQUIREMENTS

DOCUMENTS   The U.S. State Department has a **Visa Waiver Pilot Program** allowing citizens of certain countries to enter the United States without a visa for stays of up to 90 days. At press time, these included Andorra, Austria, Belgium, Brunei, Denmark, Finland, France, Germany, Iceland, Ireland, Italy, Japan, Liechtenstein, Luxembourg, Monaco, the Netherlands, New Zealand, Norway, San Marino, Spain, Sweden, Switzerland, and the United Kingdom. Citizens of these countries need only a valid passport and a round-trip air or cruise ticket in their possession upon arrival in the United States. Further information is available from any U.S. embassy or consulate. **Canadian citizens** may enter the United States without visas; they need only proof of residence.

Citizens of all other countries—including **Australia**—must have a **valid passport** with an expiration date at least 6 months later than the scheduled end of their visit to the United States, and a **tourist visa,** which may be obtained without charge from the nearest U.S. consulate. To obtain a visa, you must submit a completed application form (either in person or by mail) with a $1^{1}/_{2}$-inch-square photo, and demonstrate binding ties to a residence abroad. Usually you can obtain a visa at once or within 24 hours, but it may take longer during the summer rush from June through August. If you cannot go in person, contact the nearest U.S. embassy or consulate for directions on applying by mail. Your travel agent or airline office also might be able to provide you with visa applications and instructions. The U.S. consulate or embassy that issues your visa will determine the terms of your visa, including any restrictions regarding the length of your stay.

U.K. citizens can obtain up-to-date passport and visa information by calling the **U.S. Embassy Visa Information Line** at ☎ **0891/200-290** or the **London Passport Office** at ☎ **0990/210-410** (for recorded information).

Foreign driver's licenses are recognized in California, although you might want to get an international driver's license if your home license is not written in English.

CUSTOMS   Every visitor over 21 years of age may bring in, free of duty, the following: (1) 1 liter of wine or hard liquor; (2) 200 cigarettes, 100 cigars (but not from Cuba), or 3 pounds of smoking tobacco; and (3) $100 worth of gifts. These exemptions are offered to travelers who spend at least 72 hours in the United States and who have not claimed them within the preceding 6 months. It is altogether forbidden to bring into the country foodstuffs (particularly fruit, cooked meats, and canned goods) and plants (vegetables, seeds, tropical plants, and the like). Foreign tourists may bring in or take out up to $10,000 in U.S. or foreign currency with no formalities; larger sums must be declared to U.S. Customs on entering or leaving, which includes filing form CM 4790. For more specific information regarding U.S. Customs, call the Customs office at the **San Francisco International Airport** at ☎ **650/876-2816.**

MONEY

The U.S. monetary system is simple: The most common bills (all ugly, all green) are the $1 (colloquially, a "buck"), $5, $10, and $20 denominations. There are also $2 bills (seldom encountered), $50 bills, and $100 bills (the last two are usually not welcome when paying for small purchases).

There are six denominations of coins: 1¢ (1 cent, or a penny); 5¢ (5 cents, or a nickel); 10¢ (10 cents, or a dime); 25¢ (25 cents, or a quarter); 50¢ (50 cents, or a half dollar); and a $1 coin featuring Susan B. Anthony. In 2000 a new $1 coin with a portrait of Sacagawea will be put into circulation.

Though traveler's checks are widely accepted, make sure that they are denominated in U.S. dollars, as foreign-currency checks are often difficult to exchange. The three most widely recognized traveler's checks—and least likely to be denied—are **Visa, American Express,** and **Thomas Cook.** For more on traveler's-check protocol, see section 3, "Money Matters," above.

GETTING TO THE U.S.

International carriers that fly into San Francisco International include:

Airline	Phone number
Aer Lingus	☎ 01/844-4747 in Dublin
	061/415-556 in Shannon
	800/223-6537 in the U.S.
Air Canada	☎ 888/247-2262 in Canada
	800/776-3000 in the U.S.
Air New Zealand	☎ 0800/737-000 in Auckland
	64-3/379-5200 in Christchurch
	800/926-7255 in the U.S.

British Airways	☎ 0345/222-111 in London
	800/247-9297 in the U.S.
Japan Air Lines	☎ 03/5489-1111 in Tokyo
	800/525-3663 in the U.S.
Qantas	☎ 008/177-767 in Australia
	800/227-4500 in the U.S.
Virgin Atlantic	☎ 0293/747-747 in London
	800/862-8621 in the U.S.

In addition, many U.S. carriers offer international service to the United States. If they do not have direct flights to San Francisco, they can book you straight through on a connecting flight. You can make reservations by calling the following numbers in London:

Airline	Phone number
American	☎ 020/8572-5555
Continental	☎ 4412/9377-6464
Delta	☎ 0800/414-767
United	☎ 020/8990-9900

If possible, try to book a direct flight. Airlines that offer direct flights from London include **British Airways, United,** and **Virgin. Air Canada** offers direct service from Toronto, Montreal, Calgary, and Vancouver to San Francisco.

6 Getting Around

With hundreds of wineries scattered amidst Napa's 34,000 acres and Sonoma's 12,000 acres of vineyards, it's virtually impossible to explore the Wine Country without wheels. If you're arriving by air from another part of the country or abroad, see "Getting There," earlier in this chapter, for details on renting a car.

DRIVING AROUND THE WINE COUNTRY   You might be wondering: Does that mean visitors are drinking and driving up here? And how. The catch is, most of the year there's so much traffic, a major high-speed collision is virtually out of the question. Meanwhile, getting totally trashed while wine tasting is the exception and the valley has somehow avoided having a major problem with drunk-driving accidents.

Napa Valley Traffic Tip

Travel the Silverado Trail as often as possible to avoid Highway 29's traffic. Avoid passing through Main Street in St. Helena during high season. While a wintertime cruise from Napa to Calistoga can take 20 minutes, in summer you can expect the trek to take you closer to 50 minutes. Plan your time accordingly.

Of course, we're not condoning driving under the influence. But since there's no decent public transportation (other than taxis), our best recommendation is that you take it slow, monitor the amount of wine you drink, and bring along a designated driver or take a tour (see below).

DRIVING RULES   California law requires both drivers and passengers to wear seat belts. Children under 4 years or 40 pounds must be secured in approved child-safety seats. Motorcyclists must wear helmets. Auto insurance is mandatory; the car's registration and proof of insurance must be carried in the car.

You can turn right at a red light, unless otherwise indicated—but be sure to come to a complete stop first. Pedestrians *always* have the right-of-way.

TAXIS   You can avoid the driving issue altogether by calling either of Napa's two main taxi services: **Valley Cab** (☎ **707/257-6444**) or **Yellow Cab** (☎ **707/226-3731**). Sonoma is serviced by **Valley Cab** (☎ **707/996-6733**).

GUIDED TOURS   You won't have the same freedom that comes with driving yourself around, but a guided tour will allow you to meet other tourists, drink wine without worrying about getting behind the wheel, and relax while your driver deals with the traffic. Napa has a handful of good options, including the famous **Napa Valley Wine Train** and **Napa Valley Holidays,** which offers wine-tasting tours of the valley in 29-passenger minibuses; see pages 59 and 60 for details. If you're an active traveler, you might want to tour Sonoma's wineries by bike with the **Goodtime Bicycle Company;** see page 33 for information.

7 Strategies for Touring the Wine Country

We strongly suggest that you devise an itinerary before you arrive, because there's no possible way you could visit all of Napa's and Sonoma's 350-plus wineries in one visit (at least not without a few

Wine Country Orientation

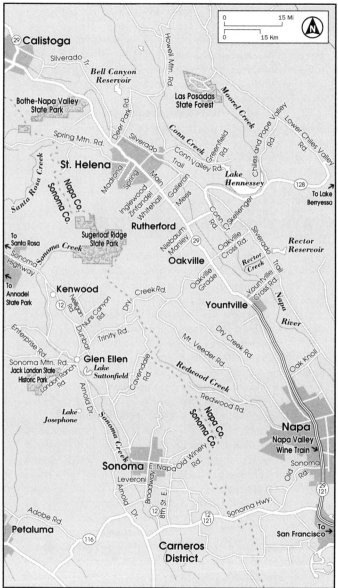

free weeks on your hands, and a mid-vacation layover at the Betty Ford clinic).

Tour smarter, not harder, is the mantra you need to chant to yourself as you pore over this book in the process of planning your trip—because the less time you spend driving in circles means more time spent sticking your schnozzle in wineglasses and saying silly things like "full bodied, yet corky."

Of course, since we don't know how long you'll be touring the Wine Country or what your level of wine knowledge is, it's impossible for us to provide you with the touring strategy that will best suit your intentions and wishes. So instead, we'll supply you with a few nuggets of Wine Country wisdom, gleaned both from experience and from picking the minds of tourist-savvy locals, and let you decide what's right for you.

NAPA VS. SONOMA: WHICH VALLEY IS RIGHT FOR YOU?

When it comes to comparing the two valleys, the most obvious distinction is size: Napa Valley dwarfs Sonoma Valley both in population, number of wineries, and sheer volume of tourism (and traffic). Napa is definitely the more commercial of the two; Sonoma still manages to maintain a backcountry ambiance thanks to its far lower density of wineries, restaurants, and hotels. Small, family-owned wineries are Sonoma's mainstay; tastings are low-key, and they come with plenty of friendly banter with the wine makers (who often will be doing the pouring themselves). But even though Sonoma lives in the shadow of far more famous Napa, its wines have actually won more awards than Napa's for the last 9 years running; don't let that "aw, shucks" attitude fool you—Sonomans know their stuff.

If it's serious R&R you're after, and you aren't too concerned with shopping outlets or visiting more than a handful of wineries each day, you'll probably be happier staying at one of Sonoma Valley's secluded inns and perhaps touring the valley by bicycle—most wineries are located down quiet, gently winding, woodsy roads. If, however, you're intent on really learning something about the wonderful world of wine making, Napa Valley may be a better choice. World-class wineries such as Sterling and Robert Mondavi offer the most interesting and edifying wine tours in North America, if not the world (though Sonoma's Benziger Winery gives them a run for their money). Compared to little brother Sonoma, Napa also has more big-name wineries, many more spas (at cheaper rates) to choose from, and a far superior selection of fine restaurants, hotels, and quintessential Wine Country activities like hot-air ballooning. To misquote Gertrude Stein, there's more there there.

Indeed, perhaps the most important distinction between Napa and Sonoma is that the Napa Valley is the undisputed cornerstone of the Wine Country. If your intention is to immerse yourself in the culture of the Wine Country, then there's no better place to start than by cruising down Napa Valley's Highway 29, the Sunset Boulevard of the Wine Country. It's along this high-rent route that all the big players in the California wine industry—Beringer, Beaulieu, Charles Krug, Niebaum-Coppola, Clos Pegase—dazzle you with their multimillion-dollar estates and pricey art collections. This is where top-notch restaurants like the French Laundry and Tra Vigne serve world-class cuisine to casually clad diners while fresh-faced Silicon Valley millionaires play croquet at the exclusive resorts just up the hill.

As you might expect, humility isn't one of Napa's strongest attributes. So don't be surprised if you encounter a bit of snobbishness at some Napa wineries, as well as a pricey tasting fee or two. On the other side of the hill, good ol' Sonomans pride themselves on their rural roots, laid-back attitude, and fee-free tasting rooms.

Is there a friendly feud between the two valleys? You betcha, which makes touring the entire Wine Country all the more interesting. If you have the luxury of time, don't just visit one: tour them both so you can compare and contrast these two very different—and very wonderful—worlds of wine making.

THE GOLDEN RULE OF WINE TASTING: LESS IS MORE

Yes, we know—they all sound great. Unfortunately, it's almost impossible to hit every winery. Actually, your best plan of action is to take it slow. **Pick three or four wineries** for a single day's outing, and really get to know not only the wines, but also the story behind each winery: its history, the types of wines they make and where they're grown, and the colorful people who make them. You can *taste* California wines just about anywhere in the world, but only by visiting the Wine Country can you learn about the painstaking, delicate, and very personal processes and years of collective experience that go into each and every bottle. Like a fine glass of wine, the Wine Country should not be rushed, but savored.

When planning your trip through the Wine Country, consider the following: Is there a specific wine you want to taste? A specific tour you'd like to take? Maybe it's the adjoining restaurant, picnic setting, or art collection that piques your interest most. Whatever your intentions may be, the best advice we can give you about visiting your chosen wineries is to **arrive early:** Most tasting rooms open at 10am, and even on the busiest of weekends, most are empty that early in the morning. "What? Start drinking at 10am?" Absolutely. First of all, you're not drinking, you're tasting and learning. Second, the staff pouring the wines will have considerably more time to discuss their product. Come one or two in the afternoon, the tasting room will probably be packed, and other visitors will be waiting in line simply to get a sample—while you're relaxing under an oak tree, finished with your wine-tasting rounds, enjoying a picnic lunch and seriously contemplating an afternoon nap. Afterwards, why not spend your time doing a little window—shopping or visiting Old Faithful while the late-birds duke it out over a sip of Chardonnay?

Another consideration when wine tasting is money. It used to be that none of the wineries charged for sampling their wares, but when the popularity of the Wine Country began to soar (along with a growing intolerance for drinking and driving), wineries—particularly those in Napa—began requesting **tasting fees.** It wasn't to make additional profit, but to discourage what the winery staffs usually refer to as "recreational drinkers": visitors who, whether they're aware of it or not, prefer quantity over quality. Nowadays, the norm at Napa Valley wineries is to charge anywhere between $2 and $8 per tasting, which usually includes the tasting glass (etched with the winery's logo) and/or a refund toward purchase. If money is a concern, consider visiting during the week: Many wineries, such as Grgich Hills, only charge a fee ($3) on the weekend.

The wineries in Sonoma, however, rarely charge for tasting wines. The exceptions are wineries offering samples of their reserve wines (usually at a separate tasting area) and champagne houses, which usually charge a few dollars for a glass of sparkling wine.

DEALING WITH THE CROWDS

Anyone who's visited the Wine Country on a sunny August weekend knows how insane the traffic can be. The Napa Valley's roads simply weren't designed to handle such an influx of vehicles, and this can turn a 30-minute drive along Highway 29 from Napa to Calistoga into 2 hours of maddening gridlock. It's ironic, of course: People arrive for a vacation in the countryside, only to be stuck in traffic for hours.

Some Wine-Buying Strategies

Just because you're buying wine directly from the people who made it doesn't mean that you'll save money by purchasing bottles in the tasting room. In fact, it's usually the other way around. You'll probably end up spending a bit more at a winery than you would at superstores that buy cases in bulk and pass the per-bottle savings on to the customer (such as **Safeway** in St. Helena, one of the best places to buy wine in Napa Valley).

If you want to save money, the smart approach is to make a list of your favorite wines as you taste at the wineries, then make your purchases when you return from your vacation. You'll not only save money on the wine, you'll save a bundle on packaging and shipping fees—but be sure to ask the winery if the release you're interested in is available in your state, and where you can purchase it.

If the selection of California wines is limited where you live, buy your wine at one of the wine shops we've recommended in the following chapters and take it to one of the shippers listed on pages 54–55, who can pack it up and ship it. Some wine shops, such as the **Wine Exchange** in Sonoma, will even do the shipping for you (and you might be able to sidestep the red tape that may accompany shipping wine to your home state; see section 8, "The Ins & Outs of Shipping Wine Home," below).

Exceptions to this strategy are wineries that offer big discounts on cases of wine, or wineries such as **Peju Province** that only sell their wines directly (that is, they have no distribution). Note: If you're able to ship your wine directly from the winery, you'll avoid having to pay sales tax; for more information, see section 8, "The Ins & Outs of Shipping Wine Home," below.

If you want to avoid the masses altogether, the solution is simple: Either **come during the off-season** (November to May) **or come midweek.** Though the optimum time to plan your trip is during the "crush"—the grape harvest season starting in late August and continuing through October when the grapes are harvested, sorted, crushed, and fermented—this is also the Wine Country's peak tourist season. This is a good time to schedule a midweek visit, if possible.

Even if your only option is to arrive on a high-season weekend, there are still ways to avoid the Napa Valley cattle drive. The smartest option is to **avoid the big wineries** such as Mondavi and

Beringer and opt for the smaller family-run places tucked into the hillsides such as Prager and Heitz. Even the wineries along the Silverado Trail, which parallels the main highway through Napa Valley, receive significantly less traffic; locals use it as their main thoroughfare during high season.

Another high-season option is to avoid Napa altogether and stick to the **Sonoma Valley.** Although it, too, suffers from traffic congestion, Sonoma usually gets far less saturated with visitors.

A FEW MORE WORDS OF WINE-COUNTRY WISDOM

Here are a few final tips that should help make your visit a more pleasant experience:

- **Chart your winery tours** on a map before venturing into the countryside. It'll save you time and traffic frustration, as well as a lot of unnecessary backtracking.
- **Plan a picnic lunch** at the last winery you're going to visit for the day (let's face it—you'll probably be too pooped to drink more wine late in the day). Many wineries offer free picnic facilities, and though few provide food, many wonderful gourmet shops in both Napa and Sonoma specialize in picnic items; see pages 127-129 and 172-173 for recommendations.
- Most wineries are open from 10am to 4:30 or 5pm and are closed on major holidays such as Thanksgiving, Christmas, and New Year's Day. Many also have restricted hours during the off-season, so **call ahead** if there's a winery you don't want to miss.
- Fine wine is a temperamental beast that hates to be mistreated. If you let that $60 bottle of Merlot cook in the back seat of your car all day, you'll probably be surprised at the new taste it has acquired. Buy a cheap Styrofoam cooler and a couple of blue ice packs, place them in the trunk of your car, and voilà!—you have a **portable wine cellar.**
- Anyone who's ever lived in a one-road town knows that you can't avoid the law for long. In our last three trips to the Wine Country, we've been bathed in a radar gun's rays twice. So there you have it: Don't speed, and for gawds sake, **don't drive while intoxicated.**

8 The Ins & Outs of Shipping Wine Home

Perhaps the only thing more complex than that $400 case of Cabernet you just purchased are the rules and regulations regarding shipping it home. Due to absurd and forever fluctuating "reciprocity laws"—which are supposedly created to protect the business of the country's wine distributors—wine shipping is limited by state regulations that vary in each of the 50 states. Shipping rules also vary from winery to winery—not to mention that, to make matters more confusing, according to at least one shipping company the list of reciprocal states (those that have agreements with California that make it no problem to ship wine there) changes almost daily! Hence, depending on which state you live in, sending even a single bottle of wine can be a truly Kafkaesque experience—and, other than the summertime traffic, one of the most frustrating aspects of a Wine Country vacation.

Sound confusing? Believe us, it is. The fact is, no one can give us the straight scoop on shipping. We've spoken to a number of agencies and each one tells us a different story. While we can't exactly outline a foolproof way to send your wine home, the following best explains what we do know about it and offers tips to help you cut through the red tape as painlessly as possible. (Note that this information was current at press time. Unfortunately, because the laws and shipping companies' procedures are ever-changing, we can't guarantee you an absolute solution; you'll have to check and see what the current situation is pertaining to your particular home state as you tour the Wine Country.)

If you happen to live in a reciprocal state and the winery you're buying from offers shipping, you're in luck. You buy, pay the postage, and the winery sends your purchase for you. It's as simple as that. If that winery doesn't ship, they will most likely be able to give you an easy shipping solution.

If you live in a nonreciprocal state, the winery may still have shipping advice for you, so definitely ask! But there's a good reason most wineries don't offer shipping to nonreciprocal states: One winery was fined big bucks (around $35,000) for breaking the law and shipping directly to Maryland, a nonreciprocal state. As this book goes to press, if you're a New York (another nonreciprocal state) resident, the odds of having your wine shipped home varies from winery to winery: Some refuse to ship at all, while others are more than accommodating ("New York has bigger fish to fry," we've been told). Do be cautious of wineries that tell you they can ship to nonreciprocal states, and make sure you get a firm commitment. When one of our New York-based editors visited Napa, a winery promised her they could, in fact, ship her purchase; but when she got home they reneged, leaving her with no way to get the wine and no potable memories of the trip.

It's possible that you'll face the challenge of finding a shipping company yourself. If that's the case, bear in mind the following:

According to the U.S. Postal Service, shipping alcoholic beverages is against the law. Of course, it's hard to imagine that anyone's getting arrested for sending a congratulatory bottle of bubbly to Aunt Myrna in Delaware, but if you tote a case labeled "Pinot Noir" into the post office, the postal clerk isn't likely to be exactly helpful. (While we're not recommending that you break the law, if you did appear with a well-packed box, they would ship it, but you'd have to declare you were shipping something other than wine—and then, of course, you'd be fibbing. Not to mention it's questionable to insure your supposed case of olive oil for $500.)

When we asked UPS about shipping, they, too, told us it was against the law. But one shipping company in the valley told us they can currently ship by either FedEx or UPS (or both, in some cases) within California and to Colorado, Idaho, Illinois, Louisiana, Maine, Minnesota, Missouri, Nebraska, New Mexico, Oregon, Virginia, Washington, and Wisconsin. (Again, don't forget the list is in constant flux.) While Airborne was lenient with shipping at one time, they seem to be buckling down after getting fined for shipping to a nonreciprocal state.

All we can really tell you about shipping is to do your homework before you buy. Talk with wineries and, if necessary, shipping companies. We've listed a few below, but you also should ask the winery from which you're buying about shipping companies; because the winery wants you to buy, they've probably done more than their fair share of shipping research and resolutions, and they should be up on the latest.

Do keep in mind that it's illegal to box your own wine and send it to a nonreciprocal state; the shippers could lose their license and you could lose your wine. However, if you do get stuck shipping illegally (not that we're recommending you do that), you might want to head to a post office, UPS, or other shipping company outside of the Wine Country area; it's far less obvious that you're shipping wine from, say, Vallejo or San Francisco than from Napa Valley.

NAPA VALLEY SHIPPING COMPANIES

Aero Packing, 163 Camino Dorado (at Highway 29), Napa (☎ 707/255-8025), will pack and ship to reciprocal states and insures the first $100 (it's 50¢ extra per hundred beyond the first). Ground shipping of one case to Los Angeles is $20 and to Florida is $45. They currently do not ship to a handful of states, including New York and Massachusetts.

The **St. Helena Mailing Center,** 1241 Adams St. (at Highway 29), St. Helena (☎ **707/963-2686**), tells us that they will pack and ship anywhere in the United States, with rates around $21 per case for ground delivery to Los Angeles and $66 to New York. While those who live in reciprocal states insure their package for up to $100 (it costs extra beyond the first $100), the Mailing Center does not insure packages shipped to nonreciprocal states. However, it's no big deal; each bottle is well-packed in Styrofoam and should make it home without a problem.

SONOMA VALLEY SHIPPING COMPANIES

Mail Boxes, Etc., 19229 Sonoma Hwy. (at Verano Street), Sonoma (☎ **707/935-3438**), which has a lot of experience with shipping wine, claims it will ship your wine to any state, either via UPS (which as of now only ships to a dozen states) or Federal Express. Prices vary from $20 to L.A. via UPS to as much as $85 to the East Coast via FedEx.

The **Wine Exchange of Sonoma,** 452 First St. E. (between East Napa and East Spain streets), Sonoma (☎ **707/938-1794**), will ship your wine, but there's a catch: You must purchase an equal amount of the same wine at their store (which they assured us would be in stock, and probably at a better rate). Shipping rates range from $20 to L.A., $45 to the East Coast.

FAST FACTS: THE WINE COUNTRY

For valley-specific information, also see the "Fast Facts" sections in chapters 4 and 5.

Area Code Both Napa and Sonoma counties use the **707** area code.

Banks Most banks are open Monday through Friday from 9am to 3pm; several stay open until about 5pm at least 1 day a week and offer limited hours on Saturday. **Bank of America** has several branches throughout the area, including locations at 1001 Adams St. in St. Helena (☎ **707/963-6807**), and 35 W. Napa St. in Sonoma (☎ **707/935-1604**); for a complete listing, call ☎ **800/348-5202.** You'll also find **Wells Fargo** throughout the region, including a branch in Napa at 217 Soscol Ave., inside Raleys supermarket (☎ **707/254-8690**). The Sonoma Wells

Fargo is located at 480 W. Napa St. (☎ **707/996-2360**). For a complete listing, call ☎ **800/869-3557.** You'll find ATMs throughout both valleys, though not as many as you'd find in a big city. For information on how to locate the nearest ATM, see "Money Matters" earlier in this chapter.

Car Rentals   See "Getting Around," earlier in this chapter.

Emergencies   Dial ☎ **911** for police, ambulance, or the fire department. No coins are needed from a working public phone.

Liquor Laws   Liquor and grocery stores, as well as some drugstores, can sell packaged alcoholic beverages between 6am and 2am. Most restaurants, nightclubs, and bars are licensed to serve alcoholic beverages during the same hours. The legal age for purchase and consumption is 21; proof of age is required.

Safety   Considering the Napa Valley's 5.1 million and Sonoma's 2.4 million annual visitors, the Wine Country still has a remarkably safe, sleepy-town atmosphere. The only safety consideration you will need to heed is your own basic common sense.

Taxes   A 7.25% sales tax is added at the register for all goods and services purchased in the Napa Valley; it's 7.5% in Sonoma. (Note that you won't have to pay sales tax if you have your purchases shipped directly from the store out of state.) Napa hotel taxes range from 10% to 12%; in Sonoma, hotel tax is 10%.

Time   The Wine Country is in the Pacific standard time zone, which is 8 hours behind Greenwich mean time and 3 hours behind eastern standard time. For the local time, call ☎ **707/ 767-8900.**

Weather   Though a general weather recording does not exist, there's an emergency number, which is only in operation during very wet weather. For information on flood conditions, contact the **Travel Advisory** at ☎ **888/854-NAPA.**

4

The Napa Valley

*C*ompared to its sister valley, Sonoma, Napa is a bit farther from San Francisco, encompasses hundreds more wineries, and has more of an overall touristy, big-business feel to it. You'll still find plenty of rolling, mustard flower–covered hills and vast stretches of vineyards, but they come hand in hand with large, upscale restaurants; designer discount outlets; rows of hotels; and, in summer, plenty of traffic. Even with hordes of visitors year-round, Napa Valley is still pretty sleepy, with a focus on daytime attractions—wine tasting, outdoor activities, and spas—and fabulous food. Nightlife is very limited, but after indulging all day, most visitors are ready to turn in early anyway.

1 Orientation & Getting Around

Napa Valley is relatively compact. Just 25 miles long, it claims 34,000 acres of vineyards, making Napa the most densely planted wine-growing region in the U.S. It's an easy jaunt from one end to the other: you can drive it in less than half an hour—closer to 50 minutes during high season.

Conveniently, most of the large wineries—as well as most of the hotels, shops, and restaurants—are along a single road, **Highway 29,** which starts at the mouth of the Napa River, near the north end of San Francisco Bay, and continues north to Calistoga and the top of the growing region. All of the Napa Valley coverage in this chapter—every town, winery, hotel, and restaurant—is organized below from south to north, beginning in the village of Napa, and can be reached from this main thoroughfare.

ALONG HIGHWAY 29: NAPA'S TOWNS IN BRIEF

While it's virtually impossible to tell when you cross from one town into the next, each does have its own distinct personality. The **village of Napa** serves as the commercial center of the Wine Country and the gateway to Napa Valley—hence the high-speed freeway that whips you right past it and on to the "tourist" towns of St. Helena and Calistoga. However, if you do veer off the highway, you'll be surprised to discover a small but burgeoning community of 70,000 residents with the most cosmopolitan (relatively) atmosphere in the county, and some of the most affordable accommodations in the valley. Unfortunately, any charm Napa exudes is all but squelched by the used-car lots and warehouse superstores surrounding the quaint neighborhoods.

Heading north on either Highway 29 or the Silverado Trail leads you to Napa's wineries and the more idyllic pastoral towns beyond.

Yountville, population 3,700, was founded by the first white American to settle in the valley, George Calvert Yount. While it lacks the small-town charm of neighboring St. Helena and Calistoga—primarily because it has no rambunctious main street—it does serve as a good base for exploring the valley, and it's home to a handful of excellent wineries, inns, and restaurants, including James Beard's 1997 top dining spot in the nation, the French Laundry.

Driving farther north on the St. Helena Highway (Hwy. 29) brings you to **Oakville,** most easily recognized by Oakville Cross Road and the Oakville Grocery (see p. 127), one of our favorite places to pick up gourmet picnic fare and one of the only indications that you've reached the small town. If you so much as blink after Oakville, you're likely to overlook **Rutherford,** the next small town that borders on St. Helena. Each has spectacular wineries, but you won't see most of them while driving along Highway 29.

Next comes **St. Helena,** located 17 miles north of Napa on Highway 29. St. Helena is a former Seventh Day Adventist village that manages to maintain a pseudo-Old West feel while simultaneously catering to upscale shoppers with deep pockets and its generally wealthy resident population of 6,000 and growing. This quiet, attractive little town is home to a slew of beautiful old houses, as well as great restaurants, first-rate accommodations, and many exceptional wineries.

Calistoga, the last tourist town in Napa Valley, was named by Sam Brannan, entrepreneur extraordinaire and California's first millionaire. After making a bundle supplying miners during the gold rush, he went on to take advantage of the natural geothermal springs at the north end of the Napa Valley by building a hotel and spa in 1859. Flubbing up a speech in which he compared this natural California wonder to New York State's Saratoga Springs resort, he serendipitously coined the name "Calistoga" and it stuck. Today, this small, simple resort town with 5,000 residents and an old-time main street (no building along the 6-block stretch is more than two stories high) is popular with city folk who come here to unwind. Calistoga is a great place to relax and indulge in mineral waters, mud baths, Jacuzzis, massages, and, of course, wine. The vibe is more casual—and a little groovier—than you'll find in neighboring towns to the south.

VISITOR INFORMATION

Even if you plan to skip the town of Napa, you may want to stop at the **Napa Valley Conference and Visitors Bureau,** 1310 Town Center Mall (off First Street), Napa, CA 94559 (☎ **707/ 226-7459**), to pick up a variety of local information and money-saving coupons.

All over Napa and Sonoma you can pick up a very informative, free weekly called the *Wine Country Review,* which provides the most up-to-date information on the area's wineries and related events.

WINE-TASTING TOURS

Let's say you've had your fill of driving from winery to winery. Or you already know that family dynamics get a little stressed when that certain back-seat driver tries to navigate through traffic. Or the whole point of this vacation is to drink too much, eat too much, and avoid all mental exertion. If any of these scenarios ring true, you may want to consider letting one of the companies below figure out the details of your Wine Country tour.

RIDING THE NAPA VALLEY WINE TRAIN   You don't have to worry about drinking and driving if you tour the Wine Country aboard the **Napa Valley Wine Train,** a rolling restaurant that makes a leisurely 3-hour, 36-mile journey through the vineyards of Napa, Yountville, Oakville, Rutherford, and St. Helena. You'll love riding in the vintage-style cars, each finished with polished Honduran mahogany paneling and etched-glass partitions.

During the trip, an attentive staff serves optional gourmet meals complete with all the finery—damask linen, bone china, silver flatware, and etched crystal. The fixed menus consist of three to five courses, which might include a salmon dish or Black Angus filet mignon served with a Cabernet and Roquefort sauce. In addition to the dining rooms, the train pulls a Wine Tasting Car, a Deli Car, and four 50-passenger lounges. A recent add-on to the daytime rides is an optional stop in Yountville and at the Grgich Winery in Rutherford for a tour of the barreling, bottling, and wine-making process, followed by a tasting.

The train departs from the McKinstry Street Depot, 1275 McKinstry St. (near First Street and Soscol Avenue), Napa (☎ **800/427-4124** or 707/253-2111). Train fare without meals is $29.50 for daytime rides and evening rides in the Deli Car; fare with meals is $59.50 for brunch, $68.50 for lunch, and $75 for dinner. The Wine Train's latest addition, the more modern 1950s Vista Dome Car, offers only upstairs seating and has a glass top; it can only be ridden if you opt for the pricier lunch or dinner served within it. Including train fare, lunch is $81.50 for a four-course French affair; dinner, $89. Departures are Monday through Friday at 11:30am; Saturday, Sunday, and holidays at 9am, 12:30pm and 6pm. (The schedule is reduced in Jan. and Feb.) *Tip:* Sit on the west side for the best views.

BICYCLING AROUND THE WINE COUNTRY   Getaway Adventures, 620 E. Washington St., Suite 205, Petaluma, CA 94952 (☎ **800/499-2453** or 707/763-3040; **www.getawayadventures. com**), the Wine Country's only full-time operator dedicated to bicycling and adventure tours, offers a unique way to explore Napa and Sonoma. Sign up for a weekend or 6-day package and everything's taken care of—lodging, continental breakfasts, gourmet picnic lunches, dinners at local restaurants, wine tours and tastings, and unforgettable scenery in the majestic valley (bicycle, helmet, and drinking water included). On weekdays, they'll even deliver bikes to you. One-day tours, which include lunch and a visit to three to five wineries, cost $95; the downhill is a better choice for people who hate to pedal. Two-day tours start at $675 per person; a 6-day trip goes for around $1,629.

LETTING SOMEONE ELSE DO THE DRIVING   At about 4pm on any given day in the valley, there's gotta be more legally drunk drivers on the road per capita than in any other location on earth. And while traffic make high-speed collisions unlikely, why let it ruin a good buzz? That's why **Napa Valley Holidays,** 1525 Andrea Circle, Napa, CA 94558 (☎ **707/255-1050; www.charterbus.com/ napavalley.html**), has found a good niche for itself. Its regularly scheduled winery tours, conducted in 29-passenger, air-conditioned minibuses, start with pickups from two Napa locations. Passengers visit three or five wineries over 4 hours; all tasting fees are included. Tours run daily from April through November and start at $35 per individual; prices vary depending on the size of the group and the departure point.

FAST FACTS: THE NAPA VALLEY

Hospitals   Queen of the Valley Hospital, 100 Trancas St., Napa (☎ 707/257-4008), offers minor emergency care from 9am to 9pm. For after-hours emergencies, head **to St. Helena Hospital,** about 5 minutes from the town of St. Helena at 650 Sanitarium Rd., Deer Park (☎ **707/963-3611**).

Information   See "Visitor Information," above.

Newspapers/Magazines   The *Napa Valley Register* covers the entire Napa Valley; it's available at newspaper racks on the main streets in towns throughout the county. Other local town weeklies include the *Weekly Calistogan* and the *St. Helena Star,* which are both free. Essential for all visitors is the *Napa Valley Guide,* an annual, glossy 124-page magazine packed with valuable tourist information; it's sold in most shops and hotels and is also available at the **Napa Valley Conference and Visitors Bureau,** 1310 Napa Town Center Mall, off First Street (☎ **707/ 226-7459**).

Pharmacies   Smith's St. Helena Pharmacy, 1390 Railroad Ave. (at Adams St.), St. Helena (☎ **707/963-2794**), is open Monday through Friday from 9am to 6pm, Saturday from 9am to 5pm, and Sunday from 10am to 3pm. **Vasconi Drug Store,** 1381 Main St., St. Helena (☎ **707/963-1447**), is open Monday through Friday from 9am to 7pm, but its pharmacist is only part-time.

Police   Call ☎ **707/967-2850** or, in an emergency, ☎ **911.**

Post Offices   Each town has its own post office. **Napa Central,** 1625 Trancas, at Claremont (☎ **707/255-1621**), is open Monday through Friday from 8:30am to 5pm. **Napa Downtown,** 1352 Second St., between Franklin and Randolf streets (☎ **707/ 255-1268**), is open Monday through Friday from 8am to 4pm. You'll find local branches in **Yountville** at 6514 Washington St. at Mulberry (☎ **707/944-2123**), open Monday through Friday from 8am to 4pm, Saturday from 9:30am to noon; in **Oakville** at 7856 St. Helena Hwy. at Oakville Cross Road (☎ **707/ 944-2600**), open Monday through Friday from 8am to noon and 1 to 4pm, Saturday from 8am to noon; and in **Rutherford** at 1190 Rutherford Rd., at Highway 29 (☎ **707/963-7488**), operating Monday through Friday from 8am to 1pm and 2 to 4pm, Saturday from 8am to noon. The **St. Helena Post Office,** 1461 Main St., between Adams and Pine streets (☎ **707/963-2668**), is open Monday through Friday from 8:30am to 5pm and Saturday from

10am to 1pm. In **Calistoga,** head to 1013 Washington St., at Lincoln (☎ **707/942-6661**), open Monday through Friday from 9am to 4pm.

Shipping Companies **Aero Packing,** 163 Camino Dorado, at Highway 29, Napa (☎ **707/255-8025**), will pack and ship wine to reciprocal states. The **St. Helena Mailing Center,** 1241 Adams St., at Highway 29, St. Helena (☎ **707/963-2686**), will (at press time, anyway) pack and ship wine to anywhere in the United States. For more on the reciprocity laws associated with shipping wine out of California, see "The Ins & Outs of Shipping Wine Home" in chapter 3.

2 Touring the Wineries

Touring Napa Valley takes a little planning. With more than 250 wineries, each offering distinct wines, atmosphere, and experience, the best thing you can do is decide what you're most interested in and chart your path from there. (For more on this, see "Strategies for Touring the Wine Country" in chapter 3.)

The towns and wineries listed below are organized geographically, from Napa village in the south to Calistoga in the north. Bear in mind that because some wineries are on Highway 29 while others are on the Silverado Trail (which parallels Highway 29), the order in which they're listed is not necessarily the best path to follow. To save time, plan your wine tour to avoid zigzagging between the two parallel roads (see "The Napa Valley Wineries" map on p. 63 to get your bearings).

We've featured only our favorite wineries below; this portable guide would grow into a tome if we included reviews of *every* valley winery. For a complete list of local wineries, be sure to pick up one of the free guides to the valley (see "Visitor Information" and "Fast Facts," above).

While you're exploring, keep in mind that some of the most memorable Wine Country experiences aren't made on tours or in formal tasting halls, but at the mom-and-pop wineries that dot the region. These are the places where you'll discover bottles that are only sold from the proprietor's front room, and get to talk one-on-one with the people who made the wine you're buying with their own hands. Of course, the big-name wineries are not to be missed— but don't pass up the other, more personal side of the Napa Valley experience either.

The Napa Valley Wineries

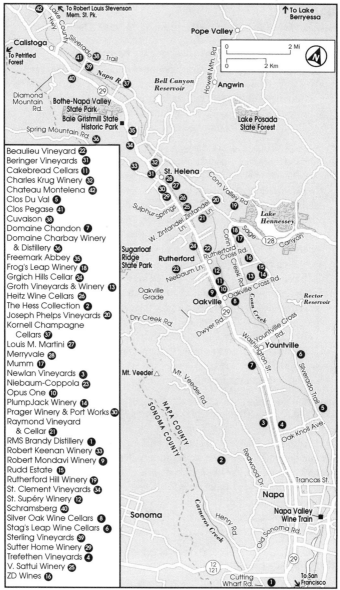

NAPA

Newlan Vineyards. 5225 Solano Ave., Napa. ☎ **707/257-2399.** www.wine.
com/nvw. Daily 10am–5pm. Tastings by appointment only. From Hwy. 29, take
Oak Knoll Ave. west to Solano Ave., turn right, and head north 1 mile.

This small, family-owned winery produces only about 10,000 cases
a year. Varieties include Cabernet Sauvignon, Pinot Noir,
Chardonnay, Zinfandel, and late harvest Johannisberg Riesling.
Wine tasting, which is offered any time during open hours, costs $3
and includes a take-home wineglass.

✪ **The Hess Collection.** 4411 Redwood Rd., Napa. ☎ **707/255-1144.**
www.hesscollection.com. Daily 10am–4pm. From Hwy. 29 north, exit Redwood
Rd. west, and follow Redwood Rd. for 6¹/₂ miles.

No place in the valley brings together art and wine better than this
combination winery/art gallery on the side of Mount Veeder. While
others strive to pair wine with food, Swiss art collector Donald Hess
went a different route: After acquiring the old Christian Brothers
winery in 1978, he continued to produce wine while funding a huge
restoration and expansion project that would honor both wine and
the fine arts. The result is a working winery interspersed with glo-
riously lit rooms that exhibit his truly stunning art collection; the
free self-guided tour takes you through these galleries as it introduces
you to the wine-making process.

For a $3 fee, you can sample the winery's current Cabernet and
Chardonnay as well as one other featured wine. If you want to take
some with you, by-the-bottle prices start at $9.95 for the second-
label Hess select brand, while most others range from $15 to $35.

Trefethen Vineyards. 1160 Oak Knoll Ave. (east of Hwy. 29), Napa. ☎ **707/
255-7700.** www.trefethen.com. Daily 10am–4:30pm. Tours by appointment
only.

Listed on the National Register of Historic Places, the vineyard's
main building was built in 1886 and remains Napa's only wooden,
gravity-flow winery. Although Trefethen is one of the valley's oldest wineries, it didn't produce its first Chardonnay until 1973—but
thank goodness it did. Their whites and reds are both award-
winners and a pleasure to the palate. Tastings are free, but if you
want to sample a reserve wine, it'll cost you $5.

Clos Du Val. 5330 Silverado Trail (north of Oak Knoll Ave.), Napa. ☎ **707/
259-2200.** Daily 10am–5pm. Tours by appointment only.

If you're starting your tour in Napa along the Silverado Trail, this
is a good place to stop. The beautiful ivy-covered building and

House of the Spirits

When you've had it with wine tasting for the day and you can no longer tell your oaky Cabs from your fruity Pinots, it's time to pay a visit to the **RMS Brandy Distillery,** 1250 Cuttings Wharf Rd. (1 mile south of Highway 12/121), Napa (☎ **707/253-9055; www.rmsbrandy.com**). This replica of the brandy houses of France's Cognac region is the oldest alambic distillery in the United States, and a great place to learn about brandy.

Even if you're not a fan of brandy, you'll love this free tour. It starts with a slick presentation of a miniature-scale model of the distillery (to give you an overview of the brandy-making process), then continues to the Still House, which contains eight beautiful French-built copper stills. Next you're led to the Barrel House, an enormous building that houses nearly 4,000 barrels of aging brandy. The vapors emanating from the barrels—called the "Angel's Share"—are enough to make you heady, and the Gregorian chants piped through the sound system add to the intoxicating experience. The tour ends with not a tasting (which is illegal under U.S. law unless you buy the bottle), but rather a sniffing: Several grades of brandy are passed around as the tour guide describes the vapors of each distinct variety.

Half-hour tours are offered roughly every 45 minutes, daily from 10:30am to 5pm in summer, to 4:30pm in winter. Sorry, no picnic facilities are available.

well-manicured rose garden set the scene for a romantic wine-tasting experience before you even step foot in the door; once inside, the employees, with their French accents, authenticate the mood.

While the French have been known to make a great bottle of wine or two, here in the valley it's the exception, not the rule, when a winery is run by a Frenchman. In this case it's Bordeaux-born wine maker Bernard Portet who's responsible for the Cabernet (which makes up 45% of the winery's production), Chardonnay, Zinfandel, Pinot Noir, and Merlot. You can try them all in the rather matter-of-fact tasting room, which is refreshingly free of merchandise. There's a $5 tasting charge (refunded with purchase) for around four wines, which may include the new release Chardonnay ($22 a bottle), Cab ($25), Merlot ($28), and perhaps a library selection or two.

Lovely picnic facilities offer respite in grassy nooks along the grounds. An added bonus is the friendly, helpful staff, which happily offers directions to other wineries, along with a small map.

Stag's Leap Wine Cellars. 5766 Silverado Trail, Napa. ☎ **707/944-2020.** www.cask23.com. Daily 10am–4pm. Tours by appointment only.

From Highway 29, go east on Trancas Street or Oak Knoll Avenue, then north to the cellars. Founded in 1972, Stag's Leap shocked the oenological world in 1976 when its 1973 Cabernet won first place over French wines in a Parisian blind tasting. For $5 per person, you can be the judge of the winery's current releases, or you can fork over another fiver for one of Stag's Leap's best known wines, Cabernet Sauvignon Cask 23. The 1-hour tour runs through everything from the vineyard to production facilities and ends with a tasting. By the middle of 2000, it could also include their new caves, which are currently under construction.

YOUNTVILLE

✪ **Domaine Chandon.** 1 California Dr. (at Hwy. 29), Yountville. ☎ **707/944-2280.** www.dchandon.com. Jan–Mar Wed–Sun 10am–6pm; Apr–Dec daily 10am–8pm. Free tours every hour on the hour 11am–5pm.

The valley's most renowned sparkling winery was founded in 1973 by French champagne house Moët et Chandon. The grounds suit Domaine Chandon's reputation perfectly—this is the kind of place where the world's wealthy might stroll the beautifully manicured gardens under the shade of delicate parasols, stop at the outdoor patio for sips of the famous sparkling wine, then glide into the dining room for a luncheon.

If you can pull yourself away from the bubbly (sold in tastings for $8 to $12 and served with complimentary bread and spread), the comprehensive tour of the facilities is worth the time. In addition to a shop, there's a small gallery housing artifacts from Moët et Chandon depicting the history of champagnes.

OAKVILLE

✪ **Robert Mondavi Winery.** 7801 St. Helena Hwy. (Hwy. 29), Oakville. ☎ **800/MONDAVI** or 707/226-1395. www.robertmondaviwinery.com. May–Oct daily 9:30am–5:30pm; Nov–Apr daily 9:30am–4:30pm. Reservations recommended for the guided tour (book 1 week in advance, especially for weekend tours).

If you continue on Highway 29 up to Oakville, you'll arrive at the ultimate high-tech Napa Valley winery, housed in a magnificent mission-style facility. At Mondavi, almost every variable in the wine-making process is controlled by computer—it's absolutely fascinating to watch. After the tour, you can taste the results of all this attention to detail in selected current wines (free of charge). You also can taste without taking the tour, but it will cost you: The Rose Garden (an outdoor tasting area open in summer) offers an etched Reidel glass and three wines for $10; tastings in the ToKalon Room go from $3 for a 3-ounce taste to $25 for a rare library wine.

Fridays feature an "Art of Wine and Food" program, which includes a slide presentation on the history of wine, a tour of the winery, and a three-course luncheon with wine pairing; the cost is around $60 and you must reserve in advance. Though there's no picnicking on the grounds, Mondavi does offer gourmet picnic lunches from time to time. The Vineyard Room usually features an art show, and you'll find some exceptional antiques in the reception hall. In summer, the winery also hosts some great outdoor jazz concerts. Call to learn about upcoming events.

Opus One. 7900 St. Helena Hwy. (Hwy. 29), Oakville. ☎ **707/944-9442.** www.opusonewinery.com. Daily 10:30am–3:30pm. Tours by appointment only (in high season, book a month in advance).

Unlike most other vineyard experiences, a visit to Opus One is a serious and stately affair that takes after its wine and its owners: Robert Mondavi and Baroness Phillipe de Rothschild, who, after years of discussion, embarked on this state-of-the-art collaboration. Architecture buffs in particular will appreciate the tour, which takes in both the impressive Greco-Roman-meets-20th-century building and the no-holds-barred ultra-high-tech production and aging facilities. Take note: Newcomers to wine tasting might not appreciate the haute attitude here.

This entire facility caters to one ultrapremium wine, which is offered here for a whopping $25 per 4-ounce taste (and a painful $125 per bottle). But wine lovers should happily fork over the cash: It's likely to be one of the most memorable reds you'll ever sample. Grab your glass and head to the redwood rooftop deck to enjoy the view.

RUTHERFORD

Silver Oak Wine Cellars. 915 Oakville Cross Rd. (at Money Rd.), Oakville. ☎ **707/944-8808.** www.silveroak.com. Tasting room Mon–Sat 9am–4pm. Tours Mon–Fri at 1:30pm, by appointment only.

Twenty-five years ago, an oil man from Colorado, Ray Duncan, and a former Christian Brothers monk, Justin Meyer, formed a partnership and a mission to create the finest Cabernet Sauvignon in the world. "We still haven't produced the best bottle of Cabernet Sauvignon of which Silver Oak is capable," admits Meyer, but this small winery is still the Wine Country's undisputed king of Cabernet.

A narrow tree-lined road leads to the handsome Mediterranean-style winery, where roughly 40,000 cases of 100% varietal Cab are produced annually (an additional 10,000 cases are produced annually from their Alexander Valley winery in Geyserville). The elegant tasting room is refreshingly quiet and soothing, adorned with redwood panels stripped from old wine tanks and warmed by a wood fire. Tastings and tours are $10, which includes a beautiful German-made Burgundy glass. At press time, only two wines were released: a 1995 Alexander Valley and a 1995 Napa Valley. If the $50 and $75-per-bottle price tags are a bit much, for half the price you can take home one of the winery's non-Cab releases—a velvety Meyer Family Port. No picnic facilities are available.

✪ **PlumpJack Winery.** 620 Oakville Cross Rd. (just west of the Silverado Trail), Oakville. ☎ **707/945-1220.** www.plumpjack.com. Daily 10am–4:30pm.

If most wineries are like a traditional and refined Brooks Brothers suit, PlumpJack stands out as the Todd Oldham of wine tasting: chic, colorful, a little wild, and popular with a young, hip crowd. Like the franchise's PlumpJack restaurant and wine shop in San Francisco and their resort in Tahoe, this playfully medieval winery is a welcome diversion from the same old, same old. But with Getty bucks behind what was once Villa Mt. Eden winery, the budget covers far more than just atmosphere. There's also some serious wine making going on here, and for $5 you can sample the Cabernet, Petite Sirah, Riesling, and Chardonnay—each an impressive product from a winery that's only been open to the public since mid-1997. The few vintages for sale currently range from $25 to $45. There are no tours or picnic spots, but this refreshingly stylized and friendly facility will make you want to hang out for a while nonetheless.

Groth Vineyards & Winery. 750 Oakville Cross Rd. (off Hwy. 29 or the Silverado Trail), Oakville. ☎ **707/944-0290.** www.grothwines.com. Mon–Sat 10am–4pm. Production tours and tasting available by appointment only: Mon–Fri 11am and 2pm and Sat 11am.

Dennis Groth first made it big as Atari's CFO; his contemporaries must have thought he was nuts when he declared "Game Over" and went into the wine business. But when his 1985 Cabernet Sauvignon

Reserve received a perfect score of 100 from wine critic Robert Parker—who had never before given an American wine such high marks—his name was back up among the highest-scoring players.

Recognition may be reward enough, but Groth's latest trophy is his stunning mission-style building, a big salmon palace surrounded by 121 acres of vineyards. The formal—and sometimes stuffy—setting is the kind of place where you're inclined to whisper. You must make an appointment to visit, and then fork over $5 to taste his $45-a-bottle Cab (which is still one of the most revered in the state), $20 Chardonnay, and $14 Sauvignon Blanc. (Tasting fees are refunded with a purchase.) Unfortunately, no picnicking is allowed, but you can enjoy your wine out on the terrace or in the charming garden on sunny days, or in front of the fireplace during winter.

Rudd Estate (formerly Girard Winery). On the Silverado Trail at Oakville Cross Rd., Oakville. ☎ **707/944-8577.** Daily 11am–4pm.

While the tasting room staff is welcoming, there's no denying that this serious winery will appeal most to serious wine drinkers. For 17 years straight, Girard's Cabernet has consistently received 90 points (out of 100) or better by the country's top wine aficionados. And despite all the hoopla, the winery has intentionally kept its production down to around 15,000 per year and continues to use only estate-grown grapes; the combination guarantees better quality control (and also explains why most bottles go for $18 to $40). Since Dean & DeLuca's owner, Mr. Leslie Rudd, purchased the winery in 1996, a 2-year renovation project has been completed and brand new tasting room added. Samples are free, but swigs of older wines cost around $5 for two or three varieties. Picnic facilities and tours are not currently offered.

Cakebread Cellars. 8300 St. Helena Hwy. (Hwy. 29), Rutherford. ☎ **800/588-0298** or 707/963-5221. www.cakebread.com. Daily 10am–4pm. Tours by appointment only.

This winery's moniker is actually the owners' surname, but it suits the wines produced here, where the focus is on making wine that pairs well with food. They've done such a good job that 85% of their 85,000 annual cases go directly to restaurants, which means only a select few wine drinkers get to take home a bottle. Even if you've found their label in your local wine store, your choice has been limited: Just three varieties are distributed nationally. Here you can sample the Sauvignon Blanc, Chardonnay, Cabernet, Merlot, Zinfandel, Pinot Noir, Rubaiyat-blend wine, and their dry rosé Vin de Porche, which are all made from Napa Valley grapes. Prices range from an affordable $15 for a bottle of the 1998 Sauvignon Blanc to a pricey $80 for the 1996 Reserve Cab, but the average bottle sells for just a little more than $20. In the tasting room, a large barnlike space, the hospitable hosts pour either a $5 or $10 sampling; both include a keepsake wineglass.

✪ **St. Supéry Winery.** 8440 St. Helena Hwy. (Hwy. 29), Rutherford. ☎ **800/ 942-0809** or 707/963-4507. www.stsupery.com. Daily 9:30am–5pm (6pm during summer). Tours every hour on the hour.

The outside may look like a modern corporate office building, but inside you'll find a functional and welcoming winery that encourages first-time wine tasters to learn more about oenology. On the self-guided tour, you can wander through the demonstration vineyard where you'll learn about growing techniques. Inside, kids gravitate toward "SmellaVision," an interactive display that teaches you how to identify different wine ingredients. Adjoining is the Atkinson House, which chronicles more than 100 years of wine-making history. For $3 you'll get lifetime tasting privileges, and though they probably won't be pouring their ever-popular Moscato dessert wine, the Sauvignon Blanc and Chardonnay flow freely. Even the prices make visitors feel at home: Many bottles go for around $8, although their 1995 Meritage Cabernet will set you back $40.

Niebaum-Coppola. 1991 St. Helena Hwy. (Hwy. 29), Rutherford. ☎ **707/ 968-1100.** www.niebaumcoppola.com. Daily 10am–5pm. Memorial Day–Labor Day 10am–6pm. Tours offered daily at 11am and 2pm.

In March 1995, Hollywood met Napa Valley when Francis Ford Coppola bought historic Inglenook Vineyards. Although the renowned film director has been dabbling in wine production for years, Niebaum-Coppola (pronounced *Nee*-bomb *Coh*-pa-la) is his biggest endeavor yet. He plunked down millions to renovate the beautiful 1880s ivy-draped stone winery and restore the surrounding property to its historic dimensions, gilding it with the glamour you'd expect from Tinseltown in the process. On display are Academy awards and memorabilia from such Coppola films as *The Godfather* and *Bram Stoker's Dracula;* the Centennial Museum chronicles the history of the estate and its wine making as well as Coppola's filmmaking.

Despite the Hollywood hullabaloo, the wine is not forgotten. Available for tasting are a Rubicon (a blend of estate-grown Cabernet, Cabernet Franc, and Merlot, aged for more than 5 years),

Cabernet Franc, Merlot, Chardonnay, Zinfandel, and others, all made from organically grown grapes and ranging from around $10 to more than $80. There's also a wide variety of both expensive and affordable gift items. Speaking of expensive, the steep $7.50-per-person tasting fee might make you wonder whether a movie is included in the price—it's not (but you'll at least get to keep the souvenir glass). And at $20 a pop for the château and garden tour, you'll wonder whether you're *funding* his next film. But the grounds are indeed spectacular, and the $1^1/_2$-hour journey includes private tasting and glass.

Don't let the prices deter you; if nothing else visit the grounds—they're absolutely stunning and it costs nothing to stroll. You're welcome to picnic at any of the designated garden sites.

Beaulieu Vineyard. 1960 St. Helena Hwy. (Hwy. 29), Rutherford. ☎ **707/967-5230.** www.bvwine.com. Daily 10am–5pm. Tours daily 11am–4pm.

Bordeaux native Georges de Latour founded the third-oldest continuously operating winery in Napa Valley in 1900, and, with the help of legendary oenologist André Tchelistcheff, produced world-class, award-winning wines that have been served by every president of the United States since Franklin D. Roosevelt. The brick-and-redwood tasting room isn't much to look at, but with Beaulieu's (pronounced *Bowl*-you) stellar reputation, they have no need to visually impress. They offer tastings for $5 as well as a variety of bottles under $20. The Private Reserve Tasting Room offers a "flight" of reserve wines to taste for $18, but if you want to take a bottle to go, it may cost as much as $75. A free tour explains the wine-making process and the vineyard's history.

Grgich Hills Cellar. 1829 St. Helena Hwy. (Hwy. 29, north of Rutherford Cross Rd.), Rutherford. ☎ **707/963-2784.** Daily 9:30am–4:30pm. Free tours by appointment only, Mon–Fri 11am and 2pm, Sat–Sun 11am and 1:30pm.

Yugoslavian émigré Miljenko (Mike) Grgich made his presence known to the world when his Château Montelena Chardonnay bested the top French White Burgundies at the famous 1976 Paris tasting. Since then, this master vintner has teamed up with Austin Hills (of the Hills Brothers coffee fortune) and started this extremely successful and respected winery in Rutherford.

The ivy-covered stucco building isn't much to behold, and the tasting room is even less appealing, but people don't come here for the scenery: As you might expect, Grgich's (pronounced *Grr*-gitch) Chardonnays are legendary—and priced accordingly. The smart buys, however, are the outstanding Zinfandel and Cabernet Sauvignon, which are priced at around $20 and $45, respectively. The winery also produces a fantastic Fumé Blanc for as little as $18 a bottle. Before you leave, be sure to poke your head into the barrel-aging room and inhale the divine aroma. Tastings cost $3 on weekends, which includes the glass, and are free on weekdays. No picnic facilities are available.

ZD Wines. 8383 Silverado Trail (between Oakville Cross and Rutherford Cross rds.), Rutherford. ☎ **800/487-7757** or 707/963-5188. www.zdwines.com. Daily 10am–4:30pm. Tours by appointment only, daily 10:30am–4:30pm.

What began in 1968 as little more than a hobby of two former aerospace engineers, Norman de Leuze and Gino Zepponi, has become a serious (and successful) family operation, as its fancy new digs along the Silverado Trail attest. Now owned and operated by the de Leuze family, ZD's wines have garnered more than 340 awards of excellence in prestigious competitions around the world. ZD is well known among the wine world's cognoscenti for their barrel-fermented Chardonnay, intense Pinot Noir, and fruity Cabernet Sauvignon. They recently added a fourth wine to the family: a ZD Merlot from the mountainous Atlas Peak area of the Napa Valley. These are carefully crafted wines in limited supply, so expect to pay at least $25 to $30 for their most recent releases. Tastings are $5, which is credited toward your wine purchase. Also offered is a $10 private tour and tasting, which includes freshly baked bread and artisan cheeses. The moniker ZD, by the way, stands for both the original founders' initials, as well as an engineering term for Zero Defects—a fitting mantra for their wine-making process. No picnic facilities are available.

Mumm Napa Valley. 8445 Silverado Trail (just south of Rutherford Cross Rd.), Rutherford. ☎ **800/686-6272** or 707/942-3434. www.mumm.com. Daily 10am–5pm. Tours offered every hour daily 10am–3pm.

At first glance, Mumm, housed in a big redwood barn, looks almost humble. But once you're in the front door, you'll know that they mean business—big business. Just beyond the extensive gift shop (filled with all sorts of namesake mementos) is the tasting room, where you can purchase sparkling wine by the glass ($3.50 to $6) or the bottle ($15 to $50, with most closer to $15), and take in the breathtaking vineyard and mountain views. Unfortunately, there's no food or picnicking here, but during warm weather, out on the open patio with a glass of champagne in hand, you'll forget all about nibbling. Mumm also offers a 45-minute educational tour and an art gallery with exhibits of Ansel Adams photographs of the Wine Country as well as rotating exhibits year round.

Frog's Leap Winery. 8815 Conn Creek Rd. (west of the Silverado Trail), Rutherford. ☎ **800/959-4704** or 707/963-4704. E-mail: Ribbitt@frogsleap. com. Mon–Sat 10am–4pm. Tastings and tours by appointment only. From Hwy. 29, take Rutherford Cross Rd. and turn left at the fork.

One of the valley's leaders in organic farming, Frog's Leap is known for its kick-ass Zinfandels (not to mention the Sauvignon Blancs, Merlots, Cabernets, and Chardonnays). The entrance is confusing, so bear in mind that the beautifully restored 1884 big red barn is where the action takes place; the small gift shop behind the barn on the left is the best place to locate an employee if you don't find someone immediately. It's here that you'll find gifts featuring the winery's motto—"Time's fun when you're having flies"—and where you'll start your tour. The 45-minute expedition gives "a scintillating history" of how Frog's Leap began, a tour of the barn, and wine tasting, which may even be poured directly from the tanks. If there's action on the vines, you may get to pick and eat fresh grapes.

Considering that Frog's Leap is a favorite on restaurant wine lists and has a small annual production of 48,000 cases, the wine is well priced. At press time, the following had been released (expect new releases due out in May and June of 2000): 1997 Zin goes for $18 a bottle; the 1998 Sauvignon Blanc, $14. The only current releases are the Cab ($30) and Merlot ($27).

Rutherford Hill Winery. 200 Rutherford Hill Rd. (off the Silverado Trail), `Rutherford. ☎ **800/MERLOT-1** or 707/963-7194. www.rutherfordhill.com. Daily 10am–5pm. Tours daily at 11:30am, 1:30, and 3:30pm (Sat–Sun also at 12:30 and 2:30pm).

Though Rutherford Hill Winery offers a wide array of wines—Chardonnay, Cabernet, Zinfandel Port, Sangiovese, Cabernet Sauvignon—it's best known for its Merlot. In fact, Rutherford Hill is Napa Valley's leading producer of premium Merlots, committing 75% of its entire wine production to this popular fruity varietal. Using massive drilling machinery imported from England, nearly a mile has been carved into the limestone slopes behind the winery, where more than 8,000 barrels of wine are stored in a naturally temperature-controlled environment. Half-hour tours include a trip through the caves (including a rare barrel tasting) and take you into the bowels of the immense wooden structure that houses the fermentation tanks and tasting room ($4, including wineglass).

Perched high above the valley, Rutherford Hill is also the Wine Country's premier picnicking site, offering the same superb views of the valley that guests of Auberge du Soleil (see section 4, "Where to Stay," below) pay big bucks for. Prices for current wines range from $13.50 for their 1998 Gewürztraminer to $44 for the exceptional 1996 Zinfandel Port, sold exclusively at the winery and quickly sold out of stock.

ST. HELENA

Raymond Vineyard & Cellar. 849 Zinfandel Lane (off Hwy. 29 or the Silverado Trail), St. Helena. ☎ **800/525-2659** or 707/963-3141. www.raymondwine.com. Daily 10am–4pm. Tours by appointment only.

As fourth-generation vintners from Napa Valley and relations of the Beringers, brothers Walter and Roy Raymond have had plenty of time to develop terrific wines—and an excellent wine-tasting experience. The short drive through vineyards to reach Raymond's friendly, unintimidating cellar is case in point: Passing the heavy-hanging grapes makes you feel you're really in the thick of things before you even get in the door. Then comes the spacious, warm room, complete with dining table and chairs—a perfect setting for sampling the four tiers of wines, most of which are free for the tasting and well priced to appeal to all levels of wine drinkers: The Amber Hill label starts at $6 a bottle for the Chardonnay and $11 for the Cab; the reserves are priced in the low twenties, while the "Generations" Cab costs $50.

Along with the overall experience, we also liked the great gift selection, which includes barbecue sauces, mustard, a chocolate wine syrup, and a gooey hazelnut Merlot fudge sauce. Private reserve tastings cost $2.50. There are no picnic facilities.

✪ **V. Sattui Winery.** 1111 White Lane (at Hwy. 29), St. Helena. ☎ **707/963-7774.** www.vsattui.com. Winter daily 9am–5pm; summer daily 9am–6pm.

This combo winery and enormous gourmet deli and picnic area is a favorite for beginner wine tasters and families. Why? You can fill up on wine, pâté, and cheese samples without ever reaching for your pocketbook and you can let the kids romp the grounds while you enjoy your just-bought booty under the shade of a tree. The gourmet store stocks more than 200 cheeses, sandwich meats, pâtés, breads, exotic salads, and delicious desserts such as a white-chocolate cheesecake. (It would be an easy place to graze were it not for the continuous mob scene at the counter.)

The long wine bar in the back offers everything from Chardonnay, Sauvignon Blanc, Riesling, Cabernet, and Zinfandel to a tasty Madeira and a muscat dessert wine. Their wines aren't distributed, so if you taste something you simply must have, buy it. (If you buy a case, ask to talk with a manager, who'll give you access to the less crowded, more exclusive private tasting room.) Wine prices start at around $9, with many in the $13 range; reserves top out at around $75.

This is one of the most popular stops along Highway 29, so prepare for an enormous picnic party and you won't be disappointed. *Note:* To use the facilities, food and wine must be purchased here.

Heitz Wine Cellars. 436 St. Helena Hwy. (Hwy. 29), St. Helena. ☎ **707/963-2047.** www.heitzcellars.com. Daily 11am–4:30pm. Tours by appointment only; call ☎ **707/963-3542.**

If you're looking for a big wine-tasting hullabaloo, don't come here. At Heitz's tiny, modest tasting room, the point is the wine and the wine alone. Joe Heitz launched his winery in 1961, when there were fewer than 20 wineries in the valley. Today, he oversees the production of 40,000 cases per year, and although his reputation was built on Cabernets (such as the Martha's Vineyard Cab, which will set you back $80), he's also produced a highly-coveted 1990 Chardonnay as well as less costly Cabs, Zins, and more unusual offerings such as the Grignolino Rosé (a mere $7.50). Tastings are complimentary, but if you want to take home the fruits of Heitz's labors, count on spending upwards of $20 per bottle.

Louis M. Martini. 254 S. St. Helena Hwy. (across the street from Sutter Home), St. Helena. ☎ **800/321-WINE.** www.louismartini.com. Daily 10am–4:30pm. Tours available daily; call ahead for reservations and/or schedule.

Louis M. Martini is a comfortable stop for first-time as well as more refined wine tasters. Founded in 1922, this winery is as integral a part of the Wine Country as the Carneros region, which the Martini family developed. In fact, they actually initiated development of that area's vineyards and its production of Chardonnays and Pinot Noirs. Their large tasting room is known for its friendly atmosphere, no-charge tastings, and free-flowing Chardonnay, Cabernet, Merlot, and plenty more. (You can sample the reserve list for $6 and take home the large keepsake Cabernet glass.)

Per-bottle prices "are the best in the valley," claims one employee, who also pointed out that while they range from $6 to $35, most are closer to $15. Another bonus: the great array of gourmet gift items, including the very fun and informative Food First Tasting Kit, which helps explain the art of pairing food and wine and discusses how food affects the flavor of wine more than wine affects the flavor of food.

Merryvale. 1000 Main St. St. Helena. ☎ **800/326-6069** or 707/963-2225. www.merryvale.com. Daily 10am–5:30pm. Tours by appointment only; call ☎ **707/963-7777.**

Merryvale may be approachable and low-key, but not because it's yet to be discovered. Wines here have received plenty of attention from the likes of *Wine Spectator* and *Wine & Spirits*—especially in recent years. Actually, the winery's got a much longer history. It was originally built around the time of Prohibition. And allegedly Peter and Robert Mondavi started their wine-making careers at this site. The property's current identity (Merryvale was founded in 1983 and was previously Sunny St. Helena) celebrates its history with a tasting room within an original 2,000-gallon wooden cask that affords peeks into the Cask Room complete with century-old, 2,000-gallon casks. As for the wine, a $3 tasting fee gets you access to current "vintage" releases; it's $5 for reserve selections, and $10 for the "Connoisseur Selection." Varietals include Sauvignon Blanc, Chardonnay, Semillon, Cabernet Franc, Cabernet, and Antigua—a muscat dessert wine.

Current releases begin at $17 for the 1998 Sauvignon Blanc and top off at $75 for the delicious 1996 Profile (Cab, Merlot, and Cab Franc). Also every weekend morning at 10:30am there's a 2-hour $10 tour and wine component–tasting seminar (reserve in advance).

✪ **Joseph Phelps Vineyards.** Taplin Rd. (off the Silverado Trail), P.O. Box 1031, St. Helena. ☎ **800/707-5789.** www.jpvwines.com. Mon–Sat 9am–5pm, Sun 9am–4pm. Tours and tastings by appointment only.

Visitors interested in intimate, comprehensive tours and looking for a knockout tasting should schedule a tour at this stellar winery. A quick and discreet turn off the Silverado Trail in Spring Valley (there's no sign, so watch for Taplin Road or you'll blast right by it), Joseph Phelps was founded in 1973 and has since become a major player in both the regional and worldwide wine markets. Phelps himself is attributed with a long list of valley firsts, including launching the Syrah varietal in the valley and extending the 1970s Berkeley food revolution (led by Alice Waters) up to the Wine Country via his store, the Oakville Grocery (see p. 127).

Joseph Phelps is a favorite stop for serious wine lovers. The modern, state-of-the-art winery and big-city vibe are proof that Phelps's annual 100,000 cases prove fruitful in more ways than one. When you pass through the wisteria-covered trellis to the entrance of the redwood building, you'll encounter an air of seriousness that hangs heavier than harvest grapes. Fortunately, the mood lightens as the well-educated tour guide explains the details of what you're tasting while pouring samples of five to six wines, which may include Riesling, Sauvignon Blanc, Gewürztraminer, Syrah, Merlot, Zin, and Cab. (Unfortunately, some wines are so popular that they sell out quickly; come late in the season and you may not be able to taste or buy them.) The three excellently located picnic tables, on the terrace overlooking the valley, are available by reservation.

Sutter Home Winery. 277 St. Helena Hwy. (at Thomann Lane), St. Helena. ☎ **707/963-3104.** www.sutterhome.com. Winter daily 9:30am–4:30pm; summer daily 9am–5:30pm.

This winery's been around since 1874, but its widespread reputation stems from the early 1980s, when their introduction of White Zinfandel to the mass market made pink the prominent color in America's wineglasses. While trends have changed and the popularity of White Zin has waned, Sutter Home's department store–like tasting room is fair indication that this winery is still pouring for the people. In the friendly, bustling room, visitors surround the enormous U-shaped bar to sample a slew of wines, with Chardonnay, Cabernet, Zin, and other varieties topping out at $7 a bottle. (Alcohol-free wines are as low as $4; the Reserve Cab is $12.) Along the periphery of the room is an endless selection of food products, ranging from mustard and barbecue to pasta and chocolate sauces, as well as a complete Sutter Home wardrobe line, featuring everything from boxers to baseball-style jackets.

Tasting is free, but for $15 you can participate in a unique interactive process that allows you to blend your own wine, bottle it, and custom sign the label. No tours are offered, but you're invited to take a self-guided walk through the surrounding Victorian Gardens.

✪ Prager Winery & Port Works. 1281 Lewelling Lane (just west of Hwy. 29, behind Sutter Home), St. Helena. ☎ **800/969-PORT** or 707/963-7678. www.pragerport.com. Daily 10:30am–4:30pm.

If you want a real down-home, off-the-beaten-track experience, Prager's can't be beat. Turn the corner from Sutter Home and roll into the small gravel parking lot; you're on the right track—but when you pull open the creaky old wooden door to this shack of a wine-tasting room, you'll begin to wonder. By no means turn back! Pass the oak barrels and you'll quickly come upon the clapboard tasting room, made homey with a big Oriental rug, a cat, and, during winter, a small space heater. Most days, your host will be Jim Prager himself, a sort of modern Santa Claus in both looks and demeanor. But you won't have to sit on his lap for your wish to come true: Just fork over $5 (refundable with purchase) and he'll pour you samples of his delicious $45 Sweet Claire dessert wine, a late-harvest Johannisberg Riesling, the recently released 10-year-old port (which costs $45 per bottle and has won various awards), and a few other yummy selections like Chardonnay and Cab, which retail in the mid-30s. Also available is "Prager Chocolate Drizzle," a chocolate liqueur that tops ice creams and other desserts.

We recommend tasting here even if you can't afford to purchase; if you do want to buy, this is the only place to do it, as Prager doesn't distribute. If you're looking for a special gift, Jim's daughter custom etches bottles for around $100 in the design of your choice, plus the cost of the wine.

Robert Keenan Winery. 3660 Spring Mountain Rd. (off Hwy. 29), St. Helena. ☎ **707/963-9177.** www.keenanwinery.com. Tours and tastings daily 10am–4pm.

It's a winding, uphill drive to reach secluded Robert Keenan, but this far off the tourist track you're guaranteed more elbow room at the tasting bar and a quieter, less commercial experience. When you drive through the gate and pass a few modest homes with kids' toys out front, you'll wonder whether one of the buildings is the family winery. It's not. Keep driving (slowly—kids and dogs at play) and you'll know when you get to the main building and its redwood tasting room.

The 10,000 cases produced here per year are the result of yet another fast-paced professional who left his business behind and headed for the hills. In this case, it's native San Franciscan Robert Keenan, who ran his own insurance agency for 20 years. When he merged with another firm and was bought out in 1981, he had already purchased his "retirement property," the winery's 176 acres, and soon turned his fascination with wine making into a second career. The renovated stone building has a much older history, dating back to the old Conradi Winery, which was founded in 1890.

Today, Robert Keenan Winery is known for its big, full-bodied reds, such as the Mountain Cab. His Merlot, Chardonnay, and Cabernet Franc also range from $17 to $30 per bottle. Older vintages, which you won't find elsewhere, are for sale here as well. Take the tour to learn about their vineyards, production facilities, and wine making in general. Those looking for a pastoral picnic spot should consider spreading their blankets out here. The four tables, situated right outside the winery and surrounded by vineyards, offer stunning views.

✪ **Domaine Charbay Winery & Distillery.** 4001 Spring Mountain Rd. (5 miles west of Hwy. 29), St. Helena. ☎ **800/MDISTILL** (800/634-7845) or 707/ 963-9327. www.charbay.com. Daily (except holidays) by appointment only.

After you finally reach this mountaintop hideaway, affectionately called "the Still on the Hill," you immediately get the sense that something special is going on here. Miles Karakasevic, the owner of this family operation, considers himself more of a perfume maker than the 12th-generation master distiller he is, and it's easy to see why. The tiny distillery is crammed with bottles of his latest fragrant projects-in-the-making, such as tequila, anise liqueur (he'll name it after his wife, Susan), and habanero pepper–infused spirits. Other elixirs he's quietly becoming famous in the Valley for: black walnut liqueur, apple brandy, a line of ports, several red wines, and their charter product—Charbay (pronounced shar-BAY)—a brandy liqueur blended with Chardonnay. The tour centers around a small, 25-gallon copper alambic still; you'll be lovingly guided through an explanation of the distilling process by either Miles, his gregarious son (and apprentice) Marko, or Susan. It's all very low-key and laughter-filled at Domaine Charbay, one of the most unique and interesting places to visit in Wine Country. It's $10 per person to visit their operation and includes tastes of their various releases (what you'll get to taste depends on their mood, we suspect), which is credited toward purchases. No picnic facilities.

Beringer Vineyards. 2000 Main St. (Hwy. 29), St. Helena. ☎ **707/ 963-7115.** www.beringer.com. Off-season daily 9:30am–5pm (last tour 4pm, last tasting 4:30pm); summer 9:30am–6pm (last tour 5pm, last tasting 5:30pm). Free 45-min. tours offered every half hour 9:30am–4pm.

Follow the line of cars just north of St. Helena's business district to Beringer Vineyards, where everyone stops at the remarkable Rhine House to taste wine and view the hand-dug tunnels carved out of the mountainside. Founded in 1876 by brothers Jacob and Frederick, this is the oldest continuously operating winery in the Napa Valley—it was open even during Prohibition, when Beringer kept afloat by making "sacramental" wines. While their White Zinfandel is still the winery's most popular nationwide seller, the 1994 Chardonnay is the choice for more discerning palates: It won *Wine Spectator's* 1996 Wine of the Year award. Also noteworthy, Beringer won *Food and Wine's* winery of the year award for 1999. Three-dollar tastings of current vintages are conducted in the upstairs gift shop, where there's also a large selection of bottles for less than $20. Reserve wines are available in the Rhine House for a fee of $2 to $7 per taste.

Charles Krug Winery. 2800 St. Helena Hwy. (just north of the tunnel of trees at the northern end of St. Helena), St. Helena. ☎ **707/963-5057.** www.charleskrugwinery.com. Daily 10:30am–5:30pm. Tours daily at 11:30am, 1:30, and 3:30pm.

Founded in 1861, Krug was the first winery built in the valley, and is today owned by the family of Peter Mondavi (yes, Robert is his brother). It's worth paying your respects here with a $3 tour, which takes just under an hour and encompasses a walk through the historical redwood Italianate wine cellar, built in 1874, as well as the vineyards, where you'll learn more about grapes and varietals. The tour ends with a tasting in the retail center. But you don't have to tour to taste: Just stop by and fork over $3 to sip current releases, $5 to sample reserves; you'll also get a souvenir glass. On the grounds are picnic facilities with umbrella-shaded tables overlooking vineyards or the historic wine cellar.

St. Clement Vineyards. 2867 St. Helena Hwy. N., St. Helena. ☎ **800/331-8266** or 707/967-3033. www.stclement.com. Daily 10am–4pm. Guided tours daily 10am and 2pm; reservations required.

Perched on a knoll above Highway 29, St. Clement's tasting room is a contradictory combination of homey and corporate, comfortable and cramped. The building itself is a charming Gothic Victorian, but step inside for a sampling and you'll notice that the decor is rather businesslike. On the flip side, the staff is casual and friendly, making this a good stopover for folks who are intimidated by more stuffy scenarios. The bar has room for only three or so guests—but that's the perfect excuse to tote a glass of Merlot out onto the charming landscaped terrace.

Tours feature a walk through the cellar and/or winery plus complimentary barrel, fresh grape juice (depending on the time of year), and wine tastings. If you come just to imbibe, there's a $2 fee, which is refundable with any wine purchase (most bottles run about $25) and includes some wines that you can't get elsewhere. The picnic tables (available by appointment only) are pleasant, but the sound of Highway 29's traffic keeps the site from being entirely splendorous.

Freemark Abbey. Hwy. 29 at Lodi Lane, St. Helena. ☎ **800/963-9698.** www.freemarkabbey.com. Daily 10am–4:30pm. Tour daily at 2pm.

Set in a low-key shopping mall, Freemark Abbey's friendly tasting room has a hunting-lodge feel. The huge space features open-beamed ceilings, a roaring fire (in winter), and comfy couches. The town's only politically correct moose head on a plaque hangs above the tasting bar—check it out for yourself to see what we mean.

There's a $4 charge for tasting and a keepsake wineglass, which may be filled with a sampling of the $12 1998 Riesling, plus Chardonnay, Cabernet, and Merlot, which are priced closer to $25. During summer you can take your taste out onto the lovely outdoor terrace. While they probably won't be pouring the 1986 Bosche Cabernet, you can buy a maximum of one bottle for $65. The half-hour guided tour covers the history, viticulture, and wine cellars. No picnic facilities are available.

CALISTOGA

✪ **Frank-Rombauer Cellars.** 1091 Larkmead Lane (just off the Silverado Trail), Calistoga. ☎ **707/942-0859.** Daily 10am–5pm.

You've gotta love this place. Self-proclaimed "wine dudes"—Dennis, Bob, Chris, and Rich—will do practically anything to maintain their self-proclaimed reputation as the "friendliest winery in the valley." They'll serve you all the bubbly you want (four to six varieties: Brut, Blanc de Blanc, Blanc de Noir, and extra-dry reserve, ranging from $20 to $70 a bottle), and guarantee that you'll never wait more than 10 minutes to take the 20-minute tour of the oldest champagne cellar in the region.

Considering that the winery—formerly Kornell Champagne Cellars—is owned by former Disney president Richard Frank, it's not surprising that, as one employee pointed out, the unpretentious place is a "celebrity stopover." While the tasting room is so casual you may find yourself kicking back on a case of wine, the stone cellar (listed on the National Register of Historic Places) captures the essence of the Wine Country's history. Be sure to meander into the Back Room, where Chardonnay, Zinfandel, and Cabernet are poured. Kornell makes fewer than 500 cases of still wines a year (10,000 cases of champagne), which means if you don't try (and buy) their wine here, you may never get another chance. The same goes for their motto T-shirt: "Kiss French, Drink California." Behind the tasting room is a choice picnic area, situated under the oaks and overlooking the vineyards.

✪ **Schramsberg.** 1400 Schramsberg Rd. (off Calif. 29), Calistoga. ☎ **707/942-2414.** www.schramsberg.com. Daily 10am–4pm. Tours and tastings by appointment only.

This 200-acre champagne estate, a landmark once frequented by Robert Louis Stevenson, has a wonderful old-world feel and is one of our all-time favorite places to explore. Schramsberg is the label that presidents serve when toasting dignitaries from around the globe, and there's plenty of historic memorabilia in the front room to prove it. But the real mystique begins when you enter the champagne caves, which wind 2^1/$_2$ miles (the longest in North America, they say) and were partly hand-carved by Chinese laborers in the 1800s. The caves have an authentic Tom Sawyer ambiance, complete with dangling cobwebs and seemingly endless passageways; you can't help but feel you're on an adventure. The comprehensive, unintimidating tour ends in a charming tasting room, where you'll sit around a big table and sample several surprisingly varied selections of bubbly. Tasting prices are a bit dear at $7.50 per person, but it's money well spent. *Note:* Tastings are only offered to those who take the free tour, and you must reserve in advance.

✪ **Clos Pegase.** 1060 Dunaweal Lane (off Calif. 29 or the Silverado Trail), Calistoga. ☎ **707/942-4981.** www.clospegase.com. Daily 10:30am–5pm. Tours daily at 11am and 2pm.

What happens when a man falls in love with art and wine making, purchases more than 450 acres of prime growing property, and sponsors a competition commissioned by the San Francisco Museum of Modern Art to create a "temple to wine"? You'll find out when you visit this magnificent winery. Renowned architect Michael Graves designed this incredible oasis, which integrates art, 20,000 square feet of aging caves, and a luxurious hilltop private home. Viewing the art here is as much the point as tasting the wines—which, by the way, don't come cheap: Prices range from $13 for the 1998 Vin Gris Merlot to as much as $60 for the 1996 Hommage Artist Series Reserve, an extremely limited blend of the winery's finest lots of Cabernet Sauvignon and Merlot. Tasting all the current releases will cost $2.50 to $5 per three premium wines. The grounds at Clos Pegase (pronounced Clo Pay-*goss*) feature an impressive sculpture garden as well as scenic picnic spots.

✪ **Sterling Vineyards.** 1111 Dunaweal Lane (off Calif. 29, just south of Calistoga), Calistoga. ☎ **707/942-3300.** www.sterlingvineyards.com. Daily 10:30am–4:30pm.

No, you don't need climbing shoes to reach this dazzling white Mediterranean-style winery, perched 300 feet up on a rocky knoll. Just fork over $6 and you'll arrive via aerial tram, which offers dazzling bucolic views along the way. Once on land, follow the self-guided tour (the most comprehensive in the entire Wine Country) of the entire wine-making process. Currently owned by the Seagram company, the winery produces more than 200,000 cases per year.

Samples at the panoramic tasting room are included in the tram fare. Expect to pay anywhere from $10 to $60 for a souvenir bottle ($20 is the average), and if you can find a bottle of their 1996 Napa Valley Reserve Cabernet Sauvignon (currently going for about $60), buy it—it received a 94 in the *Wine Spectator.*

Cuvaison. 4550 Silverado Trail (just south of Dunaweal Lane), Calistoga. ☎ **707/942-6266.** www.cuvaison.com. Daily 10am–5pm. Tours at 10:30am daily with 24-hour notice or by appointment.

In 1969, Silicon Valley engineers Thomas Cottrell and Thomas Parkhill began Cuvaison (pronounced Koo-vay-*sawn,* a French term for the fermentation of wine on the skins) with a 27-acre vineyard of Cabernet, just south of Calistoga. Today, that same vineyard has expanded to 400 acres, producing 63,000 cases of premium wines every year. Known mainly for Chardonnays, wine maker John Thacher also produces a limited amount of Merlot, Pinot Noir, Cabernet Sauvignon, and Zinfandel within the handsome Spanish mission-style structure. If you're curious what an exceptional Chardonnay tastes like, beg for a sample of the award-winning 1998 Napa Valley/Carneros Chardonnay, which embodies a green apple-citrus character typical of grapes from the Carneros region.

Tastings are $4 ($5 for reserve wines), which includes a glass. Wine prices range from $19.95 for a 1998 Chardonnay to as much as $32 for a 1997 Reserve Chardonnay. *Insider Tip:* Bring back the same glass on your next visit, and the wine's free. Beautiful picnic grounds are situated amidst 350-year-old moss-covered oak trees.

Chateau Montelena. 1429 Tubbs Lane (off Calif. 29, just past the Old Faithful Geyser), Calistoga. ☎ **707/942-5105.** www.montelena.com. Daily 10am–4pm. Guided tours by appointment only at 11am and 2pm.

You've probably heard of the California Chardonnay that revolutionized the world of wine when it won the legendary Paris tasting test of 1976, beating out France's top White Burgundies. That wine was a Chateau Montelena 1973 Chardonnay, the product of Mike Grgich's (who now owns his own winery, Grgich Hills) second vintage as wine maker for Chateau Montelena. Though the tasting room is rather plain, the winery itself—housed in a replica of the great châteaux of Bordeaux—is a feast for the eyes, as are the Chinese-inspired lake and gardens behind the château. Tastings are $5, which is credited toward wine purchase; bottle prices are on the steep side, ranging from $15 for a Riesling to $45 for the Montelena Estate Cabernet Sauvignon. After sampling the winery's superb

Chardonnay, Cabernet, and Calistoga Cuvee (a blend of Cabernet Sauvignon, Cabernet Franc, and Merlot), wander around back to marvel at this classic French castle and picturesque grounds replete with wild fowl, lush foliage, and romantic walkways. Unfortunately, picnicking is not an option.

3   More to See & Do

We're not going to humor you: If days filled with wine tasting, dining on fancy food, and just lounging around in the country excite you about as much as a trip to the DMV, buy a *TV Guide* and make yourself real cozy—it's going to be one helluva long stay.

However, there are a few daytime attractions—such as golf, spectacular spas, a few wonderful shops, and museums—that will perk up anyone who simply can't take one more glass of wine; we've discussed them below.

Don't think we just forgot to mention nightlife. With few exceptions, there's more action in a 1-block ghost town than there is in Napa Valley after dark. So what do you do when it's 8pm, you've had dinner, and thumb-twiddling has already cramped your fingers? Beats us—but if you figure it out, let us know.

NAPA

If you have plenty of time and a penchant for Victorian architecture, the **Napa Valley Conference and Visitors Bureau,** 1310 Napa Town Center Mall, off First Street (☎ **707/226-7459; www. napavalley.com**), offers self-guided walking tours of the town's historic buildings.

Anyone with an appreciation for art absolutely must visit the ✪ **di Rosa Preserve,** which until recently was closed to the public. Rene and Veronica di Rosa, who have been collecting contemporary American art for more than 40 years, converted their 88 acres of prime Wine Country property into a monument to northern California's regional art and nature. Their world-renowned collection features 1,500 works in all media by more than 600 greater Bay Area artists. Their treasures are displayed practically everywhere, from along the shores of their 30-acre lake to each nook and cranny of their 110-year-old winery-turned-residence. With hundreds of surrounding acres of rolling hills protected under the Napa County Land Trust, this place is truly a must-see for both art and nature lovers. It's at 5200 Sonoma Hwy. (Highway 121/12)—look for the blue gate. Visits are by appointment only, when a maximum of 25

Up, Up & Away . . .

Admit it: Floating across lush green pastures in a hot-air balloon is something you've always dreamed of but never gotten around to actually doing. Well, here's your best chance, because believe it or not, Napa Valley is the busiest hot-air balloon "flight corridor" in the *world.* Northern California's temperate weather allows for ballooning year-round, and on summer weekends in the valley, it's a rare day when you don't see at least one of the colorful airships floating above the vineyards.

Trips usually depart early in the morning, when the air is cooler and the balloons have better lift. Flight paths vary with the direction and speed of the changing breezes, so "chase" crews on the ground must follow the balloons to their undetermined destinations. Most excursions last between 1 and 3 hours and end with a traditional champagne celebration and breakfast. Reservations are required and should be made as far in advance as possible. Prices range from $165 to $195 per person for the basic package (which includes shuttle service from your local hotel); wedding, wine-tasting, picnic, and lodging packages are also available. For more information or reservations, call Napa's **Bonaventura Balloon Company** (☎ **800/FLY-NAPA**), a highly reputable organization owned and operated by master pilot Joyce Bowen. Another good choice is **Adventures Aloft,** which runs $185 per person (☎ **800/ 944-4408** or 707/944-4408; **www.nvaloft.com**), and is Napa Valley's oldest hot-air-balloon company.

guests are guided through the preserve. Each tour lasts 2 to 2¹/₂ hours and costs $10 per person. Call ☎ **707/226-5991** for reservations.

SHOPPING   If you're looking for a trinket but don't quite know what you want, plan to spend at least an hour strolling **Red Hen's** co-op collection of antiques. You'll find everything from baseball cards to living-room sets, and prices are remarkably affordable. You can't miss this enormous red barn–style building at 5091 St. Helena Hwy., on Highway 29 at Oak Knoll Avenue West (☎ **707/ 257-0822**). It's open daily from 10am to 5:30pm. Its sister property in central Napa is the **Riverfront Antique Center,** 705 Soscol Ave., at Third Street (☎ **707/253-1966**). Here, 70 antique-art dealers exhibit their collections in stalls throughout a mazelike warehouse. During winter, bring a scarf and mittens as there's no indoor heating. Hours are daily from 10am to 5:30pm.

HITTING THE LINKS South of downtown Napa, 1.3 miles east of Highway 29 on Calif. 12, is the **Chardonnay Club** (☎ 707/257-8950), a challenging 36-hole land-links golf complex with first-class service. You pay just one fee, which makes you a member for the day. Privileges include the use of a golf cart, the practice range (including a bucket of balls), and services usually found only at a private club (such as roving snack carts and complimentary clubs cleaning). The course ambles through and around 325 acres of vineyards, hills, creeks, canyons, and rock ridges. There are three nines of similar challenge, all starting at the clubhouse so that you can play the 18 of your choice. Five sets of tees provide you with a course measuring from 5,300 yards to a healthy 7,100. Starting times can be reserved up to 2 weeks in advance. Greens fees (including mandatory cart and practice balls) from March 16 through November are $70 on weekdays (with a 2pm twilight for $45) and $90 on weekends (with a 2pm twilight for $60). Rates are discounted in winter.

RUTHERFORD

Want to bring home an unusual and beautiful handcrafted decoration for your home or yard? Seek out **Napa Valley Grapevine Wreath Company,** Hwy. 128/Rutherford Crossroad, P.O. Box 67, Rutherford, CA 94573 (☎ **707/963-8893**), which weaves big and small indoor or outdoor sculptures made out of little more than Cabernet grapevines. Call for directions—this tiny shack of a shop is hidden on a side road among Rutherford's vineyards. Hours vary during winter, but are generally Wednesday through Monday from 10:30am to 5:30pm.

ST. HELENA

Literary buffs and other romantics will want to visit the **Silverado Museum,** 1490 Library Lane (☎ **707/963-3757**), devoted to the life and works of Robert Louis Stevenson, who honeymooned here in 1880 in an abandoned Silverado Mine bunkhouse. The collection of more than 8,000 items includes original manuscripts, letters, photographs, and portraits, plus the desk he used in Samoa. Hours are Tuesday through Sunday from noon to 4pm; admission is free.

SPAS If the Wine Country's slow pace and tranquil vistas aren't soothing enough for you, St. Helena's diverse selection of spas can massage, bathe, wrap, and steam you into an overly-pampered pulp.

Should you choose to indulge, we recommend you do so toward the end of your stay—when you've wined and dined yourself to the point where you have only enough energy left to make it to and from the spa.

Unlike the cosmopolitan-chic day spas of Sonoma Mission Inn (Sonoma) and Health Spa Napa Valley (St. Helena), ✪ **White Sulphur Springs Retreat & Spa,** 3100 White Sulphur Springs Rd. (☎ **707/963-4361**), offers a more spiritual day of cleansing and pampering. Yes, you will encounter massages, aromatherapy treatments, seaweed or mineral mud wraps, and a pool and Jacuzzi for guests' use. But the most blissful benefits are not the product of some well-known architect or fancy new massage oil. Mother Nature takes the credit for the magic here: acres of redwoods, streams, grassy fields, wooded groves, and hiking trails galore. The spa treatments only make the experience that much more relaxing. The resident spotted owls, woodpeckers, raccoon, deer, and fox don't take advantage of the natural outdoor hot sulfur spring, pool, Jacuzzi, or sauna (free for spa-goers), but you might catch a glimpse of them as you bathe. Massages are given in the homey spa building or outside amidst the redwoods ($80 to $95 per hour). A day of peaceful pampering doesn't come any cheaper, but take note: This is a casual place. Five-star fanatics should stick with Sonoma Mission Inn, Spa & Country Club (see chapter 5) or Health Spa Napa Valley, which covers the other end of the spa spectrum.

If you're a fitness freak, ✪ **Health Spa Napa Valley,** 1030 Main St. (Highway 29; ☎ **707/967-8800**), is a mandatory stop after a few days of inevitable overindulgence. Sure, you can hike, bike, run the roads, or convince yourself that flexing your biceps as you raise your wineglass is enough. But if your preferred way to work off last night's umpteenth vacation dessert is to treadmill or StairMaster yourself silly, you'll want to get a temporary membership here. After a workout you can reward yourself with spa treatments: Immerse yourself in Wine Country ways with a grape-seed mud wrap ($80) or go all out with a Pancha Karma treatment—two massage therapists get out the knots with synchronized motion ($145). These are the newest facilities around and the local favorite for fitness. Memberships are $20 per day Monday through Thursday, $25 per day Friday through Sunday, and free for guests of the Inn at Southbridge.

SHOPPING   St. Helena's Main Street is the best place to go if you're suffering serious retail withdrawal. Though you'll find only a few blocks of stores that are credit-card worthy, trust us, a lot of damage can still be done. Take, for example, ✪ **Vanderbilt and Company,** 1429 Main St., between Adams and Pine streets (☎ 707/963-1010), which offers the crème de la crème of cookware, hand-painted Italian dishware, linens, and everything else you could possibly convince yourself you need for your gourmet kitchen and dining room. We did almost all our holiday shopping here last year. Open daily from 9:30am to 5:30pm.

Another great gift shop is **Oliver,** 1224-A Adams St. (☎ 707/967-8777). And no, this new shop that claims to be the number-one supplier for Williams Sonoma is not named after the famous orphan, but for everything related to delicious Napa Valley olives. Taste and pour your own oil from huge copper tanks or grab a beautifully pre-packaged bottle along with other food products galore.

We also have no bones to pick with **fideaux,** 1312 Main St. (☎ 707/967-9935), a wonderfully charming boutique known as the Eddie Bauer for dogs and cats. Hand-painted feeders, beautiful ceramic water bowls, custom-designed scratching posts, silk-screened dog and cat pillows, rhinestone collars, unique toys, and gourmet dog treats are just a few pet must-haves you'll find here. The ultimate way to bring the Wine Country home to Spot? Try a wine-barrel doghouse. Hours are 9:30am to 5:30pm daily.

Shopaholics won't be able to avoid at least one sharp turn off Highway 29 for a stop at the **St. Helena Premium Outlets,** 2 miles north of downtown St. Helena (☎ 707/963-7282). Featured designers include Donna Karan, Coach, Movado, London Fog, and more. The stores are open daily from 10am to 6pm.

Napa's best deals on wine are found not in the wineries, but in a couple of St. Helena stores. **Dean & DeLuca,** 607 S. Main St. (Highway 29; ☎ 707/967-9980), and—believe it or not—**Safeway,** 1026 Hunt Ave. (☎ 707/963-3833), have enormous wine selections; Safeway tends to have some of the best deals around.

One last favorite stop: **Napa Valley Olive Oil Manufacturing Company,** 835 Charter Oak Rd., at the end of the road behind Tra Vigne restaurant (☎ 707/963-4173; www.napavalleyoliveoilmfg.com), a tiny market that presses and bottles its own oils and sells them at a fraction of the price you'll pay elsewhere. They also have an extensive selection of Italian cooking ingredients, imported snacks, and the best deals on exotic mushrooms we've ever seen. You'll also love their age-old method for totaling the bill, which you simply must find out for yourself. They are open daily 8am to 5pm.

BICYCLING The quieter northern end of the valley is an ideal place to rent a bicycle and ride the Silverado Trail. **St. Helena Cyclery,** 1156 Main St. (☎ **707/963-7736**), rents bikes for $7 per hour or $25 a day, including rear rack and picnic bag.

CALISTOGA

Calistoga Depot, 1458 Lincoln Ave. (on the site of Calistoga's original 1868 railroad station) has a variety of shops, some of which are housed in six restored passenger cars dating from 1916.

NATURAL WONDERS Old Faithful Geyser of California, 1299 Tubbs Lane (☎ **707/942-6463**), is one of only three "old faithful" geysers in the world. It's been blowing off steam at regular intervals for as long as anyone can remember. The 350°F water spews at a height of about 60 feet every 40 minutes, day and night. The performance lasts about a minute, and you can bring along a picnic lunch to munch on between spews. An exhibit hall, gift shop, and snack bar are open every day. Admission is $6 for adults, $5 for seniors, $2 for children 6 to 12, free for children under 6. Open daily from 9am to 6pm (to 5pm in winter). To get there, follow the signs from downtown Calistoga; it's between Calif. 29 and Calif. 128.

You won't see thousands of trees turned into stone, but you'll still find many interesting petrified specimens at the **Petrified Forest,** 4100 Petrified Forest Rd. (☎ **707/942-6667**). Volcanic ash blanketed this area after the eruption of Mount St. Helena three million years ago. As a result, you'll find redwoods that have turned to rock through the slow infiltration of silicas and other minerals, as well as petrified seashells, clams, and marine life indicating that water covered this area before the redwood forest appeared. Admission is $4 for adults, $3 for seniors and children 12 to 17, $1 for children 4 to 11, and free for children under 4. Open daily from 10am to 5:30pm (to 4:30pm in winter). Heading north from Calistoga on Calif. 128, turn left onto Petrified Forest Road, just past Lincoln Street.

BICYCLING Cycling enthusiasts can rent bikes from **Getaway Adventures BHK,** 1117 Lincoln Ave. (☎ **800/499-BIKE** or 707/942-0332; **www.getawayadventures.com**). Full-day tours cost $95 and include lunch and a visit to four or five wineries; downhill cruises are available for people who hate to pedal.

HORSEBACK RIDES If you like horses and venturing through cool, misty forests, then $50 will seem like a bargain for a 1¹/₂-hour ride with a friendly tour guide from **Napa Valley Trail Rides** (☎ **707/996-8566; www.thegridnet/trailrides/**). After you've been saddled and schooled in the basics of horse handling at the stable, you'll be led on a leisurely stroll (with the occasional trot thrown in for excitement) through beautiful Bothe-Napa Valley State Park off Highway 29 near Calistoga. We've taken the trip ourselves and loved every minute of it—sore butts and all.

✪ **MUD BATHS**   The one thing you should do while you're in Calistoga is what people have been doing here for the last 150 years: Take a mud bath. The natural baths are composed of local volcanic ash, imported peat, and naturally boiling mineral hot-springs water, all mulled together to produce a thick mud that simmers at a temperature of about 104°F.

After you've overcome the hurdle of deciding how best to place your naked body into the mushy stone tub, the rest is pure relaxation as you soak with surprising buoyancy for about 10 to 12 minutes. A warm mineral-water shower, a mineral-water whirlpool bath, and a mineral-water steam-room visit follow. Afterward, a relaxing blanket wrap will slowly cool down your delighted body followed by a half-hour muscle-melting massage. All of this takes about 2 hours and costs about $99 (we recommend you add another half-hour's worth of massage for an additional $20). The outcome is a rejuvenated, revitalized, squeaky-clean you. *Note:* Mud baths aren't recommended for those who are pregnant or have high blood pressure.

The spas also offer a variety of other treatments, such as hand and foot massages, herbal wraps, acupressure face-lifts, skin rubs, and herbal facials. Prices range from $35 to $150, and appointments are necessary for all services; call at least a week in advance, and as far in advance as possible during the busy summer season.

Indulge yourself at any of these Calistoga spas:

Spa	Address	Telephone Number
Dr. Wilkinson's Hot Springs	1507 Lincoln Ave.	707/942-4102
Lincoln Avenue Spa	1339 Lincoln Ave.	707/942-5296
Golden Haven Hot Springs Spa	1713 Lake St.	707/942-6793
Calistoga Spa Hot Springs	1006 Washington St.	707/942-6269
Calistoga Village Inn & Spa	1880 Lincoln Ave.	707/942-0991
Eurospa & Inn	1202 Pine St	707/942-6829
Indian Springs Resort	1712 Lincoln Ave.	707/942-4913

Lavender Hill Spa	1015 Foothill Blvd.	800/528-4772 or 707/942-4495
Mount View Spa	1457 Lincoln Ave.	707/942-5789
Nance's Hot Springs	1614 Lincoln Ave.	707/942-6211
Roman Spa Motel	1300 Washington St.	707/942-4441

4 Where to Stay

With more than 2,500 hotel rooms available throughout the county, you'd think it'd be a snap to secure a room. Unfortunately, choosing and reserving accommodations—especially from April through November—can be a challenge, and to add to the frustration is that ever-burdening 2-night minimum.

Because the Napa Valley is so small, it really doesn't much matter which town you base yourself in; everything's within a half-hour or 45-minute drive from everything else. There are, however, a number of other things you should think about when deciding where to stay. Consider whether you want to be in a modern hotel with all the expected conveniences or a quaint turn-of-the-century B&B; surrounded by acres of vineyards or closer to the highway; in the company of the more conservative wealthy or those leading alternative lifestyles. Accommodations here run the gamut—from motels and B&Bs to world-class luxury retreats—and all are easily accessible from the main highway. While we recommend shacking up in the more romantically pastoral areas such as St. Helena, there's no question you're going to find better deals in the towns of Napa or laidback Calistoga. As always, the primary determining factor will come down to one question: how much are you willing to spend?

We've arranged the listings below first by area and then by price, using the following categories: **Very Expensive,** more than $250 per night; **Expensive,** $200 to $250 per night; **Moderate,** $150 to $200 per night; and **Inexpensive,** less than $150 per night (sorry—the reality is that anything less than $150 a night qualifies as inexpensive 'round these parts).

When planning your trip, keep in mind that during the high season—between June and November—most hotels charge peak rates and sell out completely on weekends; many have a 2-night minimum. Always ask about discounts. During the off-season, you have far better bargaining power and may be able to get a room at almost half the summer rate. Also note that while the valley is reasonably small and condensed, tourist traffic makes it beneficial to stay as close to the attractions you want to visit as possible.

RESERVATIONS SERVICES   A number of companies offer help with hotel and B&B reservations at no charge. **Accommodation Referral Bed & Breakfast Exchange** (☎ **800/240-8466,** 800/499-8466 in California, or 707/963-8466), which also represents hotels and inns, will ask you which dates you're traveling, your price range, and what kind of accommodation you're looking for before coming up with recommendations. **Bed & Breakfast Inns of Napa Valley** (☎ **707/944-4444**), an association of 26 Napa Valley B&Bs, provides inn descriptions and makes reservations. **Napa Valley Reservations Unlimited** (☎ **800/251-NAPA** or 707/252-1985) is also a source for everything from hot-air balloon and glider rides to wine-tasting tours by limousine.

NAPA

Wherever tourist dollars are to be had, you're sure to find big hotels with familiar names catering to independent vacationers, business travelers, and groups. **Embassy Suites,** 1075 California Blvd., Napa, CA 94559 (☎ **800/362-2779** or 707/253-9540), offers 205 of their usual two-room suites, which include a kitchenette, coffeemaker, modem capabilities, and two TVs; extras include a complimentary cooked-to-order breakfast, indoor and outdoor pools, and restaurant; rates range from $190 to $280. The 191-room **Napa Valley Marriott,** 3425 Solano Ave., Napa, CA 94558 (☎ **800/228-9290** or 707/253-7433), offers lighted tennis courts, an exercise room, a heated outdoor pool and spa, and two restaurants; rates range from $189 to $249.

VERY EXPENSIVE

Silverado Country Club & Resort. 1600 Atlas Peak Rd., Napa, CA 94558. ☎ **800/532-0500** or 707/257-0200. Fax 707/257-2867. www.silveradoresort. com. 280 suites. A/C MINIBAR TV TEL. $255 junior suite; $325 1-bedroom suite; $435–$535 2- or 3-bedroom suite. Golf and spa promotional packages available. AE, DC, DISC, MC, V. Drive north on Hwy. 29 to Trancas St.; turn east to Atlas Peak Rd.

If you long for the opulence of an East Coast country club, bring your racquet and golf clubs to this 1,200-acre resort in the Napa foothills, where the focus is on the sporting life. The spacious accommodations range from very large studios with king-size bed, kitchenette, and a roomy, well-appointed bathroom to one-, two-, or three-bedroom cottage suites. Each comes with a wood-burning fireplace. Cottage suites are in private, low-rise groupings tucked away in shared courtyards along peaceful walkways. All rooms are individually

Napa Valley Accommodations

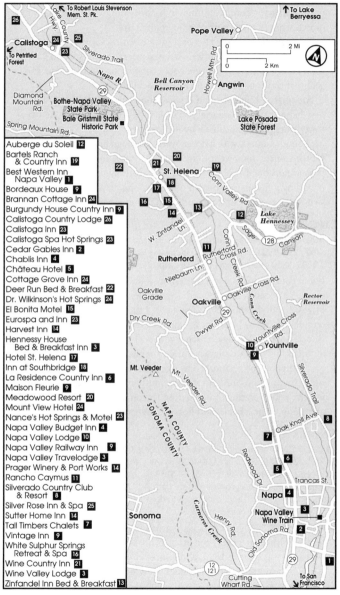

Auberge du Soleil **12**
Bartels Ranch & Country Inn **19**
Best Western Inn Napa Valley **1**
Bordeaux House **9**
Brannan Cottage Inn **24**
Burgundy House Country Inn **9**
Calistoga Country Lodge **26**
Calistoga Inn **23**
Calistoga Spa Hot Springs **23**
Cedar Gables Inn **2**
Chablis Inn **4**
Château Hotel **5**
Cottage Grove Inn **24**
Deer Run Bed & Breakfast **22**
Dr. Wilkinson's Hot Springs **24**
El Bonita Motel **15**
Eurospa and Inn **23**
Harvest Inn **14**
Hennessy House Bed & Breakfast Inn **3**
Hotel St. Helena **17**
Inn at Southbridge **18**
La Residence Country Inn **6**
Maison Fleurie **9**
Meadowood Resort **20**
Mount View Hotel **24**
Nance's Hot Springs & Motel **23**
Napa Valley Budget Inn **4**
Napa Valley Lodge **10**
Napa Valley Railway Inn **9**
Napa Valley Travelodge **3**
Prager Winery & Port Works **14**
Rancho Caymus **11**
Silverado Country Club & Resort **8**
Silver Rose Inn & Spa **25**
Sutter Home Inn **14**
Tall Timbers Chalets **7**
Vintage Inn **9**
White Sulphur Springs Retreat & Spa **16**
Wine Country Inn **21**
Wine Valley Lodge **3**
Zinfandel Inn Bed & Breakfast **13**

decorated with country home-style furnishings, and manage to offer a sense of privacy despite the resort's size.

Dining/Diversions: There's a quintessential steak-and-seafood restaurant, as well as a garden-view restaurant serving superb California and Pacific Rim cuisine and a large indoor/outdoor bar and grill that serves breakfast, lunch, and cocktails.

Amenities: Limited room service, concierge, dry cleaning, laundry, baby-sitting, secretarial services, valet parking. There are two cleverly designed golf courses by Robert Trent Jones, Jr.—the 6,500-yard South Course, with a dozen water crossings, and the 6,700-yard North Course, somewhat longer but a bit more forgiving; a staff of pros are on hand (greens fee $115 for 18 holes on either course, including a mandatory cart). Full-service spa, tennis courts, several swimming pools, tour desk, conference rooms, and business center.

EXPENSIVE

La Residence Country Inn. 4066 St. Helena Hwy., Napa, CA 94558. ☎ **707/253-0337.** Fax 707/253-0382. www.laresidence.com. 20 units. A/C TEL. $195–$350 double; lower rates Dec–Apr. AE, DC, MC, V.

If you consider a B&B too homespun and a luxury hotel too impersonal, La Residence is a good alternative. Set on 2 acres just off Highway 29, the inn's 20 rooms are in either the late-18th-century-revival-style main house or the newer French barn–style building. Rooms are individually decorated with wall-to-wall carpeting, period antiques, armoires, designer fabrics, fireplaces (in most), CD players, and patios or verandas. The pool-area spa is secluded and well manicured. A full breakfast is served in the attractive dining room, which is often warmed by a roaring fire on chilly mornings; in the afternoon, wine, cheese, and hors d'oeuvres are offered.

MODERATE

✪ **Cedar Gables Inn.** 486 Coombs St., Napa, CA 94559. ☎ **800/309-7969** or 707/224-7969. Fax 707/224-4838. www.CedarGablesInn.com. E-mail: info@cedargablesinn.com. 9 units. $139–$259 double ($10 less in winter). Rates include full breakfast and complimentary port. AE, DISC, MC, V. From Hwy. 29 north, exit onto First St. and follow signs to downtown; turn right onto Coombs St.; the house is at the corner of Oak St.

Innkeepers Margaret and Craig Snasdell have developed quite a following with their grand, romantic B&B in Old Town Napa. The Victorian was built in 1892, and rooms reflect the era with rich tapestries and stunning gilded antiques. Five rooms have fireplaces; five have whirlpool tubs; and all feature queen-size brass, wood, or iron beds. Guests meet each evening in front of the roaring fireplace in the family room for complimentary wine and cheese. At other times, it's a perfect place to cuddle up and watch the large-screen TV.

INEXPENSIVE

Best Western Inn Napa Valley. 100 Soscol Ave., Napa, CA 94559. ☎ **800/528-1234** or 707/257-1930. Fax 707/255-0709. 68 units. A/C TV TEL. Apr–Nov $140–$160 double; Dec–Mar $98–$140 double. AE, CB, DC, DISC, JCB, MC, V.

Let's face it, this motel and its location—at the industrial southern edge of Napa—are about as fashionable as jug wine. But when frilly B&Bs with smaller rooms and noisy neighbors are charging two or three times what you'll pay here, a view of the 24-hour Denny's downstairs starts looking pretty good. Many of the traditional motel-style rooms at this Best Western have small balconies, but not much in the way of views—keep your gaze focused inward on the basic but clean and spacious accommodations. The loftlike suites are perfect for families and come with amenities aplenty: two TVs, two phones, coffeemaker, fridge, and decent toiletries.

Chablis Inn. 3360 Solano Ave., Napa, CA 94558. ☎ **707/257-1944.** Fax 707/226-6862. www.chablisinn.com. 34 units. A/C TV TEL. Apr to mid-Nov $80–$130 double; mid-Nov to Mar $70–$100 double. AE, DC, DISC, MC, V.

There's no way around it. If you want to sleep cheaply in a town where the *average* room goes for upward of $200 per night in high season, you're going to have to motel it. But look on the bright side: Because your room is likely to be little more than a crashing pad after a day of eating and drinking, a clean bed and a remote control are all you'll really need anyway. But Chablis offers much more than that. Each of the superclean motel-style rooms has a new mattress, refrigerator, and coffeemaker; some even boast kitchenettes and/or whirlpool tubs. Guests have access to an outdoor heated pool and hot tub, plus a basic continental breakfast. Friendly owner Ken Patel is on hand most of the time and is constantly upgrading his tidy highway-side hostelry.

Château Hotel. 4195 Solano Ave., Napa, CA 94558. ☎ **800/253-6272** in California or 707/253-9300. Fax 707/253-0906. 115 units. A/C TV TEL. Apr–Oct $110–$140 double; Nov–Mar $100 double. AAA, government, corporate, senior-citizen, and other discounts available. AE, CB, DC, MC, V. From Hwy. 29 north, turn left just past Trower Ave., at the entrance to the Napa Valley wine region.

This contemporary two-story motel complex tries to evoke the aura of a French country inn, but it isn't fooling anybody—a motel's a motel. However, the rooms and bathrooms are spacious and have separate vanity/dressing areas, and most units have refrigerators. Ten rooms are specially designed for guests with disabilities. If you're used to a daily swim, the Château also has a heated pool and spa. Bargain travelers: Be sure to ask about discounts; some special rates will knock the price down by $20.

The Hennessy House Bed & Breakfast Inn. 1727 Main St. (between Lincoln and First sts.), Napa, CA 94559. ☎ **707/226-3774.** Fax 707/226-2975. www.hennessyhouse.com. 10 units. A/C TEL. Mid-Mar to mid-Nov $125–$250 double; mid-Nov to mid-Mar $105–$230 double. Rates include full breakfast, afternoon tea and cookies, and nightly wine-and-cheese hour. AE, CB, DC, DISC, MC, V.

This Eastlake-style Queen Anne Victorian may be old enough to be on the National Register of Historic Places, but its antiquity is contrasted by the fresh hospitality of owners Alex and Gilda Feit. Since the couple took over the B&B in late 1997, they've been on a mission to satisfy each and every guest. Their genuine concern makes a stay here very personable. Rooms in the main house are quaint, with a combination of antique furnishings, queen-size bed, fireplace, and/or a claw-foot bathtub. Carriage-house accommodations, located just off the main house, are larger but less ornate and feature whirlpool tubs (a bummer to climb into if you're not agile); all have fireplaces. Because walls are thin throughout both structures, TVs are out of the question (except for a few rooms where additional insulation was recently added), and if your neighbor's a snorer, you'll know it firsthand. But it'll make for fun conversation over breakfast, when guests meet in the dining room for an impressive full meal. The adjoining living room allows TV junkies to stay tuned. The small garden is a nice spot for a bit of morning sun and is also the access point for the sauna.

Napa Valley Budget Inn. 3380 Solano Ave., Napa, CA 94558. ☎ **707/257-6111.** Fax 707/252-2702. 58 units, all with bathroom (shower only). A/C TV TEL. May–Oct from $70 double; Nov–Apr from $56 double. Rates include continental breakfast. AE, DC, DISC, MC, V. From Hwy. 29 north, turn left onto the Redwood Rd. turnoff and go 1 block to Solano Ave.; then turn left for half a block.

This no-frills lodging has an excellent location and simple, clean, comfortable rooms. Local calls are free, and guests can enjoy the complimentary coffee in the lobby and the small pool on the premises (heated summers only).

Napa Valley Travelodge. 853 Coombs St., Napa, CA 94559. ☎ **800/578-7878** or 707/226-1871. Fax 707/226-1707. 45 units. A/C TV TEL. $54–$189 double. CB, DC, DISC, JCB, MC, V.

Rarely does so much come so cheaply. This Travelodge has been around for a while, but even if you've stayed here before you won't recognize it. In early 1998, the owners gutted the entire place with the intent of turning it into a "New Orleans-style" motel (including a cobblestone center courtyard/parking area). And while there are no wild partyers hanging over the balconies throwing beads, there's still plenty to celebrate. Every room has a VCR, 36-inch TV, coffee, ironing board, and hair dryer; some feature a Jacuzzi tub. Guests have access to coin-operated laundry facilities, a pool, a video library, and for a nominal fee, a fitness center 2 blocks away. If you're lucky enough to secure a room, you will have gotten one of the best deals around.

Tall Timbers Chalets. 1012 Darms Lane, Napa, CA 94558. ☎ **707/252-7810.** Fax 707/252-1055. www.talltimberscottages.com. 8 cottages. A/C MINIBAR TV. Mar–Oct Sun–Thurs $116 double, Fri–Sat and holidays $125–$150 double; Nov–Feb Sun–Thurs $75 double, Fri–Sat and holidays $90–$150 double. Extra person $20. AE, MC, V. Free parking. From Hwy. 29 north, turn left onto Darms Lane before you reach Yountville.

While many hotels' prices skyrocket during the high season, Tall Timbers—a group of eight whitewashed, roomy cottages surrounded by pines and eucalyptus—remains cute, centrally located, and affordable. Each cottage is nicely decorated and includes a toaster oven and coffeemaker, as well as a basket of fresh fruit on your arrival. Other nice touches include a basic breakfast of muffins and fruit drinks in the refrigerator and a complimentary bottle of champagne. Each cottage sleeps up to four (there's a bedroom plus a queen-size sofa bed in the living room) and two have sundecks (though you cannot be guaranteed one).

Mary, who runs the place, requires a check in advance to reserve a room, and when the valley is booked, she may even rent out her own room adjoining the office. If you come expecting some of the cheapest, simple lodgings in the area rather than the Ritz, you'll be pleased with your stay. There are no phones in the cottages, but you can use the one in the main office. Tall Timbers isn't particularly difficult to find, but to be on the safe side, ask for specific directions. Smoking is not allowed.

Wine Valley Lodge. 200 S. Coombs St. (between First and Imola sts.), Napa, CA 94558. ☎ **707/224-7911.** 53 units. A/C TV TEL. $69–$119 double; $120–$165 deluxe rooms. AE, CB, DC, DISC, MC, V.

Dollar for dollar, the Wine Valley Lodge offers the most for the least in all of Wine Country. Located at the south end of town in a quiet residential neighborhood, the mission-style motel is extremely well kept and accessible, just a short drive from Hwy. 29 and the wineries to the north. The reasonably priced deluxe rooms are family style with two bedrooms connected by a bathroom. The $500,000 room renovation, beginning in February 2000, promises continued improvements by year's end.

YOUNTVILLE

In addition to hotels, try the **Villagio Inn and Spa** (6481 Washington St., near California St.; ☎ **707/944-8877; www.villagio.com**), a large and quite attractive, although corporate, property. The modern rooms range from $225 to $335.

EXPENSIVE

Vintage Inn. 6541 Washington St. (between Humboldt St. and Webber Ave.), Yountville, CA 94599. ☎ **800/351-1133** or 707/944-1112. Fax 707/944-1617. www.vintageinn.com. 80 units. A/C TV TEL. $150–$350 double; $225–$350 minisuites and villas. Additional person $25. Rates include continental breakfast and afternoon tea. AE, CB, DC, DISC, MC, V. Free parking. Pets $25. From Hwy. 29 north, take the Yountville exit and turn left onto Washington St.

This contemporary, French-country hotel is situated on an old 23-acre winery estate in the heart of up-and-coming Yountville. The complex feels far more corporate than "inn" would suggest, and the staff is professional. Rooms are bright and cozy; each has a fireplace or private veranda, oversize beds, and a coffeemaker, plus a Jacuzzi tub and plush bathrobes. If you're looking for a workout, you may rent a bike, reserve one of the two tennis courts, or take a dip in the 60-foot swimming pool or outdoor whirlpool, both heated year-round. A continental champagne breakfast and afternoon tea are served daily in the Vintage Club. Services include concierge and laundry/valet.

MODERATE

✪ **Maison Fleurie.** 6529 Yount St. (between Washington St. and Yountville Crossroad), Yountville, CA 94599. ☎ **800/788-0369** or 707/944-2056. Fax 707/944-2056. www.foursisters.com. 13 units. A/C TV TEL. $110–$260 double. Rates include full breakfast and afternoon hors d'oeuvres. AE, DC, MC, V.

Maison Fleurie is one of the prettiest hotels in the Wine Country, a trio of beautiful 1873 brick-and-fieldstone buildings overlaid with ivy. Seven rooms are located in the main house—a charming Provençal replica complete with thick brick walls, terra-cotta tile, and paned windows—while the remaining rooms are split between the old bakery building and the carriage house. All have private baths, and some feature private balconies, patios, sitting areas, Jacuzzi tubs, and fireplaces. Breakfast is served in the quaint little dining room; afterwards, you're welcome to wander the landscaped grounds, use the pool or outdoor spa, or borrow a mountain bike (free of charge) to ride around town. It's impossible not to enjoy your stay at Maison Fleurie.

✪ **Napa Valley Lodge.** 2230 Madison St., Yountville, CA 94599. ☎ **800/ 368-2468** or 707/944-2468. Fax 707/944-9362. www.woodsidehotels.com. 55 units. A/C MINIBAR TV TEL. $212–$525 double. Rates include champagne breakfast buffet. AE, CB, DC, DISC, MC, V.

Many frequent visitors compare this contemporary hotel to the Vintage Inn, noting that it's even more personable and accommodating. The lodge is just off Highway 29, though they do a good job of disguising it. Facilities include a pool, redwood sauna, and small exercise room; the newly upgraded guest rooms are large, ultraclean, and better appointed than many in the area. Many have vaulted ceilings and 33 have fireplaces. All come with a king- or queen-size bed, wicker furnishings, coffeemaker, robes, and either a private balcony or a patio. They were updated in 1999. The cheapest rooms at ground level are smaller and get less sunlight than those on the second floor. Extras include concierge, on-demand video, afternoon tea and cookies, Friday-evening wine tasting, and a full champagne breakfast—with all this, it's no wonder AAA gave the Napa Valley Lodge the four-diamond award for excellence. Ask about winter discounts—they can be as high as 30%.

INEXPENSIVE

Bordeaux House. 6600 Washington St., Yountville, CA 94599. ☎ **707/ 944-2855.** Fax 707/944-2855. www.bordeauxhouse.com. 7 units. A/C TV. Sun–Thurs $125 double, Fri–Sat $155 double. Additional person $25 extra. 2-night minimum during high season. Rates include full breakfast. MC, V.

Considering the name, we were expecting this centrally located hotel on a quiet Yountville street to be some kind of romantic, antique-French-style structure. We were way off. How far? Try 1970s two-story brick. Nonetheless, there are seven ultratidy rooms here, each renting for what in this neck of the woods is a very reasonable price. Each has a private entrance; six have fireplaces and private patios. Whoever took a stab at the interior design didn't have the best aim (although the grass cloth walls are pretty cool). However, new bedskirts, spreads, and window coverings are a step in the right direction. Added bonuses include port and sherry, which are available in the common area.

Burgundy House Country Inn. 6711 Washington St. (P.O. Box 3175), Yountville, CA 94599. ☎ **707/944-0889.** www.bbinternet.com/burgundy. 6 units, all with bathroom (shower only). A/C. $145–$160 double. Rates include breakfast. MC, V. From Hwy. 29 north, take the Yountville exit and turn left onto Washington St.

This distinctly French country inn, built of local fieldstone and river rock in the early 1890s as a brandy distillery, is tiny but impressive. The interior features thick stone walls and hand-hewn post and lintel beams, enhanced today by antique country furnishings. The six cozy guest rooms (all nonsmoking) have colorful quilted spreads and comfortable beds along with very small bathrooms. Delightful touches include fresh flowers in each of the rooms, a full breakfast, and complimentary port and sherry in the common area. The breakfast can be taken inside or outdoors in the pretty garden.

Napa Valley Railway Inn. 6503 Washington St. (adjacent to the Vintage 1870 shopping complex), Yountville, CA 94599. ☎ **707/944-2000.** 9 units. A/C TV. $75–$140 double. AE, MC, V.

This is one of our favorite places to stay in the Wine Country: it's inexpensive and it's cute as all get out. Looking hokey as heck from the outside, the Railway Inn consists of two rows of sun-bleached cabooses and railcars sitting on a stretch of Yountville's original track and connected by a covered wooden walkway. Things get considerably better, though, as you enter your private caboose or railcar, each sumptuously appointed with comfy love seats, queen-size brass beds, and tiled full baths. The coups de grâce are the bay windows and skylights, which let in plenty of California sunshine. The railcars are all suites, so if you're looking to save your pennies, opt for the cabooses. Adjacent to the inn is Yountville's main shopping complex, with wine tastings and some good low-priced restaurants.

OAKVILLE & RUTHERFORD
VERY EXPENSIVE

✪ **Auberge du Soleil.** 180 Rutherford Hill Rd., Rutherford, CA 94573. ☎ **707/963-1211.** Fax 707/963-8764. www.aubergedusoleil.com. 50 units. A/C MINIBAR TV TEL. $350–$535 double. Rates discounted Dec–Mar. AE, CB, DC, DISC, JCB, MC, V. From Rutherford, turn right on Calif. 128 and go 3 miles to the Silverado Trail; turn left and head north about 200 yd. to Rutherford Hill Rd.; turn right.

This spectacular Relais & Châteaux member is the kind of place you'd imagine movie stars frequenting for clandestine affairs or weekend retreats. Set high above the Napa Valley in a 33-acre olive grove, it's quiet, indulgent, and luxuriously romantic. The

Mediterranean-style rooms are large enough to get lost in—and you might want to once you discover all the amenities. The bathtub alone, an enormous hot tub with a skylight overhead, will tempt you to grab a glass of California red and settle in. A wood-burning fireplace is surrounded by oversized, cushy furniture; it's an ideal place to relax and listen to CDs or watch a movie on the VCR. Fresh flowers, original art, terra-cotta floors, and natural-wood and leather furnishings whisk you out of the Wine Country and into the Southwest. Each sun-washed private deck has spectacular views of the valley. Those with money to burn should opt for the $2,000-per-night cottage suite; the 1,800-square-foot hideaway's got two fireplaces, two full baths, a den, and a patio Jacuzzi. Now *that's* living. All guests have access to a celestial swimming pool and a tiny exercise room with one of the grandest views around, plus an array of spa services. All in all, this is one of the best places we've ever stayed.

Dining: See "Where to Dine," below.

Amenities: Concierge, newspaper delivery, valet parking, 24-hour room service, twice-daily maid service, laundry/valet, complimentary shoe shine. Outdoor pool with sundeck, massage rooms, three tennis courts, exercise room, beauty salon. Sculpture and nature trail with picnic areas.

MODERATE

Rancho Caymus. 1140 Rutherford Rd. (P.O. Box 78), Rutherford, CA 94573. ☎ **800/845-1777** or 707/963-1777. Fax 707/963-5387. 26 suites. A/C MINIBAR TV TEL. $155–$205 double. Rates include continental breakfast. AE, CB, DC, MC, V. From Hwy. 29 north, turn right onto Rutherford Rd./Calif. 128 E.; the hotel is ahead on your left.

This Spanish-style hacienda, with two floors opening onto wisteria-covered balconies, was the creation of sculptor Mary Tilden Morton (of Morton Salt). Morton hired skilled craftspeople to make each room in the hacienda a work of art. She designed the adobe fireplaces herself, and wandered through Mexico and South America purchasing artifacts for the property.

Guest rooms surround a whimsical garden courtyard with an enormous outdoor fireplace. The mix-and-match interior decor is on the funky side, with overly varnished dark-wood furnishings and braided rugs. The inn is cozy, however, and rooms are decent-sized, split-level suites with queen beds. Other amenities include wet bars, sofa beds in the sitting areas, and small private patios. Most of the suites have fireplaces, and five have kitchenettes and whirlpool tubs. Since chef Ken Frank's La Toque opened here, this funky inn has also become a dining destination (see "Where to Dine," for complete details).

ST. HELENA
VERY EXPENSIVE

Harvest Inn. 1 Main St., St. Helena, CA 94574. ☎ **800/950-8466** or 707/963-9463. Fax 707/963-4402. www.harvestinn.com. 54 units. A/C TV TEL. May–Nov $249–$289 double; Dec–Apr $149–$189 double. AE, DC, DISC, MC, V.

If you like your accommodations loaded with 20th-century luxuries yet suggestive of Olde England, you'll like the Harvest Inn. Ornate brick walkways lead through beautifully landscaped grounds to this Tudor-style inn. Each of the immaculate rooms is furnished with dark-oak beds and dressers, black leather chairs, and antique furnishings; most have brick fireplaces, wet bars, and refrigerators, and all were recently upgraded with new textiles and CD players, feather beds, down comforters, and 25-inch TV with VCR. (Videos are for rent on the property.) Facilities include a wine bar, heated pools, and outdoor spas. A word of caution: This is a large, big-business hotel, and though it does its best to set a charming stage, you can't help but notice the corporate vibe and accoutrements permeating the place.

✪ **Meadowood Napa Valley.** 900 Meadowood Lane, St. Helena, CA 94574. ☎ **800/458-8080** or 707/963-3646. Fax 707/963-3532. www.meadowood. com. 85 units. A/C MINIBAR TV TEL. $320–$465 double. Ask about promotional offers and off-season rates. 2-night minimum on weekends. AE, DISC, DC, MC, V.

This ultra-luxurious resort, tucked away on 256 acres of pristine mountainside amidst a forest of madrone and oak trees, is quiet and reclusive enough to make you forget that the busy wineries are just 10 minutes away. Rooms are furnished with American country classics and have beamed ceilings, private patios, stone fireplaces, and forested views; many are individual suite-lodges that are so far removed from the common areas that you must drive to get to them (lazier folks can opt for more centrally located accommodations).

The resort offers a wealth of activities: You can spend your days playing Meadowood's challenging 9-hole golf course, any of the seven championship tennis courts, or croquet on two international regulation lawns. Other options include an incredible new full-service spa, private hiking trails, a health spa, and heated pools and a whirlpool. Those who might actually want to leave here (we certainly never did) to do some wine tasting can check in with John

Thoreen, the resort's wine tutor, whose sole purpose is to help guests better understand and enjoy Napa Valley wines.

Dining: See "Where to Dine," below.

Amenities: Concierge, room service, dry cleaning and laundry, full-service spa, newspaper delivery, secretarial service, baby-sitting. Golf course, croquet lawns, pools with sundeck, massage rooms, tennis courts, exercise room, hiking trails, and executive conference center.

EXPENSIVE

Bartels Ranch & Country Inn. 1200 Conn Valley Rd., St. Helena, CA 94574. ☎ **707/963-4001.** Fax 707/963-5100. www.bartelsranch.com. 4 units. A/C TV TEL. $165–$425 double. AE, DC, DISC, JCB, MC, V. From downtown St. Helena, turn east on Pope St., cross Silverado Trail, and continue onto Howell Mountain Rd.; bear right onto Conn Valley Rd.; the inn is 2 miles ahead on the left.

Perched on 60 acres of rolling meadows studded with fig trees, cypress, old oaks, and a recently planted vineyard, this palatial retreat is run by ebullient innkeeper Jami Bartels. She also designed and decorated the 7,000-square-foot stone ranch house. The four individually decorated rooms provide every comfort—fireplaces, VCRs (with video library), CD players, balconies—plus conveniences like ironing boards, hair dryers, and private baths; a couple of the rooms even have their own Jacuzzis. Our personal favorite is the Niagara, with adjustable beds and blue heart-shaped Jacuzzi tub. There's a communal sundeck and newly renovated pool, as well as a book-filled game room with pool and Ping-Pong tables. The bountiful breakfasts are served on the patio on warm mornings; complimentary wine, fruit, and cheese are served each afternoon. Other treats include evening dessert, and coffee, tea, and cookies are always on hand. Forever aiming to please, Jami provides her guests with picnic supplies and bicycles, and will arrange as much or as little of your vacation as you wish; she's also the ultimate source regarding the valley. A bocce-ball court, croquet lawns, and access to horseback riding and tennis are other outdoor options.

MODERATE

Hotel St. Helena. 1309 Main St., St. Helena, CA 94574. ☎ **888/478-4355** or 707/963-4388. www.napavalley.com/napavalley/lodging/hotels/sthelena. 18 units, 14 with private bathroom. A/C TEL. $145 double without bathroom; $165–$195 double with bathroom. Rates discounted in winter. Rates include continental breakfast. AE, DC, MC, V.

This downtown hotel occupies a historic 1881 building, the oldest wooden structure in St. Helena. The hotel keepers celebrated the building's 100th birthday with a much-needed renovation; now it's more comfortable than ever. The hallways are cluttered with stuffed animals, wicker strollers, and other memorabilia. Most of the rooms have been decorated with brass beds, wall-to-wall burgundy carpeting, and oak or maple furnishings. There's a garden patio and wine bar, and TVs are available upon request. Smoking is discouraged.

Prager Winery & Port Works. 1281 Lewelling Lane, St. Helena, CA 94574. ☎ **707/963-3720.** Fax 707/963-7679. www.pragerport.com. 2 units. A/C. $200–$300 double. Rates include a full breakfast en suite and unlimited tastings in the tasting room. MC, V.

Until we wrote about them, the two suites at Prager Winery were one of the best-kept secrets in the valley. Its incognito location—on a residential side street behind Sutter Home—gives no indication of the affordable accommodations within. The smaller suite, which is still huge, is perched above one of our favorite tasting rooms (See "Touring the Wineries," above), up a flight of stairs. It boasts a bedroom with a queen bed, living room with fireplace, fridge, coffeemaker, and a lovely private sundeck. The garden cottage is also enormous and immaculate, and has a bedroom, living room with piano, fireplace, and private garden. Both are homey, sleep up to four, and come with a full, delivered breakfast and unlimited wine tastings.

Sutter Home Inn. At the Sutter Home Winery, 277 St. Helena Hwy. S., P.O. Box 248, St. Helena, CA 94574. ☎ **707/963-3104,** ext. 4100 weekdays 8am–4pm, ext. 4130 evenings and weekends. Fax 707/963-5397. www.sutterhome.com. 9 units. TV TEL. $190 double. Rates include full breakfast. AE, DISC, MC, V.

Yes, it's on the grounds of Sutter Home's wine-tasting and sales building, but don't expect to be surrounded by vineyards. The building that houses the nine guest rooms is flanked by a Victorian garden, but take a few steps further west and you'll be playing chicken on Highway 29. Still, considering its St. Helena location, handsome Victorian-style rooms (nonsmoking, impeccably clean), and moderate price, Sutter Home offers a darn good deal. But there is a catch: Since the winery holds over half its rooms for wine-industry professionals, reservations are hard to come by. On the flip side, if they don't fill the reserved spaces and you're looking for last-minute accommodations, you might get lucky (especially during the off-season). Another plus: There's no 2-night minimum.

✪ **Wine Country Inn.** 1152 Lodi Lane, St. Helena, CA 94574. ☎ **707/ 963-7077.** Fax 707/963-9018. www.wine-country-inn.com. E-mail: romance@ winecountryinn.com. 24 units, all with bathroom (12 with shower only). A/C TEL. $130–$258 double. Rates include full buffet breakfast. MC, V.

Just off the highway behind Freemark Abbey vineyard, this attractive wood-and-stone inn, complete with a French-style mansard roof and turret, overlooks a pastoral landscape of Napa Valley vineyards. The individually decorated rooms are furnished with iron or brass beds, antique furnishings, and handmade quilts; most have fireplaces and private terraces overlooking the valley, while others have private hot tubs. One of the inn's best features is the outdoor pool (heated year-round), which is attractively landscaped into the hillside. Another favorite is the selection of suites, which come with stereos, plenty of space, and lots of privacy. Wine and plenty of appetizers are served nightly, along with a big dash of hotel-staff hospitality in the inviting living room. Five new cottages are slated to open in late 2000.

Zinfandel Inn Bed & Breakfast. 800 Zinfandel Lane (off Hwy. 29), St. Helena, CA 94574. ☎ **707/963-3512.** Fax 707/963-5310. www.zinfandelinn. com. 3 units. A/C TV TEL. Mar–Nov $175–$363 double; Dec–Feb $100–$250 double. Rates include full breakfast, plus champagne and truffles on arrival. MC, V.

Frilly romantics, get ready to break out your credit cards. Within the walls of this English Tudor are three rooms guaranteed to charm anyone into lace and old-world elegance. A rock-work fireplace comes with the price of the Chardonnay Room (along with an old TV and very soft mattress). The newly remodeled and very romantic Zinfandel Suite now includes a Jacuzzi and king-size four-poster bed with huge private deck, enormous bathroom (with a window overlooking the deck), and double shower and sink. The Petit Sirah room, styled in French Victorian fashion, is appropriately named— it's hardly bigger than a shoe box. It does have a private bathroom, but you'll have to step out of your room to get to it.

Sun worshipers will appreciate the manicured, grassy, and secluded backyard—a peaceful and expansive spot with a large aviary, small pool, gazebo, and canopied hot tub. Rates also include a delicious, full-service breakfast. *Note:* While this place is sweet, we also consider it a bit overpriced.

INEXPENSIVE

✪ **Deer Run Bed & Breakfast.** 3995 Spring Mountain Rd., P.O. Box 311, St. Helena, CA 94574. ☎ **800/843-3408** or 707/963-3794. Fax 707/ 963-9026. 4 units, all with bathroom (shower only). A/C TV. $150–$195 double. AE, MC, V. Rates include full breakfast.

Regardless of your budget, if romantic solitude is a big part of your vacation plan, Deer Run should be on your itinerary. Situated $4^{1}/_{2}$ miles (10 min. by car) from downtown St. Helena along a winding mountain road, this four-room B&B is the ultimate heavenly hideaway. Each of the wood-paneled rooms looks onto owners Tom and Carol Wilson's 4 acres of forest, and all feature gorgeous antiques, feather beds, a private entrance, deck, decanter of brandy, fridge, coffee and tea, robes, hair dryer, and access to hiking trails. One unit adjoins the cedar-shingled main house and boasts a king bed, Laura Ashley textiles, wood-burning fireplace, and open-beam ceiling. The Carriage House Suite offers an antique queen bed, Spanish tile floors, gas stove, and huge bathroom. The Studio Bungalow is fashioned after Ralph Lauren, with Spanish tile, a cathedral ceiling, and whitewashed cedar. Deer meander by the Honeymoon Suite (the most secluded), a sweet split-level cottage with a separate bedroom and gas fireplace; its price includes breakfast delivered to your doorstep. Outside, Cody, the resident chocolate Lab, hangs out by the very small pool.

✪ **El Bonita Motel.** 195 Main St. (at El Bonita Ave.), St. Helena, CA 94574. ☎ **800/541-3284** or 707/963-3216. Fax 707/963-8838. www.elbonita.com. 41 units. A/C MINIBAR TV TEL. May–Oct $109–$239 double; Mar and Nov $99–$199 double; Dec–Feb $85–$159 double. AE, CB, DC, DISC, MC, V. Rates include continental breakfast.

This 1930s art-deco motel was built a bit too close to Hwy. 29 for comfort, but the $2^{1}/_{2}$ acres of beautifully landscaped gardens behind the hotel (away from the road) help even the score. The rooms, while small, are spotlessly clean and decorated with new furnishings; all have microwaves and coffeemakers, and some have kitchens or whirlpool baths. Families, attracted to the larger bungalows with kitchenettes, often consider El Bonita one of the best values in Napa Valley—especially considering the heated outdoor pool, Jacuzzi, sauna, and massage facility.

✪ **White Sulphur Springs Retreat & Spa.** 3100 White Sulphur Springs Rd., St. Helena, CA 94574. ☎ **800/593-8873** (in CA) or 707/963-8588. Fax 707/963-2890. www.whitesulphursprings.com. 28 units, 9 cottages. Carriage House (shared bathroom) $85–$105 double; The Inn $105–$125 double; Creekside Cottages $135–$195. Additional person $15 extra. Discounts available during off-season and midweek. Single-night stays accepted in Carriage House rooms; cottages require 2-night minimum weekends Apr–Oct and all holidays. MC, V.

If your idea of the ultimate vacation is a cozy cabin set among 330 acres of creeks, waterfalls, hot springs, hiking trails, and redwood, madrone, and fir trees, paradise is a short winding drive away from downtown St. Helena. Established in 1852, Sulphur Springs claims to be the oldest resort in California. Seward "Buzz" and Betty Foote have been gradually upgrading the property while retaining its natural rustic charm. Guests stay at the inn or in small and large creekside cabins. Each is decorated with simple but homey furnishings; some have fireplaces or wood-burning stoves, and/or kitchenettes. The most luxurious are the newly renovated cabins, but the well-worn, wood-paneled ones seem more suitable to the natural surroundings. You can't help but feel at peace here. Venture off on a hike; take a dip in the natural hot sulphur spring; lounge by the pool; sit under a tree and watch for woodland creatures; or schedule a day of spa treatments. Just don't book a room here if you're the type who needs superluxury accommodations—this place will be too earthy for you. *Note:* No RVs are allowed without advance notice. A full service restaurant serves three primarily vegetarian menus daily.

CALISTOGA
EXPENSIVE

✪ **Cottage Grove Inn.** 1711 Lincoln Ave., Calistoga, CA 94515. ☎ **800/ 799-2284** or 707/942-8400. Fax 707/942-2653. www.cottagegrove.com. 16 cottages. A/C TV TEL. $215–$275 double. Rates include continental breakfast and evening wine and cheese. AE, CB, DC, DISC, MC, V.

Standing in two parallel rows at the end of the main strip in Calistoga is the perfect retreat—new cottages that, though located on a residential street, seem well-removed from the action once you've stepped across the threshold. Each compact guest house comes with a wood-burning fireplace, homey furnishings, cozy quilts, and an enormous bathroom with a skylight and a deep, two-person Jacuzzi tub, plus such niceties as gourmet coffee, a stereo with CD player, VCR (a video library is on site), wet bar, and fridge. Several major spas are within walking distance. This is our top pick if you want to do the Calistoga spa scene in comfort and style. Smoking on the small front porch only.

MODERATE

Brannan Cottage Inn. 109 Wapoo Ave., at Lincoln Ave. (P.O. Box 81), Calistoga, CA 94515. ☎ **707/942-4200.** www.bbinternet.com/brannan. 6 units. A/C. $140–$170 double. Rates include full buffet breakfast. MC, V.

This cute little 1860 cottage, complete with the requisite white picket fence, sits on a quiet side street. One of Sam Brannan's original resort cottages, the inn was restored through a community effort to salvage an important piece of Calistoga's heritage; it's now on the National Register of Historic Places. The six spacious rooms are decorated with country-style antiques, down comforters, and white lace curtains; each room also has a ceiling fan, private bathroom, and its own entrance. There's a comfortable parlor and a pleasant brick terrace furnished with umbrella tables.

Eurospa and Inn. 1202 Pine St. (between Myrtle and Cedar sts.), Calistoga, CA 94515. ☎ **707/942-6829.** Fax 707/942-1138. www.eurospa.com. 12 units. A/C TV. $149–$369 double. AE, CB, DC, DISC, MC, V. Rates include continental breakfast.

In a quiet residential section of Calistoga, this small European-style inn and spa provides a level of solitude and privacy that few other spas can match. The horseshoe-shaped inn consists of a dozen stucco bungalows, a spa center, and an outdoor patio where a light breakfast and snacks are served. The rooms, though small, are pleasantly decorated with pine furnishings and soft pastels; a few come with kitchenettes. Spa treatments range from Fango Naturium mud baths to honey-almond body scrubs, seaweed body wraps, and de-stress massage. If you're worried about going over your budget, opt for the "Wellness Packages," which include lodging, mineral bath, an hour of spa treatments, continental breakfast, and dinner voucher, for $229 per person ($319 per couple) per night.

Mount View Hotel. 1457 Lincoln Ave. (on Calif. 29, near Fairway St.), Calistoga, CA 94515. ☎ **800/816-6877** or 707/942-6877. Fax 707/942-6904. www.mountviewhotel.com. 29 units, 3 cottages. A/C TV TEL. $120–$180 double; $210–$230 cottage. Packages available. 2-night minimum on weekends. AE, DISC, MC, V.

Located on the main highway in the middle of Calistoga, this National Historical Landmark is one of the sweetest options in town. Rooms are decorated in either Victorian or art-deco style, and trimmed with beautiful hand-painted accents. There are also three self-contained cottages with queen-size bed (including featherbed and down duvet), wet bar, private deck, and hot tub—and nine suites. Almost everything in town is within walking distance, although once you settle in, you might not want to leave the quiet, sunny swimming area with heated pool. Also on the premises are a Jacuzzi and a highly rated European spa. There are plenty of great cafes within walking distance, or see "Where to Dine," below, for a review of the hotel's restaurant.

Silver Rose Inn & Spa. 351 Rosedale Rd. (off the Silverado Trail), Calistoga, CA 94515. ☎ **800/995-9381** or 707/942-9581. www.silverose.com. 20 units. A/C TEL. $145–$240 double weekdays, $165–$260 double weekends. Rates include continental breakfast. AE, DISC, MC, V.

If you like big, ranch-style spreads complete with a large wine-bottle–shaped pool, hot tub, tennis courts, and even a chipping and putting green, then you'll love the Silver Rose Inn & Spa. Situated on a small oak-covered knoll overlooking the upper Napa Valley, the inn offers so many amenities that you'll have a tough time searching for reasons to leave (other than to eat dinner, of course). Each spacious guest room is individually decorated, ranging from the peach-colored "Peach Delight" to the Oriental Room, complete with shoji screens and Oriental rugs. Several rooms come with fireplaces, whirlpool baths, and private balconies or terraces. Guests are offered exclusive on-site spa treatments, as well as an afternoon "Hospitality Hour" and a tray of fresh fruit, breads, coffee, and juice served in your room. Look for a new restaurant and winery to be completed in late 2000.

INEXPENSIVE

✪ **Calistoga Country Lodge.** 2883 Foothill Blvd. (1 mile north of Lincoln Ave.), Calistoga, CA 94515. ☎ **707/942-5555.** Fax 707/942-5864. www.countrylodge.com. 6 units, 2 with shared bathroom. $105–$160 double. Rates include breakfast and wine and cheese in the evening. AE, MC, V.

This rustic, secluded inn in the western foothills of Calistoga is one of the best bargains in the Wine Country. Where else can you get a spacious, attractively furnished room with fireplace, sitting chairs, and verdant views for as little as $105 a night? Innkeeper Rae Ellen has transformed this 1915 farmhouse into a Southwestern-style retreat, complete with cowhide rugs, bleached pine and lodgepole furniture, Indian artifacts, American antiques, and plenty of bovine accessories. It's all very tastefully—and humorously—done. In winter, the two rooms with fireplaces are the way to go (although these are the same two rooms that share a hallway bathroom). In summer, the private deck in the attic-level "Lookout Room" offers bucolic views of the surrounding century-old oak groves. Just in case you're still not convinced, Rae Ellen has recently added a pool and 24-hour hot tub to her humble estate. An extended continental breakfast is served from 7 to 10am, plus wine and cheese in the evening.

Calistoga Inn. 1250 Lincoln Ave. (at Cedar St.), Calistoga, CA 94515. ☎ **707/942-4101.** Fax 707/942-4914. www.napabeer.com. 18 units, none with bathroom. $55–$70 double includes continental breakfast. AE, MC, V.

Would the fact that the Calistoga Inn has its own brewery influence our decision to recommend it? You betcha. Here's the deal: You're probably in town for the spa treatments, but unfortunately, the guest rooms at almost every spa are lacking in the personality and warmth department. A better bet for the budget traveler is to book a room at this homey turn-of-the-century inn, then walk a few blocks up the street for your mud bath and massage. You'll have to share the bathrooms, and the rooms above the inn's restaurant can be noisy, but otherwise you get a cozy little room with a double or queen bed, washbasin, and breakfast, for a weekend rate that's half the average in these parts. What's more, there's no minimum stay, and the best beer in town is served downstairs. *Tip:* Request a room as far from the bar/restaurant as possible.

Calistoga Spa Hot Springs. 1006 Washington St. (at Gerrard St.), Calistoga, CA 94515. ☎ **707/942-6269.** www.calistogaspa.com. 57 units, 1 family unit. A/C TV TEL. Winter $70 double, $95 family unit; summer $85 double, $110 family unit. MC, V.

Very few hotels in the Wine Country cater specifically to families with children, which is why we strongly recommend the Calistoga Spa Hot Springs if you're bringing the little ones. In any case, it's a great bargain, offering unpretentious yet clean and comfortable rooms with kitchenettes, as well as a plethora of spa facilities. All of Calistoga's best shops and restaurants are within easy walking distance, and you can even whip up your own grub at the barbecues set up near the large pool and patio area.

Dr. Wilkinson's Hot Springs Resort. 1507 Lincoln Ave. (Calif. 29, between Fairway and Stevenson aves.), Calistoga, CA 94515. ☎ **707/942-4102.** www.drwilkinson.com. 42 units. A/C TV TEL. Winter $69–$109 double; summer $95–$129 double. Weekly discounts and packages available. AE, MC, V.

This spa/resort, located in the heart of Calistoga, is one of the best deals in Napa Valley. The rooms range from attractive Victorian-style accommodations with sundecks and garden patios to modern, cozy, newly renovated guest rooms in the main lodge. All rooms have coffeemakers; larger rooms have refrigerators and/or kitchens. Facilities include three mineral-water pools (two outdoor and one indoor), Jacuzzi, steam room, and mud baths. Facials and all kinds of body treatments are available in the salon, and spa service is excellent. Be sure to inquire about their excellent mid-week packages.

5 Where to Dine

Recently Napa's restaurants have been drawing as much attention to the valley as its award-winning wineries. Within the past 5 years alone, Yountville's French Laundry chef/owner Thomas Keller snagged the 1997 James Beard Award for "Chef of the Nation," and opened the more casual bistro Bouchon; L.A.'s celebrity chef

Napa Valley Dining

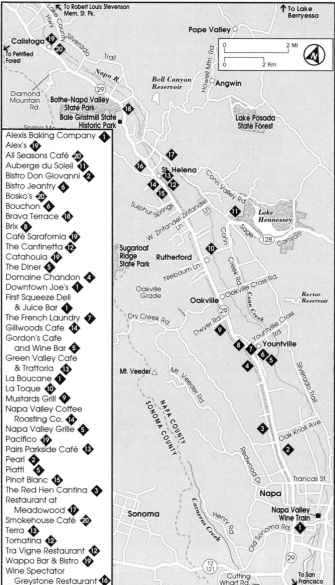

Alexis Baking Company **1**
Alex's **19**
All Seasons Café **20**
Auberge du Soleil **11**
Bistro Don Giovanni **2**
Bistro Jeantry **6**
Bosko's **20**
Bouchon **6**
Brava Terrace **18**
Brix **8**
Café Sarafornia **19**
The Cantinetta **12**
Catahoula **19**
The Diner **5**
Domaine Chandon **4**
Downtown Joe's **1**
First Squeeze Deli
  & Juice Bar **1**
The French Laundry **7**
Gillwoods Cafe **14**
Gordon's Cafe
  and Wine Bar **5**
Green Valley Cafe
  & Trattoria **13**
La Boucane **1**
La Toque **10**
Mustards Grill **9**
Napa Valley Coffee
  Roasting Co. **14**
Napa Valley Grille **5**
Pacifico **19**
Pairs Parkside Café **13**
Pearl **2**
Piatti **5**
Pinot Blanc **15**
The Red Hen Cantina **3**
Restaurant at
  Meadowood **17**
Smokehouse Café **20**
Terra **13**
Tomatina **12**
Tra Vigne Restaurant **12**
Wappo Bar & Bistro **19**
Wine Spectator
  Greystone Restaurant **16**

Joachim Splichal launched his first northern-California outpost, Pinot Blanc; the Culinary Institute of America opened its West Coast annex and an enormous restaurant; and revered chef Phillipe Jeanty departed from Domaine Chandon to open Bistro Jeanty.

Dining in the Napa Valley is a special experience on a number of levels. First off, there's the food: Nowhere else in the state are kitchens as deft at mixing fresh seasonal, local, organic produce into edible magic. Then there's the wine list: most restaurants offer fantastic wines by the glass from local boutique wineries. And finally, the ambiance: the valley's knockout dining rooms and stunning views that are second only to what's on your plate and in your glass.

The most important advice we can offer about Napa Valley's restaurants: *reserve*—especially for a seat in a more renowned room. While there's always a chance of getting in on a cancellation, there's nothing more infuriating than futilely begging someone to allow you the coveted opportunity to part with upwards of $100 in their establishment. Also bear in mind that the food is rich around here; we make a point of eating in only one restaurant a day.

Finally, if your budget can't afford the more expensive restaurants for dinner (we know, they're all expensive), have a late lunch. You might not have a heck of a lot to do after the sun goes down, but you'll be full and your wallet won't be empty.

NAPA
MODERATE

Bistro Don Giovanni. 4110 St. Helena Hwy. (on Hwy. 29, just north of Salvador Ave.), Napa. ☎ **707/224-3300.** Reservations recommended. Main courses $11–$17. AE, DC, DISC, MC, V. Mon–Thurs 11:30am–10pm, Fri–Sat 11:30am–11pm. REGIONAL ITALIAN.

Donna and Giovanni Scala serve refined Italian fare prepared with top-quality ingredients and California flair at this large, lively, Mediterranean-style restaurant. The menu features pastas, risottos, pizzas (baked in a wood-burning oven), and half a dozen other main courses such as braised lamb shank and Niman Schell bistro burgers. Less traditional appetizers include a grilled pear with a frisée-and-arugula salad with bleu cheese, caramelized walnuts, and bacon. The matchstick zucchini sprinkled with Parmesan cheese has become a signature summer dish. Pasta lovers should go for the farfalle with asparagus, porcini, wild mushrooms, pecorino cheese, and truffle oil; the seared salmon with tomato, white wine, and chive sauce is another winner. Alfresco dining among the vineyards is highly recommended on warm, sunny days.

La Boucane. 1778 Second St. (1 block east of Jefferson St.), Napa. ☎ **707/ 253-1177.** Reservations recommended. Main courses $15–$22. MC, V. Mon– Sat 5:30–10pm. COUNTRY FRENCH.

You'll be graciously welcomed into the domain of chef-owner Jacques Mokrani, who took this 1885 "Victorian lady" and refurbished her in traditional French style with antiques and lots of chintz. The dinner-only menu features such dishes as duck à l'orange and sole meunière. Try the poulet sauté Boucane, prepared with cognac, shallots, mushrooms, and sherry. To start, there are escargots and prawns Provençale, and to finish, a traditional chocolate mousse dessert, soufflés, and crème caramel. Granted, La Boucane isn't on the road to glory, but its tried-and-true French fare is better than most in the area.

Pearl. 1339 Pearl St., no. 104 (at the convergence of Franklin, Clay, and Pearl sts). ☎ **707/224-9161.** Reservations recommended. Main courses $8.75– $18.95. MC, V. Tues–Thurs 11:30am–2pm and 5:30–9pm, Fri–Sat 11:30am– 2pm and 5:30–9:30pm, Sun–Mon closed. CALIFORNIA ECLECTIC.

If you prefer to skip the destination restaurants in exchange for a casual but quality meal among the locals, pull up a chair in Pearl's warm, friendly dining room or on their lovely enclosed patio. The limited menu includes a nice selection of salads such as a whole leaf Caesar, and Asian noodle and vegetables. Main courses include sandwiches like the grilled eggplant with roasted peppers and pesto, or grilled New York steak with grilled onion on house focaccia. Also recommended are the soft polenta with sautéed seasonal veggies and the double-thick pork chops with mashed potatoes and vegetables. We always go for the grilled items and love their summer special of grilled corn bathed in sour cream with chili powder and sprinkled with manchego cheese. One bummer: when the place is jumping, service can be woefully slow.

INEXPENSIVE

✪ **Alexis Baking Company.** 1517 Third St. (between Main and Jefferson sts.), Napa. ☎ **707/258-1827.** Main courses: breakfast $3.25–$7.95; lunch $6.95– $9.95; dinner $6.75–$13. Mon–Wed 6:30am–6pm, Thurs–Fri 6:30–8pm, Sat 7:30am–3pm, Sun 8am–2pm. BAKERY/CAFE.

Alexis is a quaint, casual stop for residents and in-the-know tourists. Show up on a weekend morning and the line is out the door. But once you order from the counter and find a seat in the sunny room, you can relax, enjoy the coffeehouse atmosphere, and start your day with spectacular pastries, coffee drinks, and breakfast goodies like pumpkin pancakes with sautéed pears. Lunch also bustles with locals who come for the daily specials like fusilli pasta with roasted pumpkin, white beans, ham, and Parmesan in a cream sauce; grilled-chicken Caesar salad; roast-lamb sandwich with minted mayo and roasted shallots on rosemary bread; and lentil bulgur orzo salad. Desserts run the gamut and include a moist and magical steamed persimmon pudding during the holiday season.

Downtown Joe's. 902 Main St. (at Second St.), Napa. ☎ **707/258-2337.** Dinner main courses $8–$14. AE, DC, DISC, MC, V. Mon–Fri 8:30–11am (breakfast) and 11am–10pm, Sat–Sun 8:30am–2pm (brunch) and 2–10pm. AMERICAN BISTRO.

Working from a proven formula—good food and lots of it at a fair price—Joe's has capitalized on a prime location in downtown Napa and created what's widely regarded as the best place in town to grub and groove. The menu is all over the place, offering everything from porterhouse steaks to oysters, omelets, pasta, and seafood specials. The beers, such as the tart Lickety Split Lager, are made in-house, as are the breads and desserts. If the sun's out, request a table on the outside patio adjacent to the park. Thursday through Sunday nights, rock, jazz, and blues bands draw in the locals.

Another great reason to visit Joe's is "Hoppy Hour," from 4 to 6pm Monday through Thursday, featuring $2.50 pints and free appetizers plus a drawing every half hour to win free stuff. Every Friday is TGIF, with a giveaway (appetizers, wine, etc.) every 15 minutes.

First Squeeze Deli and Juice Bar. 1126 First St. (in Clocktower Plaza), Napa. ☎ **707/224-6762.** Deli items $3–$7. AE, DC, MC, V. Mon–Fri 7am–3pm, Sat 8am–3pm, Sun 10am–4pm. DELI/JUICE.

After you fuel up on your requisite cup of java at the **Napa Valley Coffee Roasting Co.,** located down the block at 948 Main St. (at First Street), head over here to load up on picnic supplies for the day's journey among the vineyards. Spartan furnishings (and decor to match) beg for a "to go" order, which is just as well—after one sip of a protein-powder shake, you won't be able to hold still anyway. With wheat grass, spirulina, ginseng, bee pollen, and brewer's yeast available, it's a health nut's paradise. Our favorite is the Berry Bonds, a zingy combo of blackberry, strawberry, apple juice, and frozen yogurt. Also available are full breakfasts and big, bulky sandwiches.

OAKVILLE & RUTHERFORD
EXPENSIVE

Auberge du Soleil. 180 Rutherford Hill Rd., Rutherford. ☎ **707/963-1211.** Reservations recommended. Main courses $25–$30. AE, DISC, MC, V. Daily 7–11am, 11:30am–2:30pm, and 6–9:30pm. WINE COUNTRY CUISINE.

Auberge du Soleil may be better known for its inn, but it was the restaurant that started all the fuss over this world-class resort. Alfresco dining is taken to an entirely new level here, particularly on warm summer nights when diners are rewarded with a gorgeous sunset view of the mountains. Inside, a magnificent fireplace, huge wood pillars, and fresh flowers create a warm, rustic ambiance. Chef Andrew Sutton's cooking reflects the region's produce and international influences: Pacific Rim, Southwestern, and Mediterranean styles predominate. Signature dishes include a tasting platter of truffled deviled quail egg, smoked sturgeon, Thai lobster salad, caviar, and more; and a grapevine smoked salmon with walnut-wheat croutons and roasted shallot-caper relish. Regardless of what you order, be sure to arrive before sunset and beg for terrace seating.

✪ **La Toque.** 1140 Rutherford Cross Rd., Rutherford ☎ **707/963-9770.** Reservations recommended. Fixed-price menu $65; wine $32 additional. Wed–Sat 5:30–10pm, Sun 1:30–10pm. FRENCH-INSPIRED.

Don't come here without an appetite. Renowned Ken Frank left Los Angeles's fenix at the Argyle Hotel to open one of the Wine Country's most formal dining rooms—and once you sit down to the five-course extravaganza you won't be able to refrain from gobbling up all the delicious creations that come your way. Each table at the elegant restaurant adjoining Rancho Caymus Inn is well-spaced, making plenty of room to showcase Frank's memorable and innovative French-inspired cuisine. The menu might feature an incredible Indian-spice-rubbed foie gras with Madras carrot puree, melt-in-your-mouth yellowfin tuna with braised daikon, red wine, and sautéed pea sprouts; knock-out Maine lobster with creamy orzo and lobster Cabernet sauce; and, should you find room and the extra bucks, a cheese course. For an additional $32 per person, we drank splendid and well-paired wines with each course. Alas, we did not have room for desserts of chocolate panna cotta with vanilla Anglaise and toasted pineapple fritter with vanilla bean ice cream, but after one bite we couldn't help but proceed to devour them.

YOUNTVILLE
EXPENSIVE

Brix. 7377 St. Helena Hwy. (Hwy. 29), Yountville. ☎ **707/944-2749.** Reservations recommended. Main courses $17–$24. AE, DC, DISC, MC, V. Sun–Thurs 11:30am–9:30pm, Fri–Sat 11:30am–10pm. ASIAN FUSION.

Brix is one of the largest restaurants in the Valley, which means you can choose from many different venues under one roof. In winter, for example, a table by the corner fireplace promises romantic dining; in summer, you can overlook the vineyards for a more pronounced Wine Country experience. Wherever you're positioned, the main attraction is the cuisine of newly appointed executive Chef John Wabeck. As we go to press Wabeck has yet to influence the menu, so some starters—a very tasty grilled-portobello-mushroom salad with bleu cheese and sherry walnut vinaigrette (ask them not to go too heavy on the dressing!) and main courses like a wonderful Chinese-style whole crispy fish with cilantro black-bean sauce—remained. However, we expect the chef will introduce his own creations in the coming year.

Domaine Chandon. 1 California Dr., Yountville. ☎ **707/944-2892.** Reservations suggested. Lunch $18–$21; dinner $24–$28. AE, CB, DC, DISC, MC, V. Summer daily 11:30am–2:30pm, 6–9:30pm. Winter Wed–Sun 11:30am–2:30pm and 6–9pm. Closed first 3 weeks of Jan. From Hwy. 29 north, take the Yountville exit; the restaurant is on the west side of the highway. CALIFORNIA/FRENCH.

This dining room was once the most elaborate, expensive, and formal in the region. But in the past 10 years, the competition's gotten stiff, and if Domaine wants to keep its reputation, they might want to rethink the restaurant's outdated decor. The fact remains, however, that the grounds are still fabulous, and though there's been a change of the guard in the kitchen, the food is still respectable.

As for the menu, light, contemporary dishes have replaced the heavier French fare. You aren't likely to find the once-celebrated starter of cream of tomato soup in puff pastry; instead, try the sweet white corn soup with rock crab. Other offerings might include caramelized day-boat scallops; and rack of lamb with Blue Lake beans, potato risotto, and whole grain mustard sauce. There's no question Robert Curry is a cuisine contender, but for those who've become accustomed to ex-chef Phillipe Jeanty's fare here over the past 20 years, you may suffer a brief period of adjustment.

✪ **The French Laundry.** 6640 Washington St. (at Creek St.), Yountville. ☎ **707/944-2380.** Reservations required. Vegetarian menu $80, 5-course menu $90, chef's 9-course tasting menu $105 lunch and dinner. AE, MC, V. Fri–Sun 11am–1pm; daily 5:30–9:30pm. CLASSIC AMERICAN/FRENCH.

It's almost futile to include this restaurant, since securing a reservation—or getting through on the reservation line for that matter—is about as likely as driving Highway 29 without passing a winery. (*Hint:* If you can't get a reservation, try walking in—on occasion folks don't make their reservation and tables open up—especially during lunch on rainy days.) Several years after renowned chef/

owner Thomas Keller bought the place and caught the attention of epicureans worldwide (including the judges of the James Beard Awards, who dubbed him 1997's "Chef of the Nation"), the discreet restaurant is still the hottest dinner ticket *in the world.*

Here the atmosphere is as somber and serious as the oh-so-privileged diners who quietly swoon over the ongoing parade of bite-size delights. Signature dishes include Keller's "tongue in cheek" (a marinated and braised round of sliced lamb tongue and tender beef cheeks) and "macaroni and cheese" (sweet butter-poached Maine lobster with creamy lobster broth and orzo with mascarpone cheese). Portions are small, but only because Keller wants his guests to taste as many different things as possible—nobody leaves hungry. The excellent staff is well acquainted with the wide selection of regional wines; the house charges a $30 corkage fee if you choose to bring your own bottle. On warm summer nights, request a table in the flower-filled garden.

MODERATE

✪ **Bistro Jeanty.** 6510 Washington St. (near Mulberry), Yountville. ☎ **707/ 944-0103.** bistrojeanty.com. Reservations recommended. Appetizers $4.50–$7.50, most main courses $13.75–$18.50. Daily 11:30am–10:30pm; closed Thanksgiving and Christmas. MC, V.

This casual, warm bistro is the brainchild of chef Phillipe Jeanty, who a few years back left his highly reputed 18-year post at Domaine Chandon to open one of the hottest (and most moderately priced) new restaurants in town. Jeanty was previously known for formal French cooking, but his charming and cheery bistro offers far more laid-back—but equally worship-worthy—fare. Outstanding classic French bistro fare includes everything from his legendary tomato soup in a puff pastry, and house smoked trout with potato slices basking in an olive and lite vinegar and oil bath, to daube de boeuf simmered in red wine and served with mashed potatoes, fresh peas, and baby carrots, and cassoulet with white beans, fennel sausage, pork, and duck leg. We return frequently for the decadent fall-off-the-bone coq au vin with an earthy, smoky red wine sauce, and the delicate deep-fried smelt special, which came in a wax-paper cone accompanied by a seasoned mayo dipping sauce. We, like most San Franciscans, consider this place a must-stop on the Wine Country itinerary.

Bouchon. 6534 Washington St. (at Humboldt), Yountville ☎ **707/ 944-8037.** Reservations recommended. Main courses $11.95–$16.95. AE, DC, MC, V. Daily 11:30am–2pm and 5:30–10:30pm. Late-night menu 10:45pm–1:30am. FRENCH BISTRO.

Perhaps to appease the crowds who never get a reservation at French Laundry, Thomas Keller teamed up with his brother Joseph to open a far more casual, but still delicious, French brasserie called **Bouchon.** You'll have to call in advance for an opportunity to sample the French fare, which is served in a dining room designed by Adam Tihany (who also conceptualized New York's Le Cirque 2000). Along with a raw bar, expect superb renditions of steak frite, mussels marinieres, grilled cheese sandwiches, and other heavenly French classics at far more down-to-earth prices and atmosphere.

✪ **Gordon's Cafe and Wine Bar.** 6770 Washington St., Yountville. ☎ **707/ 944-8246.** Reservations necessary for Fri dinner. Breakfast $5–$7; lunch $3.75– $8; fixed-price dinner $38. AE, DC, DISC, MC, V. Tues–Thurs and Sat–Sun 7:30am–6pm, Fri 7:30am–9pm. WINE COUNTRY CUISINE.

If you want to escape the town's highfalutin restaurants for an intimate brush with the locals, this is the place to do it. Sally Gordon opened this adorable Yountville favorite in May 1996. Part country store, part deli, and part restaurant, one wall is lined with an intriguing collection of jams, mustards, olive oils, wines, and other gourmet goods for sale; another posts the chalkboard breakfast and lunch menu above a glass display case housing a cornucopia of deli items. The floor is scuffed hardwood and fewer than a dozen tables are spaciously dispersed throughout the airy room. Breakfast (oatmeal, omelets, homemade pastries, and smoothies), lunch (soup, salads, and gourmet sandwiches), and real homemade flavor come from an open kitchen. Dinner, served only on Friday nights, is a fixed-price feast. On our visit, we opted for a velvety smooth lobster bisque; an outstanding and hearty pan-seared breast of chicken with chanterelles, shiitake mushrooms, and baby leeks over a pearl barley risotto; and the most unforgettable dessert we've had in a long, long time— a spectacular "buttermilk pie" topped with blueberries.

Mustards Grill. 7399 St. Helena Hwy. (Hwy. 29), Yountville. ☎ **707/ 944-2424.** Reservations recommended. Main courses $11–$27. CB, DC, DISC, MC, V. Apr–Oct daily 11:30am–10pm; Nov–Mar daily 11:30am–9pm. CALIFORNIA.

It's always a pleasant surprise to find a serious restaurant with a strong sense of humor; Mustards is one of those places. Housed in a convivial, barn-style space, it offers an 11-page wine list and an ambitious chalkboard list of specials. We started out with a wonderfully light seared ahi tuna that melted in our mouths. Although the tea-smoked Peking duck with almond onion sauce and grilled rabbit with potatoes, fennel, and saffron broth were tempting, we opted for a moist, perfectly flavored grilled chicken breast with mashed potatoes and fresh herbs. The menu includes something for everyone, from gourmands and vegetarians to good old burger lovers.

Napa Valley Grille. 6795 Washington St. (on Hwy. 29 at Madison St.), Piatti. 6480 Washington St. (between Washington and Oak sts.), Yountville. ☎ **707/ 944-2070.** Reservations recommended. Main courses $7–$16. AE, DC, MC, V. Mon–Thurs 11:30am–10pm, Fri–Sat 11:30am–11pm, Sun 11:30am–10pm. ITALIAN.

This local favorite—the first (and best) of a swiftly growing northern-California chain—is known for its excellent, reasonably priced food served in a rustic Italian-style setting. Chef Peter Hall, a seasoned Napa Valley cook who honed his culinary art at Tra Vigne and Mustards before taking over the helm here, performs to a mostly sold-out crowd nightly. For the perfect meal, start with a salad of morning-cut field greens mixed with white corn and Napa Valley strawberry crostini, accompanied by a bowl of the spaghetti squash and sweet-potato soup. Though Hall offers a wide array of superb pastas and pizzas, it's the wood oven–roasted duck—basted with a sweet cherry sauce and served over a bed of citrus risotto—that brings back the regulars. There are far fancier and more intimate restaurants in the valley, but we can't think of any that can fill you up on such outstanding fare at these prices.

INEXPENSIVE

The Diner. 6476 Washington St., Yountville. ☎ **707/944-2626.** Reservations not accepted. Breakfast $4–$8; lunch $6–$10; dinner $8–$13.25. MC, V. Tues– Sun 8am–3pm and 5:30–9pm. From Hwy. 29 north, take the Yountville exit and turn left onto Washington St. AMERICAN/MEXICAN.

Funky California meets roadside eatery at this popular diner, decorated with a collection of vintage diner water pitchers and a rotating art exhibit. The fare is far from that of a regular greasy spoon— the "home-style" menu is extensive, portions are huge, and the food is very good. Breakfasts feature good old-fashioned omelets, French toast, and German potato pancakes. Lunch and dinner dishes include a host of Mexican and American dishes such as chicken picatta with veggies and rice, grilled fresh fish, giant burritos, and thick sandwiches made with house-roasted meats and homemade bread.

ST. HELENA
EXPENSIVE

✪ **Restaurant at Meadowood.** At the Meadowood Napa Valley, 900 Meadowood Lane, St. Helena. ☎ **707/963-3646.** Reservations recommended. À la carte menu $21.50–$28; fixed-price $54, $80 with wine pairings; vegetarian prix-fixe $35, $56 with wine pairings. Sun brunch $35, including buffet of salads, seafood, and dessert, plus 1 hot entree. AE, DISC, DC, MC, V. Daily 6–10pm; Sun brunch 10am–2pm. CALIFORNIA WINE COUNTRY.

Chef Maria del Pilar Sanchez presides over one of Napa Valley's finest restaurants, located in the gazebo-style clubhouse dining room of the ultraluxurious Meadowood Resort. Though à la carte selections are offered, most guests prefer one of the prix-fixe menus. When we last dined here, dinner started with a flavorful grilled day boat of scallops with foie gras and balsamic vinaigrette. Next came a persimmon lacquered guinea hen with puree blanc-superb. Chocolate crème brûlée with caramelized bananas finished the evening, thank goodness, because we couldn't eat another bite. Though we didn't have room to try it, the four-course vegetarian meal sounded wonderful: couscous layered with zucchini flavored with anise seeds, accompanied by a crispy strudel of artichokes, onions, and wild mushrooms. A popular après-dinner pastime is to retire to the small, romantic lounge and nurse a snifter of brandy as you warm your bones in the glow of the large stone fireplace.

MODERATE

Brava Terrace. 3010 St. Helena Hwy. (Hwy. 29), St. Helena. ☎ **707/ 963-9300.** Reservations recommended, especially for weekend lunch. Main courses $8–$21. AE, DC, DISC, MC, V. Nov–Apr Thurs–Tues noon–9pm; May–Oct daily noon–9pm. CALIFORNIA/MEDITERRANEAN.

Fred Halpert earned acclaim as the head chef at the Portman Hotel in San Francisco; in 1991, he set up his own shop in the Wine Country, where he became a hit almost immediately. Halpert is always searching for new taste sensations; fortunately, thorough training in the cuisines of Provence and other locales backs up that experimentation. The food is both good and reasonably priced: Try a simple sandwich of roasted vegetables with sun-dried-tomato butter, or go whole hog with such main courses as coq au vin or crusted pan-seared sea bass with oven-roasted tomatoes and thyme. There's always a fish, pasta, and risotto of the day. Be sure to try the spicy fries (a heartburn special). If your stomach can handle the wild and robust mix of flavors and food, finish your meal with the chocolate-chip crème brûlée. A dozen wines by the glass are available.

Pairs Parkside Café. 1420 Main St., St. Helena. ☎ **707/963-7566.** Reservations recommended on weekends. Lunch $7–$9; dinner $12–$18. AE, DC, JCB, MC, V. Thurs–Mon 11:30am–3pm and 5:30–9pm. CALIFORNIA/ASIAN.

This restaurant's name refers to the *pairing* of complementary foods and wines. Hence the sophisticated menu recommends a Chardonnay with the sorrel-crusted salmon fillet, a Merlot to accompany the rosemary lavender grilled lamb chops, and a Sauvignon Blanc to wash down the lemon basil steamed halibut with fennel jasmine rice. (Vegetarian specials also are available.) Owners Craig (chef de cuisine) and Keith (pastry chef and dining-room manager) Schaueffel also seem to have a handle on matching food with atmosphere. The restaurant's 50 seats are well spaced, and the warm gold-textured walls, hardwood floors, and soft jazz set the tone for a casual evening of fun. And if the wine board's 16 by-the-glass selections have you stumped, enlist the help of the friendly staff; they know their wine. Cocktailers will have to curb their desire: No hard booze is served.

✪ **Pinot Blanc.** 641 Main St., St. Helena. ☎ **707/963-6191.** Lunch $9–$20; dinner $16–$24. AE, DC, DISC, JCB, MC, V. Daily 11:30am–3pm and 5–9pm; Fri–Sun 11:30am–3pm and 5:30–9pm; limited bar menu 3–5:30pm. Extended summer hours. FRENCH BISTRO.

Reviews were mixed as L.A. celebrity-chef Joachim Splichal's formal new restaurant settled in over the past 2 years. But when we dined here, nothing could be more clear: Pinot Blanc rocks! The beautiful dining room, recently renovated to evoke a country French atmosphere, is the perfect spot to sample the gastronomic glories of executive chef Sean Knight. Lunch offerings might include potato lasagna with forest shrooms and chanterelle jus or curry chicken salad with sun-dried Napa grapes and apples. Dinner features such entrees as coq au vin, cannelloni with roasted vegetables, and planked Atlantic salmon with shallot and apple smoked-bacon crust. The wine list features over 200 selections.

✪ **Terra.** 1345 Railroad Ave. (between Adams and Hunt sts.), St. Helena. ☎ **707/963-8931.** Reservations recommended. Main courses $18.50–$26. CB, DC, MC, V. Sun–Mon and Wed–Thurs 6–9pm, Fri–Sat 6–10pm. CONTEMPORARY AMERICAN.

St. Helena's restaurant of choice is the creation of Lissa Doumani and her husband, Hiro Sone, a master chef who hails from Japan. Sone makes full use of the region's bounty, coaxing every nuance of flavor from his fine local ingredients. The simple dining room is a perfect foil for this extraordinary food. Among the appetizers, the terrine of foie gras with fig and endive salad and the home-smoked salmon with potato latkes, sour cream, and crème fraîche are the stars of the show. The main dishes successfully fuse different cooking styles: try the grilled salmon with Thai red-curry sauce or the sake-marinated sea bass with shrimp dumplings in shiso broth. A recommended finale? The chocolate truffle cake with espresso ice cream.

✪ **Tra Vigne Restaurant.** 1050 Charter Oak Ave., St. Helena. ☎ **707/ 963-4444.** Reservations recommended. Main courses $12.50–$22; Cantinetta $4–$8. CB, DC, DISC, MC, V. Daily 11:30am–10pm; Cantinetta daily 11:30am– 6pm. ITALIAN.

Tra Vigne's combination of good food, high-energy atmosphere, and "reasonable" prices (reasonable being a relative term) makes this restaurant a longstanding favorite. The enormous dining room packs 'em in every night—and whether seated on the veranda (heated on cold nights) or in the center of the bustling scene, diners are usually thrilled just to have a seat. Even though the wonderful bread served with house-made flavored olive oils is tempting, save room for the robust California dishes, cooked Italian-style. The menu features about five pizzas, including a succulent caramelized onion, thyme, and Gorgonzola version. The dishes of the day might include grilled Sonoma rabbit with teleme-layered potatoes, oven-dried tomatoes, and mustard pan sauce, and a dozen or so antipasti. Equally tempting are the pastas, including ceppo with sausage, spinach, potatoes, sun-dried tomatoes, and pecorino, and the delicious desserts. When ordering, plan wisely: Most dishes are very rich.

The adjoining Cantinetta offers a small selection of sandwiches, pizzas, and lighter meals (see below).

Wine Spectator Greystone Restaurant. At the Culinary Institute of America at Greystone, 2555 Main St., St. Helena. ☎ **707/967-1010.** Reservations strongly recommended. Tastings (food) daily $4.50–$7; lunch and dinner $14–$24. AE, CB, DC, MC, V. Daily 11:30am–10pm. WINE COUNTRY CUISINE.

This place offers a combination visual and culinary feast that's unparalleled in the area, if not the state. The room itself is an enormous stone-walled former winery, but the festive decor and heavenly aromas warm the space up. Cooking islands—complete with scurrying chefs, steaming pots, and rotating chicken—provide edible entertainment. The "tastings" (appetizer) menu features seasonally-inspired dishes, including a perfect calamari sautéed with smoked paprika garlic and rosemary (wonderful every time we come, regardless of the preparation!), a fine seafood and white bean salad, and an unimpressive mushroom piroshki. Portions are small but affordable; pastas and salads are a bit heftier. Main courses, such as a crispy fried lamb shank with cranberry beans, cherry tomatoes, and spinach, are well portioned and good, but we recommend you opt for a barrage of appetizers to share. Also order the "Flights of Fancy," where for $14 to $20 you can sample three 3-ounce pours of local wines. (Wines by the glass are from the same selection, which, annoyingly, does not list by-the-glass prices.) While the food is serious, the atmosphere is playful—casual enough that you'll feel comfortable in jeans or shorts. For a meal here, reserve far in advance. We prefer to stop by, have a snack at the bar, and eat our big meals elsewhere.

INEXPENSIVE

✪ **The Cantinetta.** Tra Vigne Restaurant, 1050 Charter Oak Ave., St. Helena. ☎ **707/963-8888.** Main courses $4–$8. CB, DC, DISC, MC, V. Daily 11:30am–6pm. ITALIAN.

Regardless of where we dine while in the valley, we always make a point of stopping at the Cantinetta for an espresso and a snack. Part cafe, part shop, it's a casual place with a few tables and a counter. The focaccias (we've never had better in our lives!), pasta salads, and pastries are outstanding, and there's also a selection of cookies and other wonderful treats, flavored oils (free tastings), wines, and an array of gourmet items, many of which were created here. You also can get great picnic grub to go.

Gillwoods Cafe. 1313 Main St. (at Spring St.), St. Helena. ☎ **707/963-1788.** Breakfast $4.60–$8; lunch $6–$9. AE, MC, V. Daily 7am–3pm. AMERICAN.

In a town like this—where if you order mushrooms on your burger, the waiter's likely to ask, "What kind?"—a plain old American restaurant can be a godsend. In St. Helena, the land of snobs and fancy rabes, Gillwoods is that place. At this homey haunt, with its wooden benches and original artwork, it's all about the basics. You'll find a breakfast of bakery goods, fruit, pancakes, omelets (with pronounceable ingredients), and a decent eggs Benedict; and a lunch menu of burgers, sandwiches, lots of salads, veggie lasagna, chicken-fried steak, and meat loaf. Lunch is available starting at 10:30am, but late risers can order breakfast until 3pm.

Green Valley Cafe & Trattoria. 1310 Main St. (between Hunt Ave. and Adams St.), St. Helena. ☎ **707/963-7088.** Reservations recommended. Lunch $5.75–$7; dinner $9–$12. MC, V. Daily 11:30am–3pm, 5:30–9:30pm. ITALIAN.

When locals want a casual, inexpensive night out, they convene at this small Italian restaurant. Its long green bar and row of tightly arranged tables have a casual neighborhood feel that many of the valley's restaurants lack, and chef/owner Delio's cooking is backed by big-city experience at hole-in-the-wall prices. One St. Helena store owner simply must have the lasagna once a week. Others lean toward the eggplant topped with tomato and béchamel sauce and Parmesan, fried calamari with garlic mayo, braised lamb shank with polenta, or freshly made ravioli. Lunch offerings include a spinach salad and a few other appetizers, a selection of cold and hot sandwiches (Italian sausage; burger; and grilled eggplant, tomato, cheese, peppers, onions, and olives), and, of course, a few pasta dishes.

Tomatina. At The Inn at Southbridge, 1016 Main St., St. Helena. ☎ **707/967-9999.** Pasta $6–$8; pizza $8–$19. DC, DISC, MC, V. Daily 11:30am–10pm. ITALIAN.

After we've been in the Wine Country for about a week, we usually can't stand the thought of one more decadent wine and foie-gras meal. That's when we race to Tomatina for a $3.50 chopped salad, a welcome respite. Families and locals come here for another reason: Though the menu is limited, it's a total winner for anyone looking for freshly prepared, wholesome food at atypically cheap Wine Country prices. A Caesar salad, for example, costs a mere $4.50. "Apizzas"—pizzas folded like a soft taco—are the house specialty, and come filled with such delights as fresh Maine clams and oregano. Pizzas are of the build-your-own variety with gourmet toppings like sautéed mushrooms, fennel sausage, baby spinach, sun-dried tomatoes, and homemade pepperoni. The 26 respectable local wines are served by the glass at a toast-worthy cost of $3.75, or $18 per bottle. Everything is ordered at the counter and brought to the tables in the very casual dining area or the outdoor patio. Kids especially like the pool table and big-screen TV.

CALISTOGA
MODERATE

Alex's. 1437 Lincoln Ave. (between Washington and Main sts.), Calistoga. ☎ **707/942-6868.** Main courses $12–$25. MC, V. Tues–Fri 4–10pm, Sat 2–10pm, Sun 1–9pm (3–9pm in winter). CONTINENTAL.

Alex's is for those non-cholesterol-counting red-meat eaters who get excited at the sight of a big double-cut of prime rib oozing with au jus and served with the requisite side of pungent horseradish, mashed potatoes, and plenty of French bread. Sure, the menu has the standard pasta, seafood, and poultry dishes, but they're all done far, far better at Catahoula or All Seasons Café down the street. Nope, none of that fancy-schmancy stuff for you; it's the perfectly aged, hand-cut God Bless America New York steak you're hankering for, served on a plain white tablecloth slightly soiled by your second glass of scotch. In an era in which the life expectancy of most restaurants is counted in months, Alex's has been around since 1969, so you know it must be doing something right.

All Seasons Café. 1400 Lincoln Ave. (at Washington St.), Calistoga. ☎ **707/942-9111.** Reservations recommended on weekends. Lunch $7.50–$13; dinner $10.25–$19. MC, V. Mon–Tues and Thurs–Fri 11am–3pm; daily 5:30–10pm. Wine shop, Thurs–Tues 11am–7pm. CALIFORNIA.

Wine Country devotees often wend their way to the All Seasons Café in downtown Calistoga because of its extensive wine list and knowledgeable staff. The trick here is to buy a bottle of wine from the cafe's wine shop, then bring it to your table; the cafe adds a corkage fee of around $7.50 instead of tripling the price of the bottle (as they do at most restaurants). The diverse menu ranges from pizzas and pastas to such main courses as braised lamb shank "osso bucco" in an orange, Madeira, and tomato sauce. Anything with the house-smoked salmon or spiced sausages is also a safe bet. Chef John Coss saves his guests from any major *faux pas* by matching wines to his dishes on the menu, so you know just what's right for smoked salmon and Crescenza cheese pizza.

✪ **Catahoula.** 1457 Lincoln Ave. (between Washington and Fairway sts.), Calistoga. ☎ **707/942-2275.** Reservations recommended. Main courses $11–$20. MC, V. Winter 5:30–10:30pm daily; summer Fri–Sun 8:30–10am; Sat–Sun noon–3:30pm; daily 5:30–10:30pm. AMERICAN/SOUTHERN.

The domain of chef Jan Birnbaum, formerly of New York's Quilted Giraffe and San Francisco's Campton Place, this restaurant is the town's current favorite. And for good reason: It's the only place in Napa where you can get a decent rooster gumbo. And you'd have to travel all over Louisiana to find another pan-fried jalapeño-pecan catfish like this one. Catahoula's funky and fun, and the food that comes out of the wood-burning oven—like the roast duck with chili cilantro potatoes or the whole roasted fish with lemon broth, orzo, and escarole—is exciting (and usually spicy).

INEXPENSIVE

Bosko's. 1364 Lincoln Ave. (between Cedar and Washington sts.), Calistoga. ☎ **707/942-9088.** Main courses $6–$11. MC, V. Daily 11am–10pm. ITALIAN.

It's hard not to like a place with sawdust on the floor, because you immediately know that you won't encounter any snooty waiters or jacked-up prices. Bosko's formula is simple: Serve good, cheap Italian food, hot and fast. It's a homey place, with red-and-white-checkered tablecloths, an exposed beam ceiling, and a huge U-shaped counter. All 16 versions of pasta are cooked to order, as are the 10 or so pizzas and hot sandwiches. Order at the counter, scramble for a table, and then wait for your food to be delivered. The lunch special is a great deal: half a sandwich or plate of pasta, salad, and a good bowl of minestrone soup. Even more brilliant is the method of wine selection: Simply choose a bottle from the wine rack, pay retail for it at the counter, and drink it with your meal. There's no corkage fee for bottles bought from Boskos, but there's a $5 fee for bottles brought into the restaurant.

Café Sarafornia. 1413 Lincoln Ave. (at Washington St.), Calistoga. ☎ **707/ 942-0555.** Main courses $3–$9. AE, MC, V. Mon–Fri 7am–3pm, Sat–Sun 7am– 4pm. AMERICAN.

When Calistoga locals want a quick, inexpensive fix for breakfast or lunch, this is where they come. Café Sarafornia is pleasantly homey, a clean, bright, cheery bastion for late risers like us who prefer to eat their huevos rancheros at noon (breakfast is served all day). The cafe consists of little more than a U-shaped counter, a few booths, wood and tile floors, and a series of bucolic wall murals. The menu is a lesson in simplicity—burgers, hot dogs, pastas, sandwiches, salads, and requisite small-town specials like chicken-fried steak with red-eye gravy. And if you like to sweat and holler, be sure to sample the five-alarm chili. The cafe also offers kids' meals for a mere $3.95.

Pacifico. 1237 Lincoln Ave. (between Myrtle and Cedar sts.), Calistoga. ☎ **707/942-4400.** Main courses $6.75–$14.50. MC, V. Mon–Fri 11am– 10pm, Sat–Sun 10am–10pm. MEXICAN.

If you're in the mood for Mexican food, Pacifico is the place. The rather mundane-looking facade opens up into a surprisingly festive interior, complete with brilliantly colorful Mexican artwork and pottery, huge potted palm trees, and a south-of-the-border bar complete with faux tile roof and waterfall. The menu is *muy grande,* covering just about every conceivable region in Mexico from Tacos de Oaxaquenos (grilled, marinated chicken tacos topped with guajillo chile salsa) to Enchiladas del Ray (filled with Chihuahua cheese and covered with chile verde sauce). Fiesta Hour, Monday through Friday from 4:30 to 6pm, features special prices on margaritas and tacos. Pacifico also has the best selection of beers on tap in town.

Smokehouse Café. 1458 Lincoln Ave., Calistoga. ☎ **707/942-6060.** Main courses $8–$21. MC, V. Daily 7:30am–10pm (closed for dinner Tues–Wed Jan– Feb). REGIONAL AMERICAN BBQ.

Who would have guessed that some of the best spareribs and house-smoked meats in northern California would come from this little kitchen in Calistoga? Here's the winning game plan: Start with the Sacramento delta crawfish cakes and husk-roasted Cheyenne corn, then move on to the slow pig sandwich, a half slab of ribs, or homemade sausages—all of which take up to a week to prepare (not while you wait, luckily). The clincher is the fluffy all-you-can-eat cornbread dipped in pure cane syrup, which comes with every full-plate dinner. Kids are especially catered to—a rarity in these parts—and patio dining is available in summer.

Wappo Bar & Bistro. 1226B Washington St. (off Lincoln Ave.), Calistoga. ☎ **707/942-4712.** Main courses $8.50–$14.50. AE, MC, V. Wed–Mon 11:30am–2:30pm and 6–9:30pm. GLOBAL.

One of the best alfresco dining experiences in the Wine Country is under Wappo's honeysuckle-and-vine-covered arbor, but you'll also be comfortable inside this small bistro at one of the well-spaced, well-polished tables. The menu offers a wide range of choices, from Chilean sea bass with mint chutney to roast rabbit with oven tomato tagliarini. Desserts of choice are the black-bottom coconut cream pie and the strawberry rhubarb pie.

6 Where to Stock Up for a Picnic & Where to Enjoy It

You could easily plan your whole trip around restaurant reservations. But put together one of the world's best gourmet picnics, and the valley's your oyster. There are myriad places to spread your blanket, from grassy meadows to picnic tables at the foot of the vineyards. Best of all, you don't have to count on the maître d' for the best seat in the house. Go ahead, break out that bottle of your newfound favorite Cabernet, indulge in truffle-flavored pâté, hand-feed imported chocolates to your picnic partner. The cost will be a fraction of what it would cost to eat in most Wine Country restaurants, and the overall experience will be unforgettable.

One of the finest gourmet-food stores in the Wine Country, if not all of California, is **the Oakville Grocery Co.,** 7856 St. Helena Hwy. at Oakville Cross Road (☎ **707/944-8802**). Here you can put together the provisions for a memorable picnic, or, if you give them at least 24 hours' notice, the staff can prepare a picnic basket for you. You'll find shelves crammed with the best breads and the choicest selection of cheeses in the northern Bay Area, as well as pâtés, cold cuts, crackers, top-quality olive oils, fresh foie gras (domestic and French, seasonally), smoked Norwegian salmon, fresh caviar (Beluga, Sevruga, Osetra), and, of course, an exceptional selection of California wines. The Grocery Co. is open daily from 9am to 6pm; it also has an espresso bar tucked in the corner (open daily from 7am to 3pm), offering breakfast and lunch items, house-baked pastries, and 15 wines available by the glass or for tasting.

Another of our favorite places is **Dean & DeLuca,** 607 S. Main St. (Highway 29), north of Zinfandel Lane and south of Sulphur Springs Road in St. Helena (☎ **707/967-9980**). This ultimate gourmet grocery store is more like a world's fair of foods, where everything is beautifully displayed and often painfully pricey. As you pace the barn-wood plank floors, you'll stumble upon more high-end edibles than you've ever seen under one roof: local organic produce; 200 domestic and imported cheeses (with an on-site aging room to ensure proper ripeness); shelves and shelves of tapenades, pastas, oils, hand-packed dried herbs and spices, chocolates, sauces, and cookware; an espresso bar; one hell of a bakery section; and more. Along the back wall you can watch the professional chefs prepare gourmet take-out—try the fresh seared salmon with chanterelle mushrooms at $7.50 per 6-ounce serving, or order a to-go fireside dinner, a four-course meal which ranges from $7.50 to $9.50 and may include a Caesar salad, rotisserie pork loin with mustard and apricot glaze, French green lentils, sun-dried tomatoes, and root veggies (two-person minimum). Wine master John Hardesty presides over the 1,200-label collection. Adjoining the wine room is a walk-in cedar humidor with over 200 cigars to choose from. Hours are Monday through Saturday from 10am to 7pm (the espresso bar opens at 8am), and Sunday from 10am to 6pm.

Also see page 74 for details on **V. Sattui Winery,** 1111 White Lane (at Hwy. 29), St. Helena (☎ **707/963-7774**). Besides an enormous selection of wines and gourmet deli items—including 200 kinds of cheeses and desserts such as a sumptuous white-chocolate cheesecake—you'll also find extensive picnic facilities, making this winery one of the most popular stops along Highway 29.

If you crave a quieter, more pastoral picnic spot, head for one of the four picnic tables at **Robert Keenan Winery** in St. Helena (see p. 78), located right outside the winery and surrounded by vineyards, offering stunning views. Or try the beautiful picnic grounds situated amidst 350-year-old moss-covered oak trees at **Cuvaison** in Calistoga (see p. 83); the spectacular grounds at **Niebaum-Coppola** in Rutherford (see p. 70); or the Wine Country's premier picnicking site, **Rutherford Hill Winery** (see p. 73), which boasts superb views of the valley.

5

The Sonoma Valley

Sonoma Valley is often thought of as the "other" Wine Country, forever in the shadow of the Napa Valley. Truth is, even though there are far fewer wineries here, Sonoma wines have actually won more awards than any other California wine-growing region for 9 years running (much to the chagrin of Napa vintners, no doubt).

The Sonoma Valley is also far more rural and less traveled than its neighbor to the east, offering a more genuine away-from-it-all experience than its classier cousin. The roads are less crowded, the pace slower, and the whole valley still relatively free of slick tourist attractions and big-name hotels. Commercialization has, for the most part, not yet taken hold. Small, family-owned wineries are still Sonoma's mainstay, just as in the old days of wine making, when everyone started with the intention of going broke and loved every minute of it (as the saying goes in these parts, "It takes two million to make a million").

Unlike Napa Valley, you won't find palatial wineries with million-dollar art collections, aerial trams, and Hollywood ego trips (read: Niebaum-Coppola). Rather, the Sonoma Valley offers a refreshing dose of reality, where modestly sized wineries are integrated *into* the community rather than perched on hilltops like corporate citadels. If the Napa Valley feels more like a fantasyland, where everything exists to service the almighty grape and the visitors it attracts, then the Sonoma Valley is its antithesis, an unpretentious gaggle of ordinary towns, ranches, and wineries that welcome tourists but don't necessarily *rely* on them. The result, as you wind your way through the valley, is a chance to experience what Napa Valley must have been like long before the Seagrams and Moët et Chandons of the world turned the Wine Country into a major tourist destination.

1 Orientation & Getting Around

Sonoma Valley is some 17 miles long and 7 miles wide, and is bordered by two mountain ranges: the Mayacamas to the east and the Sonoma Mountains to the west. There is only one road, Highway

12 (also known as the Sonoma Highway), that passes through the valley, starting at the northern edge of the Carneros District, leading though the communities of Sonoma, Glen Ellen, and Kenwood, and ending at the southern boundary of Santa Rosa. Conveniently, most of the wineries—as well as most of the hotels, shops, and restaurants—are either in the town of Sonoma, along Highway 12, or a short distance from it. Of the numerous side roads that branch off Highway 12, only Bennett Valley Road to the west and Trinity Road (a.k.a. Oakville Grade) to the east lead over the ranges and out of the valley, and neither is easy to navigate. If you're coming from Napa, we strongly suggest you take the leisurely southern route along Highway 12/121 rather than Trinity Road, which is a real brake-smoker.

ALONG HIGHWAY 12: SONOMA'S TOWNS IN BRIEF

As you approach the Wine Country from the south, you must first pass through the **Carneros District,** a cool, windswept region that borders the San Pablo Bay and marks the entrance to both Napa and Sonoma valleys. Until the latter part of the 20th century, this mixture of marsh, sloughs, and rolling hills was mainly used as sheep pasture (*carneros* means sheep in Spanish). After experimental plantings yielded slow-growing yet high-quality grapes—particularly Chardonnay and Pinot Noir—several Napa and Sonoma wineries expanded their plantings here, eventually establishing the Carneros District as an American Viticultural Appellation. Though about a dozen wineries are spread throughout the region, there are no major towns or attractions—just plenty of gorgeous scenery as you cruise along Highway 121, the major junction between Napa and Sonoma.

At the northern boundary of the Carneros District along Highway 12 is the centerpiece of Sonoma Valley, the midsized town of **Sonoma,** which owes much of its appeal to Mexican general Mariano Guadalupe Vallejo. It was Vallejo who fashioned this pleasant, slow-paced community after a typical Mexican village—right down to its central plaza, Sonoma's geographical and commercial center. The plaza sits at the top of a T formed by Broadway (Highway 12) and Napa Street. Most of the surrounding streets form a grid pattern around this axis, making Sonoma easy to negotiate. The plaza's Bear Flag Monument marks the spot where the crude Bear Flag was raised in 1846, signaling the end of Mexican rule; the symbol was later adopted by the state of California and placed on its flag. The 8-acre park at the center of the plaza, complete with two ponds populated with ducks and geese, is perfect for an afternoon siesta in the cool shade. Our favorite attraction, however, is the gaggle of brilliantly feathered chickens that roam unfettered through the streets of Sonoma—a sight you'll *definitely* never see in Napa.

About 7 miles north of Sonoma on Highway 12 is the town of **Glen Ellen,** which, though just a fraction of the size of Sonoma, is home to several of the valley's finest wineries, restaurants, and inns. Aside from the addition of a few new restaurants, this charming Wine Country town hasn't changed much since the days when Jack London settled on his Beauty Ranch, about a mile west. Other than the wineries, you'll find few real signs of commercialism; the shops and restaurants, located along one main winding lane, cater to a small, local clientele—that is, until the summer tourist season, when traffic nearly triples on the weekends. If you're as yet undecided where you want set up camp during your visit to the Wine Country, we highly recommend this lovable little town.

A few miles north of Glen Ellen along Highway 12 is the tiny town of **Kenwood,** the northernmost outpost of the Sonoma Valley. Though Kenwood Vineyards' wines are well known throughout the United States, the town itself consists of little more than a few restaurants, wineries, and modest homes recessed into the wooded hillsides. The nearest lodging, the luxurious Kenwood Inn & Spa, is located about a mile south. Kenwood makes for a pleasant day trip—lunch at Café Citti, a tour of Château St. Jean, dinner at Kenwood Restaurant—before returning to Glen Ellen or Sonoma for the night.

A few miles beyond Kenwood is **Santa Rosa,** the county seat of Sonoma and home to more than 139,000 residents. Historically, it's best known as the hometown of horticulturist Luther Burbank, who produced more than 800 new varieties of fruits, vegetables, and plants during his 50-year tenure here. Unless you're armed with a map, however, it's best to avoid exploring the large, sprawling city, as it's easy to get lost; plus, it has little more to offer than what you'll find in Sonoma Valley proper.

VISITOR INFORMATION

While you're in Sonoma, stop by the **Sonoma Valley Visitors Bureau,** 453 1st St. East in the Carnegie Library Building (☎ **707/ 996-1090; www.sonomavalley.com**). It's open daily from 9am to 7pm in summer and from 9am to 5pm in winter. An additional visitors bureau is located a few miles south of the square at 25200

Arnold Dr. (Highway 121), at the entrance to Viansa Winery
(☎ **707/996-5793**); it's open daily from 9am to 5pm.

TOURING THE SONOMA VALLEY BY BIKE

Sonoma and its neighboring towns are so small, close together, and
relatively flat that it's not difficult to get around on two wheels. In
fact, if you're in no great hurry, there's no better way to tour the
Sonoma Valley than via bicycle. You can rent a bike at the
✪ **Goodtime Bicycle Company,** 18503 Sonoma Hwy. (Calif. 12),
Sonoma (☎ **888/525-0453** or 707/938-0453). They'll happily
point you to easy bike trails, or you can take one of their organized
excursions to Kenwood-area wineries or to south Sonoma wineries.
Not only do they provide a gourmet lunch featuring local Sonoma
products, they'll also carry any wine you purchase for you and help
with shipping arrangements. Lunch rides start at 10:30am and end
at around 3pm. The cost, including food and equipment, is $65 per
person (that's a darn good deal). Rentals cost $25 a day or $5 per
hour, and include helmets, locks, and everything else you'll need
(delivery is a $25 flat day rate). Bikes are also available for rent from
Sonoma Valley Cyclery, 20093 Broadway, Sonoma (☎ **707/
935-3377**), for $20 a day, or $6 per hour.

FAST FACTS: THE SONOMA VALLEY

Hospitals   The **Sonoma Valley Hospital,** 347 Andrieux St. in
downtown Sonoma (☎ **707/935-5000**), is a district hospital that
provides inpatient, outpatient, and continuing care to the public.
Its emergency room is supported by state-of-the-art equipment and
is staffed 24 hours a day by physicians and nurses specifically
trained in emergency treatment. SVH also has an intensive care
unit, pediatric center, and surgical services

The **Santa Rosa Memorial Hospital,** 1165 Montgomery Dr.
in Santa Rosa, about a 30-minute drive north from Sonoma
(☎ **707/546-3210**), offers 24-hour emergency service, as well as
complete inpatient and outpatient services, a cardiac center, pedi-
atrics, and a dental clinic.

Information   See "Visitor Information," above.

Newspapers/Magazines   The main newspaper in Sonoma Valley is the *Press Democrat,* a New York Times publication printed
daily and distributed at newsstands throughout Sonoma, Lake,
Napa, and Mendocino counties. Sonoma's local paper is the

Sonoma Index Tribune; published twice a week and available at newsstands around town, it covers regional news, events, and issues. Also available around town is the *Sonoma Valley Visitors Guide,* a slender $2 publication listing just about every sightseeing, recreation, shopping, lodging, and dining option in the valley, as well as a winery map.

Pharmacy   The pharmacy at **Long's Drugs,** 201 W. Napa St., Sonoma (☎ **707/938-4730**), is open Monday through Saturday from 9am to 9pm, Sunday from 10am to 6pm. If you prefer a more personable place to get your prescription filled, **Adobe Drug,** 303 W. Napa St., Sonoma (☎ **707/938-1144**), a locally owned drugstore, claims to be Sonoma's "Prescription Specialists" and will even make deliveries; it's open Monday through Friday from 9am to 8pm, Saturday from 9am to 7pm.

Police   For the local police, call ☎ **707/996-3601** or ☎ **707/ 996-3602,** or, in an emergency, ☎ **911.**

Post Offices   In **downtown Sonoma,** the post office is at 617 Broadway, at Patton Street (☎ **707/996-2459**). The **Glen Ellen** post office is at 13720 Arnold St., at O'Donnel Lane (☎ **707/ 996-9233**). Both branches are open Monday through Friday from 8:30am to 5pm.

Shipping Companies   **Mail Boxes, Etc.,** 19229 Sonoma Hwy., at Verano Street, Sonoma (☎ **707/935-3438**), which has a lot of experience with shipping wine, claims it will ship your wine to any state, either via UPS or Federal Express. They're open Monday through Friday from 9am to 6pm and Saturdays until 3pm. The **Wine Exchange of Sonoma,** 452 First St. E. (between East Napa and East Spain streets), Sonoma (☎ **707/938-1794**), will ship your wine as well—*if* you purchase an equal quantity of the same wine at their store (which they assured us would be in stock, and probably at a better price). For more on the reciprocity laws associated with shipping wine out of California, see "The Ins & Outs of Shipping Wine Home" in chapter 3.

Taxis   Call **A-C Taxi** at ☎ **707/526-4888.**

2 Touring the Wineries

Sonoma Valley is currently home to about 35 wineries (including California's first winery, Buena Vista, founded in 1857) and 13,000 acres of vineyards, which produce roughly 25 types of wines totaling more than five million cases a year. Chardonnay is the varietal for which Sonoma is most noted, and it represents almost one-quarter of

---

Touring Tip

If you'd rather leave the driving to someone else during your wine-tasting journey, call **Valley Wine Tours** at ☎ **707/975-6462** (**www.valleywinetours.com**) and reserve a seat on one of their guided tours of Sonoma Valley's most popular wineries, including Ravenswood, Buena Vista, Benziger, and Arrowood. Learn the history of the various family-owned wineries while traveling in air-conditioned comfort (they even provide lunch). A Champagne Tour and an Art & Wine Tour are available as well. Prices range from $60 to $125 per person for group tours. Private tours run $250 per couple.

---

the valley's vine acreage. Unlike the rigidly structured tours at many of Napa Valley's corporate-owned wineries, tastings and tours on the Sonoma side of the Mayacamas Mountains are usually free and low-key, and come with plenty of friendly banter between the wine makers and their guests.

The towns and wineries covered below are organized geographically from south to north, starting at the intersection of Highway 37 and Highway 121 in the Carneros District and ending in Kenwood. The wineries here tend to be a little more spread out than they are in Napa, but they're easy to find. Still, it's best to decide which wineries you're most interested in and devise a touring strategy before you set out so you don't find yourself doing a lot of backtracking. (For more on this, see "Strategies for Touring the Wine Country" in chapter 3; and check out "The Sonoma Valley Wineries" map on p. 137 to get your bearings.)

We've reviewed our favorite Sonoma Valley wineries here. If you'd like a complete list of local wineries, be sure to pick up one of the free guides to the valley available at the **Sonoma Valley Visitors Bureau** (see "Visitor Information," above).

THE CARNEROS DISTRICT

Róche. 28700 Arnold Dr. (Calif. 121), Sonoma. ☎ **800/825-9475** or 707/935-7115. www.rochewinery.com. Daily 10am–6pm (to 5pm in winter). No tours available.

The first winery you'll encounter as you enter Sonoma Valley, Róche is typical of the area—a small, family-run operation that focuses on one or two varietals and has very limited distribution (Róche wines, in fact, are sold exclusively through the tasting room). Situated atop a gently sloping knoll, the ranch-style winery and surrounding 25 acres of vineyards are owned by Genevieve and Joe Róche (pronounced *Rósh*), who originally bought the property with no intention of starting a winery. But in the early 1980s, a colleague suggested they experiment with a few vines of Chardonnay—and the results were so impressive that they decided to go into business making estate-grown Chardonnay and Pinot Noir.

The Róches only produce about 6,000 cases per year, some of which are bought before the wine even hits the bottle. Tastings are complimentary for nonreserve wines, and prices range from $9 for a 1999 Tamarix Pinot Noir Blanc to $36 for the unfiltered 1997 Estate Reserve Pinot Noir; our favorite is the 1997 Estate Chardonnay ($31), a rich, intense wine with lingering flavors of apple, pear, and butterscotch. Picnic tables overlooking the valley are available, though you'll probably prefer lunching at neighboring Viansa Winery and Italian Marketplace (see below).

✪ **Viansa Winery and Italian Marketplace.** 25200 Arnold Dr. (Calif. 121), Sonoma. ☎ **800/995-4740** or 707/935-4700. www.viansa.com. Daily 10am–5pm. Daily self-guided tours.

The first major winery you'll encounter as you enter Sonoma Valley from the south, this sprawling Tuscany-style villa is perched atop a knoll overlooking the entire lower valley. Viansa is the brainchild of Sam and Vicki Sebastiani, who left the family dynasty to create their own temple to food and wine (*Viansa* being a contraction of Vicki and Sam). While Sam, a third-generation wine maker, runs the winery, Vicky manages the marketplace, a large room crammed with a cornucopia of high-quality preserves, mustards, olive oils, pastas, salads, breads, desserts, Italian tableware, cookbooks, and wine-related gifts.

The winery, which does an extensive mail-order business through its Tuscany Club (worth joining if you love getting mail and good wine), has quickly established a favorable reputation for its Cabernet, Sauvignon Blanc, and Chardonnay, blended from premium Napa and Sonoma grapes and sold in the sexiest-shaped bottles in Sonoma. Sam is also experimenting with Italian grape varieties such as Muscat Canelli, Sangiovese, and Ebbiolo, most of which are sold exclusively at the winery. Free tastings are poured at the east end of the marketplace, and the self-guided tour includes a trip through the underground barrel-aging cellar adorned with colorful hand-painted murals.

Viansa is also one of the few wineries in Sonoma Valley where you can purchase deli items—the focaccia sandwiches are delicious—and dine alfresco under the grape trellis while you admire the bucolic view.

The Sonoma Valley Wineries

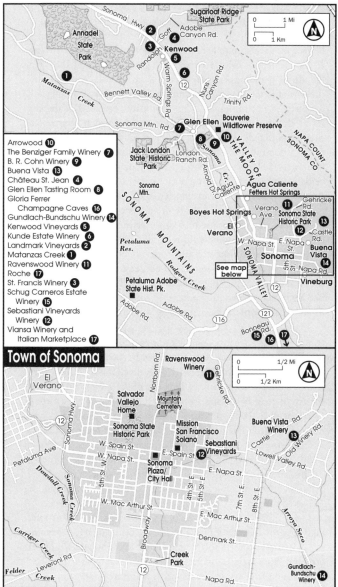

Arrowood **10**
The Benziger Family Winery **7**
B. R. Cohn Winery **9**
Buena Vista **13**
Château St. Jean **4**
Glen Ellen Tasting Room **8**
Gloria Ferrer
    Champagne Caves **16**
Gundlach-Bundschu Winery **14**
Kenwood Vineyards **5**
Kunde Estate Winery **6**
Landmark Vineyards **2**
Matanzas Creek **1**
Ravenswood Winery **11**
Roche **17**
St. Francis Winery **3**
Schug Carneros Estate
    Winery **15**
Sebastiani Vineyards
    Winery **12**
Viansa Winery and
    Italian Marketplace **17**

Town of Sonoma

⊙ **Gloria Ferrer Champagne Caves.** 23555 Carneros Hwy. (Calif. 121), Sonoma. ☎ **707/996-7256.** www.gloriaferrer.com. Daily 10am–5:30pm. Tours daily 11am–4pm.

When you have it up to here with Chardonnays and Pinots, it's time to pay a visit to Gloria Ferrer, the grande dame of the Wine Country's sparkling-wine producers. Who's Gloria, you ask? She's the wife of José Ferrer, whose family has been making sparkling wine for the past 5 centuries and whose company, Freixenet, is the largest producer of sparkling wine in the world (Cordon Negro being their most popular brand). All of which equals big bucks, and certainly a good chunk of it went into building this palatial estate. Glimmering like Oz high atop a gently sloping hill, it overlooks the verdant Carneros District; on a sunny day, enjoying a glass of dry Brut while soaking in the magnificent views is a must.

If you're unfamiliar with the term méthode champenoise, be sure to take the free 30-minute tour of the fermenting tanks, bottling line, and caves brimming with racks of yeast-laden bottles. Afterwards, retire to the elegant tasting room for a flute of Brut or Cuvée ($3 to $5.50 a glass, $16 and up per bottle), find an empty chair on the veranda, and say, "Ahhh. *This* is the life." There are picnic tables, but it's usually too windy up here for comfort; that, and you have to purchase a bottle of their sparkling wine to reserve a table.

Schug Carneros Estate Winery. 602 Bonneau Rd. (west of the junction of Calif. 116 and Calif. 121), Sonoma. ☎ **800/966-9365** or 707/939-9363. www.schugwinery.com. Daily 10am–5pm. Tours by appointment only.

A native of Germany's Rhine River valley, Walter Schug (pronounced *Shewg*) comes from a long line of Pinot Noir vintners. After graduating from the prestigious German wine institute of Geisenheim in 1959, he came to California and worked as wine maker for Joseph Phelps, where he established his reputation as one of California's top Cabernet Sauvignon and Riesling producers. In 1980, he launched his own label from a vineyard he tended at Phelps, and left soon afterwards to build this winery. Since then, Schug's wines have achieved world-class status, with an astounding 30% sold overseas.

The winery is situated on top of a rise overlooking the surrounding Carneros District, a prime region for cool-climate grapes such as Chardonnay and Pinot Noir (Schug's predominate wines). Its post-and-beam architecture reflects the Schug family's German heritage; the tasting room, however, is quite ordinary and small, designed more for practicality than pomp and circumstance (a radical contrast from neighboring Viansa and Gloria Ferrer). Typical of

Sonoma wineries, there's no tasting fee for new releases (reserve tasting $5), and bottle prices are all quite reasonable, ranging from $12 for a 1998 North Coast Sauvignon Blanc to $18 for a 1997 North Coast Merlot. The best buy, however, is the award-winning 1997 Carneros Pinot Noir, a bargain at $18. The winery has no picnic facilities, probably due to steady winds upwelling from the neighboring dairy farm.

SONOMA

✪ **Gundlach-Bundschu Winery.** 2000 Denmark St. (off Eighth St. E.), Sonoma. ☎ **707/938-5277.** Daily 11am–4:30pm. Tours last 10–20 min. and are offered daily, May–Sept only.

If it looks like the people working here are actually enjoying themselves, that's because they are. Gundlach-Bundschu (pronounced *Gun*-lock *Bun*-shoe) is your quintessential Sonoma winery—nonchalant in appearance, but obsessed with wine: The G-B clan are a nefarious lot, infamous for wild stunts such as holding up Napa's Wine Train on horseback and—egad!—serving Sonoma wines to their captives; their small tasting room looks not unlike a bomb shelter, the Talking Heads is their version of Muzak, and the "art" consists of a dozen witty black-and-white posters promoting their wines.

This is the oldest family-owned and -operated winery in California, going into its sixth generation since Jacob Gundlach harvested his first crop in 1858. What started out as a winery known for whites is now coveted among wine's cognoscenti for their reds, particularly the Zinfandels. Prices for their 17 distinct wines range from a very reasonable $10 per bottle for the Polar Bearitage (ha, ha) white table wine to $45 for the Vintage Reserve Cabernet Sauvignon, though most prices are in the mid-teens; tastings are free. Tours include a trip into their 430-foot cave.

Gundlach-Bundschu has the best picnic grounds in the valley, though you'll have to walk to the top of Towles' Hill to earn the sensational view. And the Shakespeare plays held at the winery's adjacent outdoor theater Friday through Sunday from Memorial Day to Labor Day (general admission $18) are a real blast.

Sebastiani Vineyards Winery. 389 Fourth St. E., Sonoma. ☎ **800/888-5532** or 707/938-5532. www.sebastiani.com. Daily 10am–5pm. Tours offered 10:30am–4pm, every half hour in summer, every 45 min. to an hour in winter; no reservations necessary.

The name Sebastiani is practically synonymous with Sonoma. What started in 1904, when Samuele Sebastiani began producing his first wines, has in three successive generations grown into a small empire and Sonoma County's largest winery, producing some six million cases a year. Oddly enough, the winery occupies neither the most scenic setting nor structure in Sonoma Valley, yet its place in the history and development of the region is unparalleled.

The 25-minute tour is interesting, informative, and well worth the time. You can see the winery's original turn-of-the-century crusher and press as well as the world's largest collection of oak-barrel carvings, crafted by local artist Earle Brown. If you don't want to take the tour, head straight for the charmingly rustic tasting room, where you can sample an extensive selection of wines sans tasting fee. Bottle prices are very reasonable, ranging from $8 for a 1998 White Zin to $50 for a 1997 Cabernet Sauvignon. A picnic area is adjacent to the cellars, though a far more scenic spot is located across the parking lot in Sebastiani's Cherryblock Vineyards.

Buena Vista. 18000 Old Winery Rd. (off E. Napa St., slightly northeast of downtown), Sonoma. ☎ **800/926-1266** or 707/938-1266. www.buenavistawinery. com. Daily 10:30am–5pm. Self-guided tours only.

Count Agoston Haraszthy, the Hungarian émigré who is universally regarded as the father of California's wine industry, founded this historic California winery in 1857. A close friend of General Vallejo, Haraszthy returned from Europe in 1861 with 100,000 of the finest vine cuttings, which he made available to all wine growers. Although Buena Vista's wine making now takes place at an ultramodern facility in the Carneros District, the winery still maintains a tasting room inside the restored 1862 Press House—a beautiful stone-crafted room brimming with wines, wine-related gifts, and accessories (as well as a small art gallery along the inner balcony).

Tastings are free for most wines, $3 for the really good stuff; bottle prices range from as low as $8.95 for a buttery 1998 Sauvignon Blanc to $37 for the Carneros Grand Reserve Cabernet Sauvignon. You can take the self-guided tour any time during operating hours; a "Historical Presentation," offered daily at 2pm, details the life and times of the Count. After tasting, grab your favorite bottle, a selection of cheeses from the Sonoma Cheese Factory, salami, bread, and pâté (all available in the tasting room), and plant yourself at one of the many picnic tables recessed into the lush, verdant setting.

Ravenswood Winery. 18701 Gehricke Rd. (off Lovall Valley Rd.), Sonoma. ☎ **800/NO-WIMPY** or 707/938-1960. www.ravenswood-wine.com. Daily 10am–4:30pm. Tours by reservation only.

Compared to old heavies like Sebastiani and Buena Vista, Ravenswood is a relative newcomer to the Sonoma wine scene, but it has quickly established itself as the sine qua non of Zinfandel, the versatile grape that's quickly gaining popular ground on the rapacious Cabernet Sauvignon. In fact, Ravenswood is the first winery in the United States to focus primarily on Zins, which make up about three quarters of its 150,000-case production; it also produces a Merlot, Cabernet Sauvignon, and a small amount of Chardonnay.

The winery is smartly designed—recessed into the Sonoma hillside to protect its treasures from the simmering summers. Tours follow the wine-making process from grape to glass, and include a visit into the aromatic oak-barrel aging rooms. A gourmet "Barbecue Overlooking the Vineyards" is held each weekend (from 11am to 4:40pm, Memorial Day through Sept; call for details and reservations), though you're welcome to plop your own picnic basket down at any of their tables. Tastings are free and generous, though you may not find some of the pourers to be as witty as they think they are (ours was a jerk; however, we've known people who have had great experiences here). Bottle prices range from $8.50 for a 1998 light and crisp French Colombard to $32 for a 1997 Meritage style red, but it's the kick-butt Zins—priced well in the low- to mid-teens—that you'll want to stock up on.

GLEN ELLEN

B. R. Cohn Winery. 15140 Sonoma Hwy. (Calif. 12, just north of Madrone Rd.), Glen Ellen. ☎ **707/938-4064.** www.brcohn.com. Daily 10am–5pm. Tours by appointment only.

You may not have heard of Bruce Cohn, but you've certainly heard of the Doobie Brothers, the San Francisco band he managed to fame and fortune—part of which he used to purchase this wonderfully bucolic estate with its whitewashed turn-of-the-century farmhouse and groves of rare olive trees. Cohn, a native of Sonoma County, started making his own wine in 1984 and was an immediate success. In the small, simple tasting room lined with framed gold and platinum albums, a friendly and informative staff pours free tastings of Cabernet, Pinot Noir, a delicious Chardonnay, and the occasional Merlot. Bottle prices range from the mid-teens to $35, and the winery often sells selections that aren't available elsewhere, such as the estate-grown 1997 Olive Hill Merlot ($28). Though best known for his Cabernet Sauvignon, it's a case of Cohn's reserve Chardonnay you'll want to send back home along with a bottle or two of his award-winning (and pricey) olive oil. There are a few picnic tables on the cement patio fronting the tasting room, but bring along a blanket and relax on the terraced hills of plush lawn overlooking the vineyards.

Arrowood. 14347 Sonoma Hwy. (Calif. 12), Glen Ellen. ☎ **707/938-5170.**
www.arrowoodvineyards.com. Daily 10am–4:30pm. Tours by appointment
only, daily at 10:30am and 2:30pm.

Richard Arrowood had already established a reputation as a master
wine maker at Château St. Jean before he and his wife, Alis Demers
Arrowood, set out on their own in 1986. Their utterly picturesque
winery is perched on a gently rising hillside lined with perfectly
manicured vineyards. Tastings take place in the Hospitality House,
the newer of Arrowood's two stately gray-and-white buildings fashioned after New England farmhouses, complete with wraparound
porches. Richard's focus is on making world-class wine with mini-
mal intervention, and his results are impressive: more than one of
his current releases has scored over 90 points. Mind you, such
excellence doesn't come cheaply: Prices start at $26 for a 1997
Chardonnay and quickly climb to the mid- to high 30s. Arrowood
is one of the very few wineries in Sonoma that charge for tastings
($3), but if you're curious what near-perfection tastes like, it's well
worth it. No picnic facilities are available.

Glen Ellen Tasting Room. 14301 Arnold Dr. (at the south end of town in Jack
London Village), Glen Ellen. ☎ **707/939-6277.** Daily 10am–5pm. Self-guided
tours available.

While most other Sonoma County wineries are knocking themselves
out to make the best wines on the planet, Glen Ellen is content with
making reasonably good wines at moderate to low prices. The story
starts with Bruno Benziger, a retired New York wine-and-spirits
importer who decided to move to Sonoma and start a winery aimed
at the middle market—and he succeeded beyond his wildest dreams:
Glen Ellen Chardonnay and Merlot became nationwide best-sellers,
and the White Zinfandel and Cabernet were among the top three.
The Benziger family eventually sold the Glen Ellen brand (along
with M. G. Vallejo) in 1993 to pursue higher-quality, lower-volume
wine (see "The Benziger Family Winery," below), though the Glen
Ellen label continues to produce about 3.8 million cases a year.

The Tasting Room, housed in the original Glen Ellen winery
built back in 1881, is a large, modern, and handsomely trimmed
room with polished woods, racks of oak wine barrels, and a wide
assortment of wine-related gifts for purchase. Tastings are free, and
bottles are value-priced at $5 for a 1998 White Zin and $7 for a
Glen Ellen Merlot; reserve wines run an affordable $12 or $18 per
bottle. Also worth a visit is the History Center, a smartly designed
self-guided tour of Glen Ellen back in its heyday (the poster-sized

black-and-white photographs are truly captivating). Picnic tables with views overlooking a creek are located behind the Tasting Room.

✪ **The Benziger Family Winery.** 1883 London Ranch Rd. (off Arnold Dr., on the way to Jack London State Historic Park), Glen Ellen. ☎ **800/989-8890** or 707/935-3000. www.benziger.com. Tasting room daily 10am–5pm. Tram tours daily (weather permitting) at 11:30am, 12:30, 2, and 3:30pm.

When Bruno Benziger moved from New York, purchased the plot next to Jack London State Park, and started the Glen Ellen label (see above), he had no idea that he would become the valley's second-largest wine producer. After the Benziger family's fast track to the top, they sold the rights to that label in order to create lower-volume, higher-quality wines under this one.

A visit here confirms that you are indeed visiting a "family" winery; at any given time, three generations of Benzigers (pronounced *Ben*-zigger) may be running around tending to chores, and you're instantly made to feel as if you're part of the clan. The pastoral, user-friendly property features an exceptional self-guided tour ("The most comprehensive tour in the wine industry," according to *Wine Spectator*), gardens, a spacious tasting room manned by an amiable staff, and an art gallery. The free 40-minute tram tour, pulled by a beefy tractor, is both informative and fun as it winds through the estate vineyards before making a champagne-tasting pit stop on a scenic bluff. (*Tip:* Tram tickets—a hot item in the summer—are available on a first-come, first-served, basis, so either arrive early or stop by in the morning to pick up afternoon tickets.)

Tastings of the standard-release wines are free, and bottle prices range from $12 for a 1998 Fumé Blanc to $21 for a 1996 Pinot Noir. The best buy, however, is the award-winning 1997 Zinfandel (Sonoma County), priced to move at $21 a bottle. You can also purchase a full glass of wine for $5 and tour the estate in style. The winery offers several scenic picnic spots.

KENWOOD

Kunde Estate Winery. 10155 Sonoma Hwy., Kenwood. ☎ **707/833-5501.** www.kunde.com. Tastings daily 10:30am–4pm. Cave tours Fri–Sun approximately every half hour 11am–4pm.

Expect a friendly, unintimidating welcome at this scenic winery, run by four generations of the Kundes since 1904. One of the largest grape suppliers in the area, the Kunde family (pronounced *Kun*-dee) has devoted 800 acres of their 2,000-acre ranch to growing ultrapremium-quality grapes, which they provide to about 30

Sonoma and Napa wineries. It's this abundance that allows them to make nothing but estate wines (wines made from grapes grown on the Kunde property, as opposed to grapes purchased from other growers).

The tasting room is located in a spiffy new 17,000-square-foot wine-making facility, which features specialized crushing equipment that enables the wine maker to run whole clusters to the press—a real advantage in white-wine production. Tastings of the dozen or so releases are free; bottle prices range from $11 for a 1999 Magnolia Lane Sauvignon Blanc to $29 for a 1994 Reserve Cabernet Sauvignon; most labels sell in the mid- to high teens. The tasting room also has a gift shop and large windows overlooking the bottling room and tank room.

The tour of the property's extensive wine caves includes a history of the winery. Private tours are available by appointment, but most folks are happy to just stop by for some vino and to relax at one of the many picnic tables placed around the man-made pond. Animal lovers will appreciate Kunde's preservation efforts; the property has a duck estuary with more than 50 species (seen by appointment only). The Kunde Estate also happens to be where actress Geena Davis and director Renny Harlin tied the knot in 1993.

Kenwood Vineyards. 9592 Sonoma Hwy. (Calif. 12), Kenwood. ☎ **707/ 833-5891.** www.kenwoodvineyards.com. Daily 10am–4:30pm. Tours at 11:30am and 2:30pm daily.

Kenwood's history dates back to 1906, when the Pagani brothers made their living selling wine straight from the barrel and into the jug. In 1970, the property was bought by the Lee family, who dumped a ton of money into converting the aging winery into a modern, high-production facility (most of it cleverly concealed within the original barnlike buildings). Since then, Kenwood's wines have earned a solid reputation for consistent quality with each of their varietals: Cabernet Sauvignon, Chardonnay, Zinfandel, Pinot Noir, Merlot, and their most popular wine, Sauvignon Blanc—a crisp, light wine with hints of melon.

Though the winery looks rather modest in size, its output is staggering: over 400,000 cases of ultrapremium wines fermented in steel tanks and French and American oak barrels. Popular with wine collectors is wine maker Michael Lee's Artist Series Cabernet Sauvignon, a limited production from the winery's best vineyards featuring labels with original artwork by renowned artists. The tasting room, housed in one of the old barns, offers free tastings of most varieties as well as gift items for sale. Wine prices are moderate, ranging from $8 for a bottle of 1995 Vintage Red table wine to $22 for a 1997 Sonoma County Merlot; the Artist Series, on the other hand, runs anywhere from $50 to $250.

Château St. Jean. 8555 Sonoma Hwy. (Calif. 12), Kenwood. ☎ **800/543-7572** or 707/833-4134. www.chateaustjean.com. Tasting room open Mon–Thurs 10am–4:30pm, Fri–Sun 10am–5pm. At the foot of Sugarloaf Ridge, just north of Kenwood and east of Hwy. 12.

Château St. Jean is notable for its exceptionally beautiful buildings, well-landscaped grounds, and elegant tasting room. Among California wineries, it's a pioneer in vineyard designation—the procedure of making wine from, and naming it for, a single vineyard. A private drive takes you to what was once a 250-acre country retreat built in 1920; a well-manicured lawn overlooking the meticulously maintained vineyards is now a picnic area, complete with a fountain and picnic tables. There's a self-guided tour with detailed and photographic descriptions of the wine-making process. When you're done, be sure to walk up to the top of the faux medieval tower for a magnificent view of the valley.

Back in the elegant tasting room—split into three areas to better handle the traffic—you can sample Château St. Jean's wide array of wines ranging from Chardonnays and Cabernet Sauvignon to Fumé Blanc, Merlot, Johannisberg Riesling, and Gewürztraminer (don't miss a rare tasting of their late-harvest wines as well—you'll be amazed what a little more time on the vine can do to a wine). Tastings are complimentary, and prices range from $9 for a Sonoma County Fumé Blanc to $30 for a Durell Vineyards Pinot Noir; most wines, though, are priced around $20. If you can find a bottle of the 1991 Sonoma County Reserve Cabernet, buy it—it's won more awards than Pete Sampras.

St. Francis Winery. 8450 Sonoma Hwy. (Calif. 12), Kenwood. ☎ **800/543-7713** or 707/833-4666. www.stfranciswine.com. Daily 10am–4:30pm. Tours by appointment only.

Although St. Francis Winery makes a commendable Chardonnay, Zinfandel, and Cabernet Sauvignon, it's their highly coveted Merlot that they're best known for. Wine maker Tom Mackey, a former high-school English teacher from San Francisco, has been hailed as the Master of Merlot by *Wine Spectator* for his uncanny ability to craft the finest Merlot in California (although we prefer the one at Matanzas Creek; see below). Seventy percent of the estate's vineyards yield Merlot grapes, used to make Mackey's Estate Reserve

Merlot—the one bottle you don't want to leave without (in fact, they'll only let you leave with one bottle).

The property itself has an interesting history: The original vineyard was planted in 1910 as part of a wedding gift to Alice Kunde (scion of the local Kunde family), but it wasn't until 1979 that Joe Martin and Lloyd Canton—two white-collar executives turned vintners—completed their long-awaited dream winery on the site and christened it after Saint Francis of Assisi. It has a small but cozy tasting room complete with the requisite wine-related gift items. Tastings are free for most wines, and $5 for the reserve reds. A good buy is the 1998 Chardonnay ($13), barrel-fermented in American and French oak for 6 months with hints of oak and fruit. Otherwise, prices range from $15 to $20 a bottle, and $39 for the reserve reds. A few picnic tables overlooking the vineyards are set out behind the tasting room.

Landmark Vineyards. 101 Adobe Canyon Rd. (off Hwy. 12), Kenwood. ☎ **800/452-6365** or 707/833-1144. www.landmarkwine.com. Daily 10am–4:30pm.

California's oldest exclusively Chardonnay estate was first founded in 1972 in the Russian River area of Sonoma County. When new housing development started encroaching on the winery's territory, proprietor Damaris Deere W. Ethridge (great-great-granddaughter of John Deere, the tractor baron) moved her operation to northern Sonoma Valley in 1990. The winery, which produces about 30,000 cases annually, is housed in a modest mission-style building set on 11 acres of vineyards. The tasting room offers complimentary samples of their award-winning Chardonnay, and for a small fee ($1.50) their Pinot Noir. (Note the wall-to-wall mural behind the tasting counter painted by noted Sonoma County artist Claudia Wagar.) Wine prices range from $11 for a 1998 Adobe Canyon Sauvignon Blanc to $22 for a 1998 Overlook Chardonnay.

The winery has a pond-side picnic area, as well as what is probably the only bocce court in the valley (yes, you can play, and yes, they provide instructions). Also available from Memorial Day to Labor Day are free Belgian horse–drawn wagon tours through the vineyards, offered every Saturday from 11am to 3pm.

JUST UP FROM THE VALLEY

✪ **Matanzas Creek.** 6097 Bennett Valley Rd. (off Warm Springs Rd.), Santa Rosa. ☎ **800/590-6464** or 707/528-6464. www.matanzascreek.com. Daily 10am–4:30pm. Tours daily by appointment only at 10:30am, 1, and 3pm. From

Hwy. 12 in Kenwood or Glen Ellen, take the Warm Springs Rd. turnoff to Bennett Valley Rd.; the drive takes 15–20 min.

Okay, so it's not technically in Sonoma Valley, but if there's one winery that's worth the detour, it's Matanzas Creek. After a wonderfully scenic 20-minute drive along Bennett Valley Road, you'll arrive at one of the prettiest wineries in California, blanketed by fields of lavender (usually in bloom near the end of June) and surrounded by rolling hills of well-tended vineyards.

The winery itself has a rather unorthodox history. In 1978, Sandra and Bill MacIver, neither of whom had any previous experience in the worlds of wine making or business, set out with one goal in mind: to create the finest wines in the country. Actually, they've overshot their mark. With the release of their Journey 1990 Chardonnay, they were hailed by wine critics as the proud parents of the finest Chardonnay ever produced in the United States, comparable to *the* finest white wines in the world.

This state-of-the-art, environmentally conscious winery produces only three varietals—the above-mentioned Chardonnay, plus Sauvignon Blanc and Merlot—all of which are available for tasting free of charge. Prices for current releases are, as you would imagine, at the higher end, ranging from $22 for a 1998 Sauvignon Blanc to a whopping $95 for the 1995 Estate Merlot—but it's easily the finest Merlot you'll sample in the Wine Country. Also available for purchase is culinary lavender from Matanzas (pronounced Mah-*tan*-zas) Creek's own lavender field, the largest outside of Provence and a breathtaking sight when it's in bloom in June. Purchase a full glass of wine and bring it outside to savor as you wander through these wonderfully aromatic gardens. Picnic tables hidden under groves of oak have pleasant views of the surrounding vineyards. On the return trip, be sure to take the Sonoma Mountain Road detour for a real backcountry experience.

3 More to See & Do

When you've had it to the gills with Sonoma Valley wineries, it's time to explore the valley's numerous other sites and attractions. The majority of activities are centered around the town of Sonoma, which is small enough to explore on foot (the picturesque town plaza is truly worth checking out). If the weather's warm, we strongly recommend a guided tour of the Sonoma Valley via horseback or bicycle, two of our favorite things to do in the Wine Country.

THE CARNEROS DISTRICT

BIPLANE RIDES For the adrenaline junkie in your group, ✪ **Vintage Aircraft Company** will help you lose your lunch on one of their authentic 1940 Boeing-built Stearman biplanes. Rides range from the "Scenic" (a leisurely flight over Sonoma Valley) and "Aerobatic" (loops, rolls, and assorted maneuvers) to—drum roll, please— the "Kamikaze," an intensely bowel-shaking aerobatic death wish that's (and we quote) "not for the faint of heart." Prices range from $70 for the Scenic to $90 for the Kamikaze. A second passenger is welcome to join the fun for an additional fee.

Safe and saner types can opt for the **glider rides,** which soar over the bay and offer breathtaking views of the Sonoma and Napa valleys and, on a clear day, the Sierra mountain range. Prices range from $80 to $145 for one passenger, $120 to $195 for two.

Reservations are recommended for both biplane and glider rides. Vintage Aircraft Company is at the Sonoma Valley Airport, 23982 Arnold Dr. (on Calif. 121, across from Gloria Ferrer Champagne Caves), Sonoma Valley (☎ **707/938-2444;** www.vintageaircraftco. com).

SONOMA

The best way to learn about the history of Sonoma is to follow the self-guided *Sonoma Walking Tour* map, provided by the Sonoma League for Historic Preservation. Tour highlights include General Vallejo's 1852 Victorian-style home; the Sonoma Barracks, erected in 1836 to house Mexican army troops; and the Blue Wing Inn, an 1840 hostelry built to accommodate travelers—including John Fremont, Kit Carson, and Ulysses S. Grant—and new settlers while they erected homes in Sonoma. You can purchase the $2.75 map at the **Vasquez House,** 414 First St. E., between East Napa and East Spain streets (☎ **707/938-0510**), open Wednesday through Sunday from 1:30 to 4pm.

Also worth a look is the **Mission San Francisco Solano de Sonoma,** located on Sonoma Plaza at the corner of First Street East and Spain Street (☎ **707/938-1519**). Founded in 1823, this was the northernmost—and last—mission built in California. It also was the only one established on the northern coast by the Mexican government, who wanted to protect their territory from expansionist Russian fur traders. It's now part of Sonoma State Historic Park. Admission is $3 for adults, $2 for children 6 to 12, and free for children 5 and under. It's open daily from 10am to 5pm except New Year's Day, Thanksgiving, and Christmas.

The Super Spa

✪ **Sonoma Mission Inn, Spa & Country Club** has always been the most complete—and the most luxurious—spa in the whole Wine Country. But with its new $20 million 27,000-square-foot facility with over 50 spa treatments, ever-popular natural mineral baths, and virtually every facility and activity imaginable, this super spa is now one of the best in the country. Within the Spanish mission-style retreat you can pamper yourself silly: soak in mineral baths, have a facial set to music, indulge in a grape seed body wrap, relax with a massage, take a sauna or herbal steam, go for a dip in the pool—the list goes on and on (and, alas, so will the bill). You can also work off those wicked wine country meals with aerobics, weights, and cardio machines; get loose in a yoga class; play tennis; or just lounge or lunch by the pool. Or you can opt for our (okay, Erika's) personal favorite—the $199 Rejuvenator, a 1-hour, 45-minute mega-treatment that includes an "oil drip" onto your hair and scalp, a scalp massage and a hair mask that smells so much like cookie dough that you'll be tempted to nibble on it, a face mask, and a glorious massage. After the treatment, take a workout in the exercise room followed by a sauna, steam, and mineral plunge, then relax poolside with a good book. Now that's living.

Of course, they have to pay for this fancy upgrade somehow, and here's how:

- Weekend day-use fee for guests: $85
- Weekday day-use fee for guests: $65
- Weekend day-use fee for non-guests: $150
- Weekday day-use fee for non-guests: $85

Steep, yes, but access to the spa facilities is free if you opt for one of the treatments, so you might as well splurge. Either way, a day at the Sonoma Mission Inn Spa is one of our favorite ways to unwind in the Wine Country (18140 Sonoma Hwy.; ☎ **800/862-4945** or 707/938-9000).

SHOPPING Most of Sonoma's shops, which offer everything from food and wine to clothing and books, are located around the plaza. **The Mercado,** a small shopping center at 452 First St. E., houses several good stores selling unusual wares. The **Arts Guild of Sonoma,** 140 E. Napa St. (☎ **707/996-3115**), showcases the works of local artists in a wide variety of styles and media. It's open

Sunday through Thursday from 11am–6pm, Friday 11am–9pm, Saturday 10am–9pm; admission is free.

Our favorite stop along the plaza, however, is the ✪ **Wine Exchange,** 452 First St. E. (☎ **707/938-1794**), which carries more than 700 domestic wines, books on wine, wine paraphernalia, olive oils, and a small selection of cigars. It's a great place to begin your wine experience: browse though the numerous racks of bottles, ask questions of the wine-savvy staff, and be sure to check out the stack of wines in open cases to the right of the front door as you enter—they're almost all priced under $10. Even the beer connoisseur who's feeling displaced in the Wine Country will be happy here, with the more than 300 beers from around the world. There are $1 wine and beer tastings daily at the small bar in back, which is occupied most evenings by a gaggle of friendly locals. The Exchange is open Monday through Saturday from 10am to 6pm, Sunday from 11am to 6pm. Shipping is available anywhere in the United States.

THE LOCAL FARMER'S MARKET   Obsessed with farm-fresh produce, Sonomans host a year-round **Sonoma Valley Farmer's Market** every Friday morning from 9am to noon at the Depot Park on First Street West (just north of East Spain Street). Dozens of growers offer fresh fruits, vegetables, flowers, homemade jams, honey, barbecued turkey, baked goods, and handmade crafts from local artists. It's such a popular gathering place for locals and visitors alike that they've added a Saturday-morning market from 1 to 3:30pm November through December, and a Tuesday-night market from 5:30pm to dusk April through October. Both Saturday and Tuesday markets are held at the plaza in front of City Hall.

GLEN ELLEN

Hikers, mountain bikers, horseback riders, and picnickers will enjoy a day spent at ✪ **Jack London State Historic Park,** 2400 London Ranch Rd. off Arnold Drive (☎ **707/938-5216**). On its 800 acres, which were once home to the renowned writer, you'll find 10 miles of trails, the remains of London's burned-down dream house (as well as some preserved structures), and plenty of ideal picnic spots. An on-site museum, called the House of Happy Walls, was built by Jack's wife to display a collection from the author's life. The park is open daily from 9:30am to 7pm in summer, from 9:30am to 5pm in winter; the museum is open daily from 10am to 5pm. Admission to the park is $6 per car, $5 per car for seniors 62 and over. Pick up the $1 self-guided tour map on arrival to help acquaint you with the grounds. In summer, golf-cart rides also are offered from noon to 4pm on weekends for those who don't want to hoof it.

SHOPPING   Gourmands might want to stop by **The Olive Press,** 14301 Arnold Dr., in Jack London Village (☎ **800/9-OLIVE-9** or 707/939-8900). With olive trees abounding in the area and the locals' penchant for gourmet foods, it's no surprise that fresh-pressed olive oil has become a lucrative business in this neck of the woods. Everyone from large commercial growers to small-volume growers and hobbyists can pile their olives in the hopper and watch the state-of-the-art Italian-made olive press in action as it conveys the fruit up a belt, cleans it, and begins the pressing process. There's also a nifty gift shop, but don't expect a bargain here; even if you bring your own bottle, a gallon of oil can go for $110 (you'd be surprised how many olives it takes to make a gallon). The Press also carries numerous varieties of olive oils, imported olive-tree varietals, cured olives, and olive-related foods, gifts, and books. Open daily from 10am to 5:30pm.

HORSEBACK RIDING   Long before the Sonoma Valley became part of the Wine Country, it was better known as cattle country—and there's no better way to explore the land's old roots than with a guided horseback tour provided by the ✪ **Sonoma Cattle Company** (☎ **707/996-8566; www.thegridnet/trailrides/**). After you've been instructed in the basics of horse handling, you'll be led on a leisurely stroll—with the occasional trot thrown in for thrills—through beautiful Jack London State Historic Park. The ride takes you past vineyards owned by London's descendants, across meadows blanketed with lupine, around a lake originally dammed by London, and up to enjoy Sonoma Mountain's panoramic views. The Sonoma Cattle Company also offers regular, sunset, and full-moon rides at Sugarloaf Ridge at the northern end of Sonoma Valley; a route that also winds through deep, shady forests and up to ridge tops with spectacular 360° views. At either location you can also opt for the Western Barbecue Ride ($75 for 3 to 4 hours) or the Gourmet Boxed Lunch Ride and Tour of the Benziger Family Winery ($55 for 3 hours).

GOLF   Thanks to the valley's mild climate, golf is a year-round pursuit. At the northern end of the Sonoma Valley is the semiprivate **Oakmont Golf Club,** 7025 Oakmont Dr., off the Sonoma Highway, Santa Rosa (☎ **707/539-0415**), which has two 18-hole championship courses, both designed by Ted Robinson, as well as a driving range, clubhouse, and locker rooms. The par 63 East course is considered the most challenging, while the par 72 West course is for higher handicapped golfers. Greens fees are $30 on weekdays, $40 on weekends; carts are $26. Reservations are recommended at least a day in advance on weekdays, and at least 1 week on weekends.

Originally designed by Sam Whiting in 1926, the **Sonoma Mission Inn Golf & County Club,** 17700 Arnold Dr., off Boyes Drive (pro shop ☎ **707/996-0300**), was completely remodeled in 1991 by Robert Muir Graves and is now owned by the Sonoma Mission Inn. Its par 72, 18-hole, 7,069-yard championship course is considered one of the top public courses in the state. It's mostly flat, with several tight doglegs around an armada of redwoods and oaks. A driving range was added in the $10-million renovation; a clubhouse and locker rooms are also provided. Greens fees ($50 Monday through Thursday, $65 Friday, $75 weekends) include cart. A strict dress code is enforced.

If you're a beginner or just want to bone up on your irons game, **Los Arroyos Golf Club,** 5000 Stage Gulch Rd. off Arnold Drive, a short drive from downtown Sonoma (pro shop ☎ **707/938-8835**), is for you. Its small, 9-hole course is fairly flat and inexpensive—$10 on weekdays, $12 on weekends. Pull carts are an extra $2; a driving range, practice greens, and club rentals are also available. It's open on a first-come, first-play basis.

4 Where to Stay

When planning your trip, keep in mind that during the high season—between June and November—most hotels charge peak rates and sell out completely on weekends; many have a 2-night minimum. Always ask about discounts, particularly during midweek, when most hotels and B&Bs drop their rates by as much as 30%. During the off-season, you will have far better bargaining power and may be able to get a room at almost half the summer rate.

HELPING HANDS   If you are having trouble finding a room, try calling the **Sonoma Valley Visitors Bureau** (☎ **707/996-1090**). They'll refer you to a lodging that has a room to spare, but they won't make reservations for you. The **Bed and Breakfast Association of Sonoma Valley** (☎ **800/969-4667**) will refer you to one of their member B&Bs, and can make reservations for you as well.

Sonoma Valley Accomodations

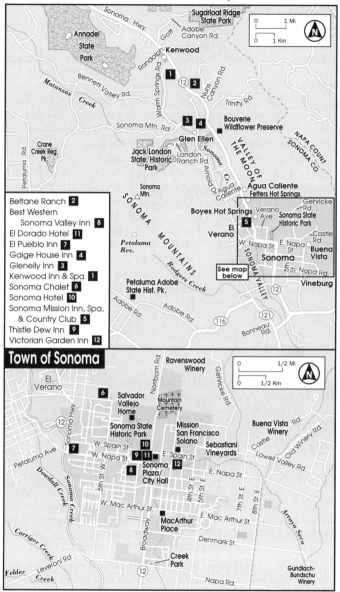

Sonoma Hwy.

Sugarloaf Ridge
State Park

0   1 Mi
0   1 Km

Annadel
State
Park

Adobe
Canyon Rd.

Goff

Randolph

Kenwood

Matanzas

Bennett Valley Rd.

Warm Springs Rd.

1

(12)   **2**

Nuns Canyon Rd.

Trinity Rd.

Creek

Sonoma Mtn. Rd.

3   **4**

Glen Ellen

Bouverie
Wildflower Preserve

NAPA COUNTY
SONOMA CO.

Crane
Creek Reg.
Pk.

Petaluma Rd.

Jack London
State Historic
Park

London
Ranch Rd.

Sonoma Cr.

Arnold Dr.

Agua Caliente

VALLEY OF THE MOON

Agua Caliente
Fetters Hot Springs

Gehricke
Rd.

Beltane Ranch **2**
Best Western
    Sonoma Valley Inn **8**
El Dorado Hotel **11**
El Pueblo Inn **7**
Gaige House Inn **4**
Glenelly Inn **3**
Kenwood Inn & Spa **1**
Sonoma Chalet **6**
Sonoma Hotel **10**
Sonoma Mission Inn, Spa,
    & Country Club **5**
Thistle Dew Inn **9**
Victorian Garden Inn **12**

Sonoma
Mtn.

SONOMA

MOUNTAINS

Petaluma
Res.

Rodgers Creek

Boyes Hot Springs

Verano Ave.

5

El
Verano

Verano

Sonoma State
Historic Park

W. Napa St.   E. Napa St.

Castle
Rd.

Buena
Vista

Sonoma

Napa Rd.

Vineburg

Petaluma Adobe
State Hist. Pk.

Adobe Rd.

Adobe Rd.

(116)

See map
below

SONOMA VALLEY

(12)

(121)

Bonneau Rd.

Town of Sonoma

0   1/2 Mi
0   1/2 Km

El
Verano

6

Salvador
Vallejo
Home

Norbom Rd.

Ravenswood
Winery

Gehricke Rd.

Mountain
Cemetery

Buena Vista
Rd.

Sonoma Hwy.

(12)

7

Sonoma State
Historic Park

W. Spain St.   **10**

W. Napa St.   **9** **11**

8

Petaluma Ave.

Doudall Creek

Sonoma Creek

5th St. W.

Mission
San Francisco
Solano

Sonoma
Plaza/
City Hall

E. Spain St.   **12**

Sebastiani
Vineyards

E. Napa St.

Buena Vista
Winery

Castle

Lowell Valley Rd.

Old Winery Rd.

4th St. E.
5th St. E.
7th St. E.
8th St. E.

Arroyo Seco

W. Mac Arthur St.

Broadway

MacArthur
Place

E. Mac Arthur St.

Denmark St.

Carriger Creek

Felder

Leveroni Rd.

Leveroni
Creek

Creek
Park

(12)

Napa Rd.

Gundlach-
Bundschu
Winery

SONOMA
EXPENSIVE

✪ **MacArthur Place.** 29 E. MacArthur St., Sonoma, CA 95476. ☎ **800/722-1866** or 707/938-2929. www.macarthurplace.com. 65 units. A/C MINIBAR TV TEL. Sun–Thurs $195–$425 double; Fri–Sat $245–$425 double. Rates include continental breakfast. AE, CB, DC, MC, V.

A highly recommended alternative to the Sonoma Mission Inn is this much smaller and more intimate luxury hotel and spa located 4 blocks south of Sonoma's plaza. Once a 300-acre vineyard and ranch, MacArthur Place has since been whittled down to an 8-acre "Country Estate" replete with landscaped gardens and tree-lined pathways, as well as a heated swimming pool and whirlpool. Most of the individually decorated guest rooms are housed within Victorian-style cottages scattered throughout the resort; all are exceedingly inviting with their custom linens, oversized comforters, and original artwork. The newer suites come with fireplaces, porches, wet bars, and whirlpool tubs. The full-service spa offers a wide array of services: fitness programs, body treatments, Indian rejuvenation treatments, skin care, astrology services, and an array of massages. Within the resort's restored century-old barn is Saddles, Sonoma's only steakhouse specializing in mesquite-grilled prime beef; and an array of other excellent restaurants—as well as shops, wineries, and bars—are a short walk away. In fact, that's where MacArthur Place has Sonoma Mission Inn beat: Once you park your car here you can *leave* it parked during your entire stay.

✪ **Sonoma Mission Inn, Spa & Country Club.** 18140 Sonoma Hwy. (Calif. 12; P.O. Box 1447), Sonoma, CA 94576. ☎ **800/862-4945** or 707/938-9000. Fax 707/935-1205. www.sonomamissioninn.com. E-mail: smi@smispa. com. 230 units. A/C MINIBAR TV TEL. $120–$380 double. AE, CB, DC, MC, V. From central Sonoma, drive 3 miles north on Hwy. 12 and turn left on Boyes Blvd.

As you drive through Boyes Hot Springs, you may wonder why someone decided to build a multimillion-dollar spa resort in this ordinary little town. There's no view to speak of, and it certainly isn't within walking distance of any wineries or fancy restaurants. So what's the deal? It's the naturally heated artesian mineral water, of course, piped from directly underneath the spa and into the temperature-controlled pools and whirlpools. Set on 12 meticulously groomed acres, the Sonoma Mission Inn consists of a massive three-story replica of a Spanish mission (well, aside from the pink paint job) built in 1927, an array of satellite wings housing numerous superluxury suites, and, of course, the world-class spa facilities. It's a popular retreat for the wealthy and the well-known, so don't be surprised if you see Barbra Streisand or Harrison Ford strolling around in skivvies. Big changes have occurred since the resort changed ownership a few years ago, including 70 new guest rooms and suites, a new $20 million spa facility (you won't even recognize the old one), and the acquisition of the Sonoma Golf Club.

The modern rooms are furnished with plantation-style shutters, ceiling fans, down comforters, and such extra amenities as bathroom scales, hair dryers, and oversize bath towels. The Wine Country rooms feature king-size beds, desks, refrigerators, and huge limestone and marble bathrooms; some offer wood-burning fireplaces, and many have balconies. The older, slightly smaller Historic Inn rooms are sweetly appointed with homey furnishings, and most have queen-size beds. For the ultimate in luxury, however, the opulently appointed (and brand new) Mission Suites are the way to go.

Dining: Mission Grill, run by chef Toni Robertson, is known for its low-calorie, low-sodium, and low-cholesterol California cuisine as well as its 200 varieties of Napa and Sonoma wines (see "Where to Dine," below). The Big 3 Diner is Mission Grill's casual cousin, serving American cuisine for breakfast, lunch, and dinner.

Amenities: Room service, concierge, laundry, dry cleaning, newspaper delivery, baby-sitting, secretarial services, valet parking, complimentary refreshments. Tennis courts. Full spa facilities (see "The Super Spa" box on p. 149 for the complete rundown).

MODERATE

✪ **El Dorado Hotel.** 405 First St. W., Sonoma, CA 95476. ☎ **800/289-3031** or 707/996-3030. Fax 707/996-3148. www.hoteleldorado.com. 26 units. A/C TV TEL. Summer $150–$210 double; winter $120–$160 double. Rates include continental breakfast and a split of wine. AE, MC, V.

This place may look like a 19th-century Wild West relic from the outside, but inside it's all 20th-century deluxe. Each modern, handsomely appointed guest room—designed by the same folks who put together the ultra-exclusive Auberge du Soleil resort in Rutherford (see chapter 4)—has French windows and tiny terraces; some offer lovely views of the plaza, while others overlook the hotel's private courtyard and heated lap pool. All rooms (except those for guests with disabilities) are on the second floor, and have private baths with plush towels and hair dryers. The two rooms on the ground floor are off the private courtyard, and each has a partially enclosed patio. Services include a concierge, laundry, in-room massage, bicycle rental, and access to a nearby health club. Breakfast, served either inside or out in the courtyard, includes coffee, fruits, and freshly baked breads and pastries. Within the hotel is Piatti, a popular restaurant serving regional Italian cuisine (see "Where to Dine," below).

Thistle Dew Inn. 171 W. Spain St., Sonoma, CA 95476. ☎ **800/382-7895.** Fax 707/996-8413. www.thistledew.com. 6 units. A/C TEL. Summer $120–$225 double; winter $110–$185 double. Rates include full breakfast and afternoon hors d'oeuvres. AE, MC, V.

Innkeepers Larry and Norma Barnett will be the first to admit that they don't run the fanciest B&B in town, but they'll just as quickly tell you that you'd be hard-pressed to find a better deal in Sonoma. Six rooms—all with private baths, queen beds, and phones with voice mail—are split between two turn-of-the-century homes, both handsomely furnished with an impressive collection of original Arts and Crafts furniture. If you're looking to save a few bucks, opt for a room in the main house; otherwise, you'll want one of the four larger and quieter rooms in the rear house. Each has its own deck overlooking Larry's cactus garden and is furnished with either a gas fireplace, a two-person whirlpool tub, or both. Look for a new second-floor two-room suite to be added in 2000. Luxury perks include breakfast (the French toast we had was excellent), which can be delivered to your room for an additional fee; afternoon hors d'oeuvres; free use of their bicycles and utensil-filled picnic baskets; passes to the nearby health club; and use of the garden hot tub. We guarantee you'll like the location—just half a block from Sonoma's plaza—as well as your hosts Larry and Norma and their very low-key, help-yourself approach toward innkeeping.

INEXPENSIVE

Best Western Sonoma Valley Inn. 550 Second St. W. (1 block from the plaza), Sonoma, CA 95476. ☎ **800/334-5784** or 707/938-9200. Fax 707/ 938-0935. www.sonomavalleyinn.com. 82 units. $89–$379 double. Rates include continental breakfast. AE, CB, DC, MC, V.

There are just two reasons to stay at the Sonoma Valley Inn: 1) it's the only place left with a vacancy, or 2) you're bringing the kids along. Otherwise, unless you don't mind staying in a rather drab room with thin walls and small bathrooms, you're probably going to be a little disappointed. Kids, on the other hand, will love the place: there's plenty of room to run around, plus a large pool and gazebo-covered spa to play in. The rooms *do* come with a lot of perks, however, such as continental breakfast delivered to your room each morning, a gift bottle of white table wine from

Kenwood Vineyards (chilling in the fridge), cable TV with HBO, and either a balcony or deck overlooking the inner courtyard. It's also in a good location, just a block from Sonoma's plaza.

El Pueblo Inn. 896 W. Napa St., Sonoma, CA 95476. ☎ **800/900-8844** or 707/996-3651. 38 units. A/C TEL. Apr–Oct $80–$95 double; Nov–Mar $65–$80 double. AE, DISC, MC, V.

Located on Sonoma's main east-west street 8 blocks from the center of town, this isn't Sonoma's fanciest hotel, but it offers some of the best-priced accommodations around. The rooms here are pleasant enough, with post-and-beam construction, exposed brick walls, light-wood furniture, and geometric prints. The coffeemaker should be a comfort to early risers, and an outdoor heated pool will cool you off in hot weather. Reservations should be made at least a month in advance for the spring and summer months.

Sonoma Chalet. 18935 Fifth St. W., Sonoma, CA 95476. ☎ **707/938-3129.** www.sonomachalet.com. 7 units including 3 cottages. Apr–Oct $95–$180 double; Nov–Mar $85–$160 double. Rates include continental breakfast. AE, MC, V.

This is one of the few accommodations in Sonoma that's truly secluded; it's on the outskirts of town, in a peaceful country setting overlooking a 200-acre ranch. The accommodations, housed in a Swiss-style farmhouse and several cottages, are all delightfully decorated by someone with an eye for color and a concern for comfort. You'll find claw-foot tubs, country quilts, Oriental carpets, comfortable furnishings, and private decks; some units have woodstoves or fireplaces. The two least expensive rooms share a bathroom, while the cottages offer the most privacy. A breakfast of fruit, yogurt, pastries, and cereal is served either in the country kitchen or in your room. If you like country rustic you'll like the Sonoma Chalet.

Sonoma Hotel. 110 W. Spain St., Sonoma, CA 95476. ☎ **800/468-6016** or 707/996-2996. Fax 707/996-7014. www.sonomahotel.com. 16 units. A/C TV TEL. Summer $95–$155 double. Winter Sun–Thurs $85–$130 double; Fri–Sat $115–$130 double. Rates include continental breakfast. AE, DC, MC, V.

This cute little historic hotel on Sonoma's tree-lined town plaza places an emphasis on 19th-century elegance and comfort. Built in 1880 by German immigrant Henry Weyl, each of the attractive guest rooms is decorated in early California style with French country furnishings, antique beds, and period decorations. In a bow to modern luxuries, recent additions include private bathrooms, well as cable TVs, phones with dataports, and (and this is crucial) air-conditioning. Perks include fresh coffee and pastries in the morning and complimentary wine and cheese in the evening. Also within the hotel is Heirloom, a popular new restaurant serving California-French cuisine (see "Where to Dine" below).

Victorian Garden Inn. 316 E. Napa St., Sonoma, CA 95476. ☎ **800/ 543-5339** or 707/996-5339. Fax 707/996-1689. www.victoriangardeninn.com. 4 units. $99–$185 double. Rates include breakfast. AE, DC, MC, V.

Proprietor Donna Lewis runs what is easily the cutest B&B in Sonoma Valley. A small picket fence and a wall of trees enclose an adorable Victorian garden brimming with bowers of violets, roses, camellias, and peonies, all shaded under flowering fruit trees. It's truly a marvelous sight in the springtime. The four guest rooms— three in the century-old water tower and one in the main house, an 1870s Greek Revival farmhouse—keep up the Victorian theme with white wicker furniture, floral prints, padded armchairs, and claw-foot tubs. The most popular rooms are the Top o' the Tower, which has its own entrance and view overlooking the garden, and the Woodcutter's Cottage, which also has its own entrance and garden view, plus a sofa and armchairs set in front of the fireplace. After a hard day's wine tasting, spend the afternoon cooling off in the pool or on the shaded wraparound porch, enjoying a mellow Merlot while soaking in the sweet garden smells.

GLEN ELLEN
EXPENSIVE

✪ **Gaige House Inn.** 13540 Arnold Dr., Glen Ellen, CA 95442. ☎ **800/ 935-0237** or 707/935-0237. Fax 707/935-6411. www.gaige.com. 15 units. A/C TEL. Summer $230–$395 double. Winter $150–$295 double. Rates include full breakfast and evening wines. AE, DC, DISC, MC, V.

When you review hotels and B&Bs for a living—and we've reviewed thousands of them—it's hard to be impressed. When we visited the Gaige House Inn, however, we were not only impressed, we didn't want to leave. The inn's owners, Ken Burnet, Jr., and Greg Nemrow, have managed to turn what was already a fine B&B into *the* finest in the Wine Country, and they've done it by offering a level of service, amenities, and decor normally associated with out-rageously expensive resorts—but without the snobbery. Breakfast, for example, is made with herbs from the inn's garden and prepared by a chef who commutes daily from San Francisco. Firm mattresses are graced with wondrously silk-soft linens and premium down comforters, and even the furniture and artwork are of museum quality.

But wait, it gets better. Behind the inn is a 1.5-acre oasis with perfectly manicured lawns, a 40-foot-long pool, and an achingly inviting creek-side hammock shaded by a majestic Heritage oak. All 15 rooms, each artistically decorated in a plantation theme with Asian and Indonesian influences (trust us, they're beautiful), have private bathrooms, direct-dial phones, and king- or queen-size beds; two rooms have Jacuzzi tubs, and several have fireplaces. The Gaige Suite is their finest room, bright and airy with large windows, a private balcony overlooking the lawn, a fireplace, and a Jacuzzi tub so large you could swim in it. Personally, we prefer Garden Room no. 10, exquisitely decorated with mahogany trim and flooring, a corner fireplace, a private deck, a huge glass-walled shower with dual heads, and a Jacuzzi tub for two. On sunny days, breakfast is served at individual tables on the large terrace. Evenings are best spent in the reading parlor sipping premium wines.

INEXPENSIVE

Beltane Ranch. 11775 Sonoma Hwy. (Hwy. 12), Glen Ellen, CA 95442. ☎ **707/996-6501.** www.beltaneranch.com. 6 units including 1 cottage. TEL. $130–$180 double. Rates include full breakfast. No credit cards (though checks are accepted).

The word "Ranch" conjures up the impression of a big ol' two-story house in the middle of hundreds of rolling acres, the kind of place where you laze away the day in a hammock watching the grass grow or pitching horseshoes in the garden. Well, friend, you can have all that and more at the Beltane Ranch, a century-old buttercup-yellow manor that's been everything from a bunkhouse to a brothel to a turkey farm. You simply can't help but feel your tensions ease away as you prop your feet up on the shady wraparound porch overlooking the vineyards, sipping a cool, fruity Chardonnay while reading *Lonesome Dove* for the third time. Each room is uniquely decorated with American and European antiques; all have private baths, sitting areas, and separate entrances. Innkeeper Deborah Mahoney serves a big country breakfast in the garden or on the porch overlooking the vineyards. For exercise, you can play tennis on the private court or hike the trails meandering through the 1,600-acre estate. *Tip:* Request one of the upstairs rooms, which have the best views.

✪ **Glenelly Inn.** 5131 Warm Springs Rd. (off Arnold Dr.), Glen Ellen, CA 95442. ☎ **707/996-6720.** Fax 707/996-5227. www.glenelly.com. 8 units. $135–$160 double. Rates include full breakfast. MC, V.

The Glenelly Inn is one of our favorite places to stay in the Wine Country. First off, the rates are reasonable, particularly when you factor in breakfast and afternoon snacks. But more important, this former 1916 railroad inn is positively drenched in serenity. Located well off the main highway on an oak-studded hillside, the peach-and-cream inn comes with everything you would expect from a country retreat—long verandas with comfy wicker chairs and views of the verdant Sonoma hillsides; a hearty country breakfast served beside a large cobblestone fireplace; and bright, immaculate rooms with old-fashioned claw-foot tubs, Scandinavian down comforters, and ceiling fans. But innkeeper Kristi Hallamore, a native San Franciscan of Norwegian descent (and a darn good cook) also understands that it's the little things that make the difference. Hence, the firm mattresses, good reading lights, and a simmering hot tub well ensconced within a grapevine- and rose-covered arbor. All rooms, decorated with antiques and country furnishings, have queen beds, private baths with showers, terry-cloth robes, and private entrances. Top picks are either the Vallejo or Jack London cottages, both with large private patios, though we also like the rooms on the upper veranda—particularly in the spring when the terraced gardens below are in full bloom.

KENWOOD

VERY EXPENSIVE

✪ **Kenwood Inn & Spa.** 10400 Sonoma Hwy., Kenwood, CA 95452. ☎ **800/ 353-6966** or 707/833-1293. Fax 707/833-1247. www.kenwoodinn. com. 12 units. Apr–Oct $255–$415 double (2-night minimum on weekends); Nov–Mar $225–$395 double. Rates include gourmet breakfast and bottle of wine. AE, MC, V.

Inspired by the villas of Tuscany, the honey-colored Italian-style buildings, flower-filled flagstone courtyard, and pastoral views of vineyard-covered hills are enough to make any northern Italian homesick. We were immediately impressed with the friendly staff who made us feel right at home. Every spacious room here is lavishly and exquisitely decorated with imported tapestries, velvets, and antiques; each has a fireplace, balcony (unless you're on the ground floor), feather bed, CD player, and down comforter—but no phone or TV, so you can relax. A minor caveat is road noise, which you're unlikely to hear from your room, but can be slightly heard over the tranquil pumped-in music around the courtyard and pool.

An impressive two-course gourmet breakfast is served poolside or in the Mediterranean-style dining room; ours consisted of a poached egg accompanied by light, flavorful potatoes, red bell peppers, and other roasted vegetables, all artfully arranged, followed by a delicious homemade scone with fresh berries and a small lemon tart.

Amenities: The inn's own full-service spa offers aromatherapy, massage (including one of the best we've had in a long time), and various skin and body treatments such as a Mediterranean salt scrub of lemon rind, rosemary, and salt.

5 Where to Dine

In the past decade, the Sonoma Valley has experienced a culinary revolution. In response to the saturation of restaurants in the Bay Area, both budding and renowned chefs and restaurateurs have pulled out their San Francisco stakes and resettled in the Sonoma Valley to craft culinary art from the region's bounty of organic produce and meats. The result is something longtime locals never dared to dream of when it came to fine dining in Sonoma: a choice.

Granted, the selection of fine restaurants in Sonoma pales in comparison to that found in Napa Valley, but the overall dining experience is certainly equivalent—enough. Yet even the big players are forced to concede to Sonoma's small-town code by keeping their restaurants simple and unpretentious, hence the absence of ostentatious eateries such as Napa's Tra Vigne or Pinot Blanc.

Instead, as you travel through the valley, you'll find a few dozen modestly sized and privately owned cafes, often run by husband-and-wife teams who pour their hearts and bank accounts into keeping their businesses thriving during the off-season. In fact, don't be surprised if the person waiting your table is also the owner, chef, host, sommelier, and retired professor from Yale. It's this sort of combination that often makes dining in Sonoma a very personable experience, and one that you'll relish long after you leave the Wine Country.

Note: Though Sonoma Valley has far fewer visitors than Napa Valley, its restaurants are often equally crowded, so be sure to make reservations as far in advance as possible. Also bear in mind that the food is usually served in large portions and washed down with copious amounts of wine—enough so that we make a point of eating at only one restaurant a day lest we explode.

SONOMA

EXPENSIVE

Depot Hotel—Cucina Rustica Restaurant. 241 First St. W. (off Spain St.), Sonoma. ☎ **707/938-2980.** www.depothotel.com. Reservations recommended. Main courses $17–$20. AE, CB, DC, DISC, MC, V. Wed–Fri 11:30am–5pm; Wed–Sun 5pm–closing. NORTHERN ITALIAN.

Michael Ghilarducci has been the chef and owner here for the past 13 years, which means he's either independently wealthy or a darn good cook. Fortunately, it's the latter. Located a block north of the plaza in a handsome, historic 1870 stone building, the Depot Hotel offers pleasant outdoor dining in an Italian garden complete with a reflection pool and cascading Roman fountain. The menu is unwaveringly Italian, filled with a plethora of classic dishes such as spaghetti bolognese and veal alla parmigiana. Start with the bounteous antipasto misto and end the feast with a dish of Michael's handmade Italian ice cream and fresh-fruit sorbets.

Mission Grill. At Sonoma Mission Inn, 18140 Sonoma Hwy., Sonoma. ☎ **707/938-9000.** Reservations recommended. Main courses $22.50–$27. AE, CB, DC, MC, V. Sun brunch 10am–2pm. Daily 6–9:30pm. CALIFORNIA/SPA.

The Grille, one of the most well-known restaurants in the Wine Country, has long suffered from a solid reputation for serving high-caliber spa cuisine. The problem, of course, is the word "spa," which conjures up visions of blue-haired ladies eating boiled vegetables and soybean salads. Fortunately, the Grille has found a solution: Toni Robertson, the former award-winning Executive Chef at the five-star Pan Pacific Hotel in Singapore (as well as stints in South Africa, Maui, Beverly Hills, and Chicago). Her emphasis is on healthy, uncomplicated cuisine that relies on fresh ingredients and natural flavors. Typical selections from the seasonally changing menu range from lean medallions of ostrich served with a ragout of fingerling potatoes, artichokes, and dried tomatoes, to roasted sea bass with saffron fettuccine and grilled Liberty duck breast in a roasted plum sauce. Service is professional yet friendly, and the wine list is extensive and expensive.

MODERATE

✪ **Café La Haye.** 140 E. Napa St., Sonoma. ☎ **707/935-5994.** Reservation recommended. Main courses $12–$16. AE, MC, V. Tues–Sat 5:30–9pm, brunch Sat–Sun 9:30am–2pm. ECLECTIC.

"Upscale comfort food" is perhaps the best way to describe what the chefs bring forth from the tiny open kitchen of this popular Sonoma cafe. Located just off the plaza, La Haye consists of a small split-level dining room (more tall than wide) that is pleasantly decorated with hardwood floors, exposed beam ceiling, and contemporary artwork. Mirroring the decor is the menu, which consists of a modest selection of simple yet appealing dishes ranging from grilled pork chop with hot sweet mustard and mashed sweet potatoes to flatiron pot roast served with fresh root vegetables over horseradish mashed

Dining in the Town of Sonoma

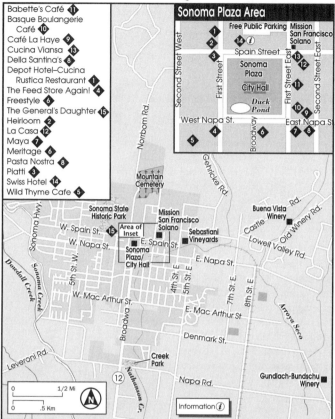

Babette's Café 11
Basque Boulangerie
   Café 10
Café La Haye 9
Cucina Viansa 13
Della Santina's 8
Depot Hotel–Cucina
   Rustica Restaurant 1
The Feed Store Again! 4
Freestyle 6
The General's Daughter 15
Heirloom 2
La Casa 12
Maya 7
Meritage 6
Pasta Nostra 8
Piatti 3
Swiss Hotel 14
Wild Thyme Cafe 5

potatoes. Appetizers we enjoyed were the house smoked salmon with potato pancake and apple-horseradish compote, and the organic mixed greens topped with spiced walnuts and roasted chioggia beets (I'm hungry just writing this). Such well-prepared and wholesomely fresh food, combined with an experienced wait staff, friendly owners, soothing atmosphere, and reasonable prices (including a modestly priced wine list and an unheard of $7 corkage fee), has made La Haye one of our favorite restaurants in Sonoma Valley for dinner and weekend brunch.

The General's Daughter. 400 W. Spain St., Sonoma. ☎ **707/938-4004.** Reservations recommended in summer. Main courses $8.75–$21.50. MC, V. Daily 11:30am–2:30pm; Sun–Fri 5–9pm, Sat 5–10pm. CALIFORNIA.

Ask almost any local about the General's Daughter and they'll give you pretty much the same answer: "It's a beautiful building, but I've never eaten there." And with good reason: This fully restored 1883 farm-house—built by General Vallejo for his daughter, Natalia—is gorgeous, a descriptor that rarely applies to the unimaginative cuisine. All the standards are here—roast chicken, grilled salmon, rib-eye steak, rack of lamb, and the requisite vegetarian dish of grilled vegetables—along with the occasional bizarre attempt at Mexican/Asian fusion (sorry, readers, but we just didn't have the stomach to sample the seared rare ahi tostada). The food isn't *bad,* really—it's just not good, and if you're going to spend $21.50 on a steak, you might as well dine at Meritage or Heirloom. The general consensus, from what we've gathered, is that the General's Daughter is best admired from a distance.

Heirloom. 110 W. Spain St., Sonoma. ☎ **707/939-6955.** Reservations recommended. Main courses $13–$17. AE, DC, MC, V. Daily 11:30am–2:30pm, 5:30–9:30pm. CALIFORNIA-FRENCH.

Heirloom Chef Michael Dotson, who honed his skills at Plumpjack's in San Francisco and Lake Tahoe, has received a plethora of kudos for his California-French cuisine at this Sonoma newcomer. Set on the first floor of the Sonoma Hotel, the 66-seat restaurant's decor follows the same theme as the hotel's guest room: a rustic, simple, early-1900s ambiance with oodles of polished wood and highlighted by the beautifully preserved mahogany bar. Dotson makes the most out of the fresh, local ingredients by letting the organic meats and vegetables shine through without dousing them in complicated sauces. The grilled organic rib eye, for example, is served with a light red wine sauce that enhances, yet doesn't overpower, the meat's natural flavors (you'll enjoy the potato gratin and Bloomsdale spinach sides as well). Other dishes on the seasonally changing menu range from pancetta-wrapped salmon in a toasted garlic thyme broth, to Zinfandel-braised lamb shank atop barley-herb risotto, and roasted Wolfe Ranch quail with Chioggia beets, kumquats, and walnuts. When making a reservation, ask for a patio table under the canopy of the beautiful maple tree or beside the outdoor fireplace. *Note:* Dotson serves a fine lunch as well.

✪ **Maya.** 101 E. Napa St., Sonoma. ☎ **707/935-3500.** Reservations recommended. Main courses $10.50–$19.50. MC, V. Mon–Sat 11:45am–9:30pm; Sun 4–9:30pm. YUCATAN CUISINE.

Gourmet Mexican might be the best way to describe this lively new restaurant on the southeast corner of Sonoma's plaza. But we're not talking about top-shelf enchiladas here. Rather, it's a winning combination of traditional Yucatan dishes prepared with ultra-fresh ingredients. Take the Salmon a la Parilla, for instance: a thick cut of fresh salmon, perfectly cooked within a banana leaf, basted with a guava-chili sauce, and served with a medley of grilled onions, sweet peppers, avocado, and cilantro. Wondrous. The Maya Pollo Rostizado—a spit-roasted half chicken that's been given a Yucatan spice rub—is commendable as well (and could easily feed two). Other menu items we considered seriously included the pan-seared monkfish in a papaya vinaigrette, the chipotle-braised lamb shank, and the grilled center-cut pork chop with a maple-balsamic demiglaze. Yes, you're probably going to pay a bit more than you planned for Mexican food, but trust us: it's worth the extra few dollars. You'll probably enjoy the faux Mayan village ambience as well: desert earth tones with bright splashes of colorful art and thick, hand-carved wood furnishings. The only caveat is the *muy fuerte* noise level, but a couple of their fantastic margaritas on the rocks and you'll soon be in a fiesta mode yourself.

✪ **Meritage.** 522 Broadway, Sonoma. ☎ **707/938-9430.** Reservations recommended. Main courses $13–$19. AE, MC, V. Wed–Mon 11:30am–9pm. SOUTHERN FRENCH/NORTHERN ITALIAN.

Learning from the mistakes made by the previous occupants—that Sonoma ain't New York City and shouldn't treat its customers as such—chef/owner Carlo Cavallo has eliminated the big-city attitude and prices at his new restaurant without diminishing style, service, and quality. The former executive chef for Giorgio Armani, Cavallo has the ability to combine the best of Southern French and Northern Italian cuisines (hence "Meritage"), giving Sonomans yet another reason to eat out. The menu, which changes twice daily, is a good read: handmade roasted pumpkin tortelloni in a parmesan cheese sauce; Napoleon of escargot in a champagne and wild thyme sauce; organic greens, strawberries, corn, and French feta salad; wild boar chops in a white truffle sauce with mashed potatoes. Such edible enticement—combined with very reasonable prices, excellent service, a stellar wine list, cozy booth seating, a handsome dining room, and Carlo's practiced charm—combine to make Meritage one of the most exciting new restaurants in the Wine Country.

Piatti. 405 First St. W., Sonoma. ☎ **707/996-2351.** Reservations recommended. Main courses $9.95–$18.95. AE, DC, MC, V. Sun–Thurs 11:30am–10pm, Fri–Sat 11:30am–11pm. ITALIAN.

Part of a northern-California chain that originated in Napa, Piatti has built a steadfast and true clientele by consistently serving large portions of good Italian food at fair prices in a festive setting. The restaurant occupies the ground floor of the El Dorado Hotel at the northwest corner of Sonoma Plaza (just follow your nose). Good pizzas and braised meats—such as the superb lamb shank flavored with a rich port-wine sauce and fresh mint—emerge from a wood-burning oven. Also offered is an array of satisfying pastas, our favorite being the cannelloni stuffed with roasted veal, spinach, porcini mushrooms, and ricotta. Other recommended dishes include a wonderful roast-vegetable appetizer, a teeming pile of fresh mussels in a tomato-and-herb broth, the rotisserie chicken with garlic mashed potatoes, and the veal scaloppini. Granted, there are fancier and more intimate restaurants in the valley, but none that can fill you up with such good food at these prices. And if the sun is out, be sure to dine alfresco on Piatti's courtyard.

Swiss Hotel. 18 W. Spain St., Sonoma. ☎ **707/938-2884.** Reservations recommended. Main courses $10–$20. AE, MC, V. Daily 11:30am–2:30pm and 5–9:30pm. (Bar, daily 11:30am–2am.) CONTINENTAL/NORTHERN ITALIAN.

With its slanting floors and beamed ceilings, the historic Swiss Hotel, located right in the town center, is a Sonoma landmark. The turn-of-the-century long oak bar at the left of the entrance is adorned with black-and-white photos of pioneering Sonomans. The bright white dining room and rear dining patio are pleasant spots to enjoy lunch specials like penne with chicken, mushrooms, and tomato cream; hot sandwiches; and California-style pizzas fired in a wood-burning oven. Dinner might start with a warm winter salad of radicchio and frisée lettuce with pears, walnuts, and bleu cheese. Main courses run the gamut; we like the linguine and prawns with garlic, hot pepper, and tomatoes; the filet mignon wrapped in a bleu-cheese crust; and the duck in an orange-honey sauce. It's all very traditional and satisfying, a style of cuisine that's becoming increasingly rare in Sonoma Valley.

INEXPENSIVE

Basque Boulangerie Cafe. 460 First St. E., Sonoma. ☎ **707/935-7687.** Menu items $3–$7. No credit cards. Daily 7am–6pm. BAKERY/DELI.

If you prefer a lighter morning meal and strong coffee, stand in line with the locals at the Basque Boulangerie Cafe, the most popular gathering spot in the Sonoma Valley. Most everything—sourdough Basque breads, pastries, quiche, soups, salads, desserts, sandwiches, cookies—is made in-house, and made well. Daily lunch specials, such as a grilled-veggie sandwich with smoked mozzarella cheese ($4.75), are listed on the chalkboard out front. Seating is scarce, and if you can score a sidewalk table on a sunny day, consider yourself one lucky person. A popular option is ordering to go and eating in the shady plaza across the street. The cafe also sells wine by the glass, as well as a wonderful cinnamon bread by the loaf that's ideal for making French toast.

✪ **Cucina Viansa.** 400 First St. E., Sonoma. ☎ **707/935-5656.** Deli items $5–$9. AE, CB, DISC, MC, V. Sun–Thurs 10am–7pm, Fri–Sat 10am–11pm. ITALIAN DELI.

Cucina Viansa is the sexiest thing going in Sonoma, a suave deli and wine bar owned by Sam and Vicki Sebastiani, who also run Viansa Winery. It's a visual masterpiece, with shiny black-and-white-checkered flooring, long counters of Italian marble, track lighting, and a center deli and wine bar where a crew of young men slice meats, pour wines, and scoop gelato. Start by sampling the preserves and jams near the entrance, then wander the aisle and choose among the armada of cured meats, cheese, fruit, pastas, salads, and breads lining the deli. Popular choices are the hefty sandwiches on herbed focaccia bread or the herb-marinated rotisserie chickens served by the half with your choice of pasta or salad. Roasted turkey, duck, pork, lamb, and rabbit also are available. Opposite the deli is the wine bar, featuring all of Viansa's current wine releases for both tasting and purchase, as well as a small selection of microbrewed beers on tap. On your way out, stop at the gelateria and treat yourself to some intense Italian ice cream. *Note:* Cucina Viansa also hosts live jazz bands every Friday and Saturday night from 6 to 11pm.

✪ **Della Santina's.** 133 E. Napa St. (just east of the square), Sonoma. ☎ **707/935-0576.** Reservations recommended. Main courses $8.95–$14.75. AE, DISC, MC, V. Daily 11:30am–3pm and 5–9:30pm. ITALIAN.

Those of you who just can't swallow another expensive, chichi California meal should follow the locals to this friendly, traditional Italian restaurant. How traditional? Just ask father/son team Dan and Robert: when we last dined here they pointed out Señora Santina's hand-embroidered linen doilies as they proudly told us about her Tuscan recipes (heck, even the dining room looks like an old-fashioned, elegant Italian living room). And their pride is merited: Every dish we tried was refreshingly authentic and well flavored—without overbearing sauces or one *hint* of California pretentiousness. Be sure to start with traditional antipasti, especially the sliced mozzarella and tomatoes or the delicious white beans. The nine pasta dishes are, again, wonderfully authentic (gnocchi lovers, rejoice!). The spit-roasted meat dishes are a local favorite (though we found them to be a bit overcooked), and for those who can't choose between chicken, pork, turkey, rabbit, or duck, there's a selection that offers a choice of three. Don't worry about breaking your bank on a bottle of wine, as most of the choices here go for under $25. Portions are huge, but save room for dessert—they're wonderful, too.

La Casa. 121 E. Spain St., Sonoma. ☎ **707/996-3406.** Reservations recommended on weekends and summer evenings. Main courses $6–$11. AE, CB, DC, DISC, MC, V. Daily 11:30am–10pm (bar appetizers until midnight). MEXICAN.

This no-nonsense Mexican restaurant, on the Sonoma Plaza across from the mission, serves great enchiladas, fajitas, and chimichangas. To start, try the black-bean soup or the ceviche made with fresh snapper, marinated in lime juice with cilantro and salsa, and served on crispy tortillas. Follow that with tamales prepared with corn husks spread with corn masa, stuffed with chicken filling, and topped with a mild red-chile sauce. Or you might opt for the delicious *suiza*-deep-dish chicken enchiladas—or fresh snapper Veracruz if it's available. On a sunny afternoon or a clear night, choose to dine patio-style, where you can sip cerveza under the warmth of heat lamps.

Wild Thyme Cafe. 165 W. Napa St., Sonoma. ☎ **707/996-0900.** Main courses $2.50–$9.50. MC, V. Tues–Fri 7am–7pm, Sat 9am–7pm, Sun 9am–3pm. GOURMET DELI.

If you're planning on a long day of wine tasting, the last you want to do is subject yourself to a large, heavy breakfast. Which is why we highly recommend that you start your day at Wild Thyme Cafe, a sort of upscale deli that serves very good yet inexpensive edibles that won't bog you down. For example, for breakfast (served 7–11am) their old-fashioned waffle with real maple syrup sure hits the spot, as does their Sonoma sourdough French toast and fresh poached eggs. For lunch, choose from an array of sandwiches (we really liked the roast turkey on focaccia with jalapeños, jack cheese, and arugula), soups, pastas, salads, and a few hearty entrees such as meat loaf, baby back ribs, and roast chicken—all best accompanied with a side of fresh green beans and garlic mashed potatoes. And, being a Wine County deli, WTC also carries the requisite Sonoma wines, cheeses, olive oils, pastries, picnic supplies, coffee drinks, and tea by-the-pot. You'll like the decor as well—soothing yellow walls, earthen tile flooring, rough-hewn wood furniture, lots of sunshine, and nary a speck of dust. On sunny days, scramble for a free table in the back patio/rose garden.

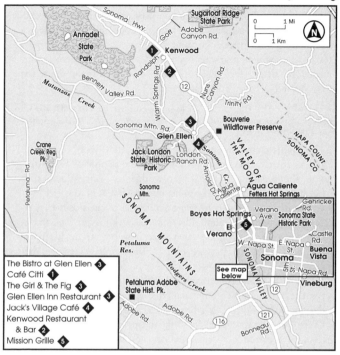

The Bistro at Glen Ellen ◆③
Café Citti ◆①
The Girl & The Fig ◆③
Glen Ellen Inn Restaurant ◆③
Jack's Village Café ◆④
Kenwood Restaurant
  & Bar ◆②
Mission Grille ◆⑤

GLEN ELLEN
MODERATE

The Bistro at Glen Ellen. 13740 Arnold Dr., Glen Ellen. ☎ **707/996-4401.**
Reservations recommended. Main courses $8–$22. AE, DISC, MC, V. Brunch
Sun 10am–3pm; lunch Mon–Sat 11am–4pm; dinner Sun–Thurs 4–10pm, Fri–
Sat 4–11pm. ECLECTIC.

There's something about really good comfort food that's satisfying
to the soul, and that's exactly what you'll find at this popular
creekside restaurant in bucolic Glen Ellen. Whether you're seated in
the handsome dining room—smartly adorned with maple floors,
dark-wood wainscoting, and a corner fireplace—or outside on the
multi-level terrace under the canopy of trees with serene views of the
adjacent Sonoma Creek, you'll be impressed with the soothing
ambiance that owner Munther Massarweh has created. The menu
is appealing as well: braised lamb shank served with saffron mushroom risotto, porterhouse pork chop accompanied with buttermilk
mashed potatoes and fig chutney, pepper-crusted ahi tuna in a

peppercorn deli glaze, sticky maple BBQ baby-back ribs, roast chicken ravioli in a yellow pepper cream sauce—all served in large portions at a fair price. The Sunday Supper—a hearty Yankee pot roast teeming with pearl onions, new potatoes, and carrots—is also worth the drive. *Hot Tip:* Locals have nothing but good things to say about The Bistro's Sunday brunch.

✪ **The Girl & The Fig.** 13690 Arnold Dr., Glen Ellen. ☎ **707/938-3634.**
Reservations recommended. Main courses $12–$19. AE, MC, V. Daily 5:30–9pm. COUNTRY FRENCH.

This modern, attractive cafe with mustard-yellow walls, tile floors, and an open kitchen is the creation of Sondra Bernstein (The Girl), who, after spending the past 4 years working at Viansa Winery and Italian Marketplace, left to open her own restaurant in August 1997. The coup de grâce was convincing San Francisco chefs/couple Gina Marie Armanini and John Gillis to come work for her. They have since moved on to open their own place; however, making his mark on Glen Ellen is their protégé John Toulze, who has taken over the kitchen with rave reviews—including one recently in the *New York Times.* The cuisine is nouveau-country with French nuances, and yes, figs are sure to be on the menu in one form or another, such as the wonderful winter fig salad made with arugula, pecans, dried figs, Laura Chenel goat cheese, and a fig-and-port vinaigrette. Garden-fresh produce and local meats, poultry, and fish are used whenever possible, in dishes such as the pork tenderloin with a potato leek pancake and roasted beets, and sea scallops with lobster-scented risotto. For dessert try the warm pear galette topped with gingered crème fraîche, a glass of the Quady Essensia Orange Muscat, and a sliver of raclette from the cheese cart. Sondra knows her wines, and will be happy to choose the best accompaniment to your meal. *Note:* Monday nights in Glen Ellen are much more fun since Sondra introduced Fondue Night.

Glen Ellen Inn Restaurant. 13670 Arnold Dr., Glen Ellen. ☎ **707/996-6409.**
Reservations recommended. Main courses $12–$22. www.glenelleninn.com.
AE, MC, V. Off-season Thurs–Tues 5:30pm–closing (depending on reservations); summer daily 5:30pm–closing. CALIFORNIA.

Christian and Karen Bertrand run this popular Glen Ellen restaurant. The dining room is so quaint and cozy that you feel as if you're dining in their home, but that's exactly the place's charm. Garden seating is the favored choice on sunny days, but the covered, heated patio is always welcoming. First courses from Christian's open kitchen might include a wild-mushroom-and-sausage "purse" served in a brandy cream sauce and warm goat-cheese croquettes. Main courses change with the seasons, but might range from linguine with artichoke hearts and feta to stellar late-harvest ravioli stuffed with pumpkin, walnuts, and sun-dried cranberries on a bed of butternut squash. Other favorites include the marinated pork tenderloin on smoked mozzarella polenta, topped with roasted pepper onion compote, and the utterly tender Nebraska corn-fed filet mignon in a foie gras-brandy reduction sauce. On our last visit, the Sonoma Valley mixed green salad, seared ahi tuna, and homemade French vanilla ice cream floating in bittersweet caramel sauce made a perfect meal. The wine list offers numerous Sonoma selections, as well as more than a dozen wines by the glass. *Tip:* There's a small parking lot behind the restaurant.

KENWOOD
MODERATE

Kenwood Restaurant & Bar. 9900 Sonoma Hwy., Kenwood. ☎ **707/833-6326.** Reservations recommended. Main courses $12.50–$24.50. MC, V. Tues–Sun 11:30am–9pm. CALIFORNIA/CONTINENTAL.

This is what California Wine Country dining should be (but what it often, disappointingly, is not). From the terrace of the Kenwood Restaurant, diners enjoy a view of the vineyards set against Sugarloaf Ridge as they imbibe Sonoma's finest at umbrella-covered tables. On nippy days you can retreat inside to the Sonoma-style roadhouse, with its shiny wood floors, pine ceiling, vibrant artwork, and cushioned rattan chairs set at white cloth–covered tables. Chef Max Schacher serves first-rate cuisine, perfectly balanced between tradition and innovation, and complemented by a reasonably priced wine list. Great starters are the Dungeness crab cake with herb mayonnaise; the superfresh sashimi with ginger, soy, and wasabi; and the wonderful Caesar salad. Main-dish choices might include poached salmon in a creamy caper sauce, prawns with saffron Pernod sauce, or braised Sonoma rabbit with grilled polenta. But the Kenwood doesn't take itself too seriously: Sandwiches and burgers also are available.

INEXPENSIVE

Café Citti. 9049 Sonoma Hwy., Kenwood. ☎ **707/833-2690.** Main courses $7–$10. MC, V. Daily 11am–3:30pm; Sun–Thurs 5:30–9pm, Fri–Sat 5–9:30pm. NORTHERN ITALIAN.

If you're this far north into the Wine Country, then you're probably doing some serious wine tasting. If that's the case, then you don't want to spend half the day at a fancy, high-priced restaurant. What you need is Café Citti (pronounced *Cheat*-ee), a roadside do-it-yourself Italian trattoria that is both good and cheap. You order from the huge menu board displayed above the open kitchen. Afterwards you grab a table (the ones on the patio, shaded by umbrellas, are the best on warm afternoons), and a server will bring your meal. It's all hearty, home-cooked Italian. Standout dishes are the green-bean salad, tangy Caesar salad, focaccia sandwiches, and roasted rotisserie chicken stuffed with rosemary and garlic. The freshly made pastas come with a variety of sauces; our favorite is the zesty marinara. Wine is available by the bottle, and the espresso is plenty strong. Everything on the menu board is available to go, which makes Café Citti an excellent resource for picnic supplies.

6 Where to Stock Up for a Picnic & Where to Enjoy It

Sure, Sonoma has plenty of restaurants, but when the weather's warm there's no better way to have lunch in the Wine Country than by toting a picnic basket to your favorite winery and basking in the sweet Sonoma sunshine. Even Sonoma's central plaza, with its many picnic tables, is a good spot to set up a gourmet picnic. But first you need grub, so for your picnicking pleasure, check out Sonoma's top spots for stocking up for an alfresco fete.

If you want to pick up some specialty fare on your way into town, stop at **Angelo's Wine Country Deli,** 23400 Arnold Dr. (☎ 707/ 938-3688), where you'll find all types of smoked meats, special salsas, and homemade mustards. The deli is known for its half-dozen types of homemade beef jerky. It's open in summer daily from 9am to 6pm; off-season, Monday through Thursday from 9am to 5pm and Friday through Sunday from 9am to 6pm.

The venerable **Sonoma Cheese Factory,** on the plaza at 2 Spain St. (☎ 707/996-1000), offers award-winning house-made cheeses and an extraordinary variety of imported meats and cheeses; a few are set out for tasting every day. The factory also sells caviar, gourmet salads, pâté, and homemade Sonoma Jack cheese. Good, inexpensive sandwiches are also available, such as fire-roasted pork loin or New York steak. While you're there, you can watch a narrated slide show about cheese making. The factory is open Monday through Friday from 8:30am to 5:30pm, Saturday and Sunday from 8:30am to 6pm.

At 315 Second St. E., a block north of East Spain Street, is the **Vella Cheese Company** (☎ **800/848-0505** or 707/938-3232), established in 1931. The folks at Vella pride themselves on making cheese into an award-winning science, their most recent victory being "U.S. Cheese Championship 1995–96" for their Monterey Dry Jack. Other cheeses range from flavorful High Moisture Jack to a razor-sharp Raw Milk Cheddar. Vella has also become famous for their Oregon Blue, made at their southern Oregon factory—it's rich, buttery, and even spreadable, one of the few premier bleus produced in this country. Any of these fine handmade, all-natural cheeses can be shipped directly from the store. Hours are Monday through Saturday from 9am to 6pm and Sunday from 10am to 5pm.

Three other highly recommended picnic outfitters include **Cucina Viansa, Wild Thyme Café,** and **Basque Boulangerie Cafe** in Sonoma; **Café Citti** in Kenwood (see "Where to Dine" above); and **Viansa Winery & Italian Marketplace,** which makes fabulous focaccia sandwiches—and has a lovely picnic area for noshing on them, too (see p. 136).

Gundlach-Bundschu (see p. 139), located on the outskirts of Sonoma, also has a wonderful picnic area perched on the side of a small hill overlooking the Sonoma countryside (though you'll have to earn the sensational view with a trek to the top). On the opposite side of the valley, our favorite picnic picks are **Château St. Jean's** (see p. 145) big, beautiful lawn overlooking the vineyards (bring a blanket) or the blissfully quiet pond-side picnic area at **Landmark Vineyards** (see p. 146), which also sports a bocce court if you're feeling restless.

If you'd rather have someone else provide the picnic grub for you, **Ravenswood Winery** (see p. 140) offers a gourmet "Barbecue Overlooking the Vineyards," held each weekend from 11am to 4:40pm, Memorial Day through the end of September. It's a great time for not much money.

Index

See also separate Accommodations and Restaurants indexes, below.

ACCOMMODATIONS

FROMMER'S® COMPLETE TRAVEL GUIDES

FROMMER'S® DOLLAR-A-DAY GUIDES

Australia from $50 a Day
California from $60 a Day
Caribbean from $70 a Day
England from $70 a Day
Europe from $60 a Day
Florida from $60 a Day

Hawaii from $70 a Day
Ireland from $50 a Day
Israel from $45 a Day
Italy from $70 a Day
London from $85 a Day
New York from $80 a Day

New Zealand from $50 a Day
Paris from $85 a Day
San Francisco from $60 a Day
Washington, D.C.,
    from $60 a Day

FROMMER'S® PORTABLE GUIDES

Acapulco, Ixtapa &
    Zihuatanejo
Alaska Cruises & Ports of Call
Bahamas
Baja & Los Cabos
Berlin
California Wine Country
Charleston & Savannah
Chicago

Dublin
Hawaii: The Big Island
Las Vegas
London
Maine Coast
Maui
New Orleans
New York City
Paris

Puerto Vallarta, Manzanillo
    & Guadalajara
San Diego
San Francisco
Sydney
Tampa & St. Petersburg
Venice
Washington, D.C.

FROMMER'S® NATIONAL PARK GUIDES

Family Vacations in the
    National Parks
Grand Canyon

National Parks of the
    American West
Rocky Mountain

Yellowstone & Grand Teton
Yosemite & Sequoia/
    Kings Canyon
Zion & Bryce Canyon

FROMMER'S® GREAT OUTDOOR GUIDES

New England
Northern California

Southern California & Baja
Washington & Oregon

FROMMER'S® MEMORABLE WALKS

Chicago
London

New York
Paris

San Francisco
Washington D.C.

FROMMER'S® IRREVERENT GUIDES

Amsterdam
Boston
Chicago
Las Vegas

London
Los Angeles
Manhattan

New Orleans
Paris
San Francisco

Seattle & Portland
Vancouver
Walt Disney World
Washington, D.C.

FROMMER'S® BEST-LOVED DRIVING TOURS

America
Britain
California

Florida
France
Germany

Ireland
Italy
New England

Scotland
Spain
Western Europe

THE UNOFFICIAL GUIDES®

Bed & Breakfast in
   New England
Bed & Breakfast in
   the Northwest
Beyond Disney
Branson, Missouri
California with Kids
Chicago

Cruises
Florida with Kids
The Great Smoky &
   Blue Ridge
   Mountains
Inside Disney
Las Vegas

London
Miami & the Keys
Mini Las Vegas
Mini-Mickey
New Orleans
New York City
Paris

San Francisco
Skiing in the West
Walt Disney World
Walt Disney World
   for Grown-ups
Walt Disney World
   for Kids
Washington, D.C.

SPECIAL-INTEREST TITLES

Born to Shop: France
Born to Shop: Hong Kong
Born to Shop: Italy
Born to Shop: New York
Born to Shop: Paris
Frommer's Britain's Best Bike Rides
The Civil War Trust's Official Guide
   to the Civil War Discovery Trail
Frommer's Caribbean Hideaways
Frommer's Europe's Greatest Driving Tours
Frommer's Food Lover's Companion to France
Frommer's Food Lover's Companion to Italy
Frommer's Gay & Lesbian Europe
Israel Past & Present
Monks' Guide to California

Monks' Guide to New York City
The Moon
New York City with Kids
Unforgettable Weekends
Outside Magazine's Guide
   to Family Vacations
Places Rated Almanac
Retirement Places Rated
Road Atlas Britain
Road Atlas Europe
Washington, D.C., with Kids
Wonderful Weekends from Boston
Wonderful Weekends from New York City
Wonderful Weekends from San Francisco
Wonderful Weekends from Los Angeles